The
Scream

The Scream

The Music, Myths & Misbehaviour of PRIMAL SCREAM

Kris Needs

Plexus, London

Copyright © 2003 by Kris Needs
Published by Plexus Publishing Limited
55a Clapham Common Southside
London SW4 9BX
Tel: 020 7622 2440
Fax: 020 7622 2441
www.plexusbooks.com

British Library Cataloguing in Publication Data

Needs, Kris
   The Scream : the music, myths and misbehaviour of Primal Scream
   1.Primal Scream (Group) 2.Rock musicians - Great Britain -
   Biography
   I.Title
   782.4'2166'0922

ISBN 0 85965 338 2

All Primal Scream songs published by EMI Publishing.

Cover photograph by Grant Fleming
Printed in and bound in Spain by Bookprint S.L., Barcelona
Cover and book design by Brian Flynn

Contents

Dedicated to the good ship Primal Scream
and all who've sailed in her,
to the everlasting memory of Joe Strummer,
and to Michelle, goddess of rabbits,
and to Abbey, Chloe, Jamie and Ellie, my new family.
And to my dear Mum.

'Yeah, take the fucking initiative, right?
Do your own stuff but don't back down. They all do.
Look, by continuing our approach,
someone sooner or later has got to pick up on it.
Someone has got to understand.
I'm afraid we don't live in history books.
We're trying to write the next chapter.'

**John Lydon talking to Kris Needs for *Zigzag* magazine in 1979,
on the eve of the release of *Metal Box*.**

'Primal Scream? I love 'em!
I did one gig with with 'em in Finland
and they were out of their minds!
For fuck's sake! All red, bleary eyes
and they all merge into this human debris.
But guess who got stripsearched
when we got off the plane at Heathrow?
Me! And one of them was on a stretcher!
They're great. How could you possibly not like them?
You've got to be anti-fun if you don't.'

John Lydon talking to Kris Needs in 2002, for *Seven* magazine.

Introduction

There always has to be someone to put the creative cat among the musical pigeons: whether it be in rock 'n' roll, soul music, jazz or even classical. And it usually seems to happen, so popular theory has it, as each decade passes its middle years and approaches old age.

The mid-to-late fifties saw the rock 'n' roll revolution kickstarted by Elvis, and followed through by the likes of Jerry Lee Lewis and Little Richard. Teenage rebellion started then and has never looked back.

In the sixties the Rolling Stones rose to notoriety as the anti-Beatles, but by 1968 they started pushing out the boundaries of the blues, their original inspiration. On *Let It Bleed* they cooked up a steaming, sexual rock ' n' blues stew that created a benchmark for many bands' music (and bad behaviour). At the same time, James Brown continued to refine and redefine funk, while George Clinton pushed out the boundaries by mixing it with drug-fuelled psychedelia. All this was changing the face of black music.

In the seventies punk rock thrust a red-hot poker 'twixt the buttocks of dreary soft rock and dull progressive boredom. The Sex Pistols turned everything upside down and created a monster movement of anger, attack and social comment, closely followed by The Clash.

By the time the eighties had passed middle-age you were wondering who was gonna do it this time around. But then along came acid house, which loved-up a whole generation. Even this movement needed its icons, and found 'em in a group of rock 'n' roll nutters from Glasgow called Primal Scream, hell-bent on hedonistic revolution, getting loaded and creating beautiful music in the process.

They've continued to inspire, confuse and confront without giving an inch. The impact created by 'Loaded', the first time Andrew Weatherall dropped 'Come Together', the supernova of *Screamadelica*, George Clinton inviting them on board the Mothership, Mani from the Stone Roses lighting a fire under the band and stoking up their energies, the punk rock future-assault of *Xtrmntr*, the latest innovations on *Evil Heat* . . . I could go on.

Here we pay tribute to Primal Scream and try and unravel the plot. There's been so much great music coursing through their veins, which have often been put to other uses. If you love the Scream, you might want to know where did *that* come from? Who do they love and why are they here? We have a cast of thousands and a bit of a guest list. It's not supposed to be a normal biography. It's the story of a band every bit as important as their influences and vice versa, told from a fan's point of view. A labour of love in line with the group's own philosophies and passions. A series of frontline bulletins from twelve years hanging out with the infamous Wild Bunch of rock 'n' roll. Time for a tribute, a doff of the hat to major influences, a few history lessons and several comedy interludes.

To coin a phrase, when they made this group they broke the mould. Or someone in the group fell over and dropped it, so they had to make a new one.

One

White Light/White Heat

'I've always loved things that other people thought were crass, gross or unlovable.'
- Bobby Gillespie

From the mid-seventies to mid-eighties I edited a magazine called Zigzag in London, and wrote the following words about The Clash when reviewing their *London Calling* album in late 1979.

'A double album from The Clash . . . but that's not the only surprise . . . Still remember anthems like 'White Man In Hammersmith Palais' and 'Stay Free', but also Stax soul, *Exile On Main Street*, Lee Perry, Gene Vincent, Phil Spector . . . Now Clash music embraces all that's vital in rock 'n' roll and black music of the last twenty years.'

How was I to know that around ten years later I'd be writing the same kind of thing about another band who became the latest upstarts to upset the applecart? And in the nineties! And probably even the double-0s!

The Clash are probably the biggest influence on Primal Scream, and I consider Primal Scream to be the 21st century equivalent of The Clash. *Screamadelica* is now lauded in the same tones as *London Calling*. Bobby Gillespie ferociously lapped up all the music press articles on The Clash and attended all the gigs he could. It inspired him to form a band. Mick Jones of The Clash and Bobby had similar upbringings, similar obsessions, and the drive and bottle to realise them.

But those similarities aside, the Scream simply had and – most importantly – *still* have that same attitude, creativity and unpredictability which set The Clash apart from everyone except Public Image Ltd. The difference is, Primal Scream have never called it a day.

Bobby Gillespie was born on 22 June, 1962, in the Springburn suburb of Glasgow. His dad was a SOGAT union official, who once stood as a Scottish MP for Labour and hung Black Panther posters on the wall. He was into books, films and especially pop music and Motown. He'd beeen part of the anti-fascist movement in the seventies and was basically anti-establishment. All this, including the politics, rubbed off on the young Bob from an early age.

'When I was young my parents would play the Stones, Beatles, Bob Dylan, soul, a lot of Motown,' Bobby told me in 1991. 'Even if you're only seven and hearing Martha Reeves, the Temptations and Ray Charles, you can't help but soak it up. When I hear the Four Tops I always think of my dad. On the radio I would hear T. Rex but also the O'Jays, Thin Lizzy and Ann Peebles. I never differentiated. I'd never think "that's rock" and "that's soul". They were just good records to me.'

Bobby says his dad never tried to indoctrinate him about politics. But Bobby was impressed

Getting 'Loaded' in '89: [left to right] Throb, Innes, Toby Toman, Bobby G, Henry Olsen.

The Clash: The original last gang in town.

by what he saw. He talked about this to Paolo Hewitt in the *Positive Energy of Madness* fanzine in 1995: 'He had a picture up on the wall of those guys giving the black power salute at the Olympics in '68. I remember saying to him, "I like that picture. What are they doing?" And him telling me about the Black Panthers and why they were doing that, but he did it in really good terms. I was about eight or nine and he was saying they're black guys who live in America but they can't go to the same school as a white guy, can't sit on the same park bench as a white guy, can't do anything the same as a white guy and that's why they're doing that. That is the way he'd do it, which was pretty cool. He'd never say, right you're going to be a socialist. He'd wait for you to ask questions and then explain it like that.'

The first record Bobby Gillespie ever bought was 'Dancing Queen' by Abba, in 1975 when he was twelve years old. In 1977 he went out and bought 'Pretty Vacant' by the Sex Pistols and Donna Summer's 'I Feel Love' on the same day. While attending Kings Park secondary school he met Alan McGee, who was in the year above, and a tearaway called Robert Young, who was a few years below. They became like a Glaswegian Three Musketeers. Bobby lived for Clash gigs and started getting the urge to form a band, but recalls that the first gig he ever went to was Thin Lizzy in 1975, the second was Dr Feelgood and the third one was The Clash. Bob and Alan would check out any happening group that came to town after that, especially of the punk variety.

Remembering his formative years, Bobby said, as we were reflecting in a Hackney café, 'I'm not trying to say I'm special, but I've always loved things that other people thought were crass, gross or unlovable. When I first saw a picture of Johnny Rotten I was transfixed. When everyone at school was listening to progressive rock, I was listening to Marc Bolan and The Clash. I've always thought that I had a different way of seeing things and that I would one day experience that.'

In 1999, *Uncut's* Michael Bonner devoted 22 pages to the Scream and got Bobby talking about those days too: 'It's what Primal Scream grew out of. Punk rock. A love of high-energy rock 'n' roll. It was the most exciting thing in our lives. It's what we lived for. I'd look at the Pistols and The Clash and wish I was involved in something like that. I didn't actually have any ambitions to be a musician then – I was just happy to buy the records and go to the gigs and have that as my world. It was what I believed in.'

Bobby and his mates would have record sessions and primitive jam sessions in their bedrooms, howling their favourite tunes while banging on the aluminum tin which housed PiL's *Metal Box*. Alan McGee ran a fanzine while Bobby bought *Zigzag*, coincidentally, when I was the editor. He still recalls my sessions with The Clash on the road, and the night John Lydon unveiled *Metal Box* for the first time, and wrote out all the lyrics. My own inspiration for writing came from Nick Kent of the *NME* and the bloke he was inspired by – the late, great speed-freak gonzo journalist Lester Bangs. Bobby and I reckon no-one came close in terms of skill, insight and attitude. Reading this shit was inspiring and made you go out and buy records. Or maybe form a band . . .

Bobby had been drawn to the noisier bands like the Rolling Stones and the Who. The rebels.

But it was punk rock which first really got him going, along with McGee and Robert Young – yet to earn the nickname 'Throb' from his exploits with the ladies – who he'd make t-shirts and tapes for. They'd listen to a Wednesday night show on Radio Clyde, which was the only place to hear the new punk records. One night McGee heard that local band the Drains were looking for a bass player. The guitarist was the fifteen-year-old Andrew Innes. McGee took the bass position and brought in Bob as singer. It would still be bedroom piss-ups with lots of punk covers and an almighty racket. Occasionally, Bobby would help out as a roadie and a drummer for another local band called Altered Images, who would later become protégés of Siouxsie and the Banshees and John Peel favourites, and score a hit with 'Happy Birthday'.

The Drains turned into Captain Scarlet and the Mysterons, with whom Bobby shouted for a few weeks. McGee recalls that together the three had about four rehearsals in January 1978. Innes also called up Malcolm McLaren's Glitterbest company, and asked him to manage them, but had no luck.

Around 1982, Bobby took a backseat when Innes and McGee decided to move to where it was all happening – London. They eventually formed a band called the Laughing Apple with pensions clerk Dick Green, and Neil Clarke, later of Lloyd Cole and the Commotions. I vaguely remember these two Scottish kids coming into the *Zigzag* offices off Portobello Road to hawk the group. They'd had a typically thankless day running round record companies and music papers, and I staggered in from the back to talk to them. I think we went to the pub over the road and they lapped up anecdotes about the Pistols, Johnny Thunders and The Clash. They were grateful just for some interest. I was just giving some time to a couple of kids from Glasgow who needed some encouragement, unlike the majority of music biz wankers at the time.

The inspiration of punk affected the Glasgow contingent in different ways. When Innes and McGee relocated to London, the latter also ran clubs and fanzines – including one called *Communication Blur*. In 1981 he opened a club called the Living Room. But the Laughing Apple failed to ripen after releasing three singles on their own label and called it a day.

In 1983 McGee got a thousand-pound bank loan and started Creation Records with Dick Green and old mate Joe Foster, once of wacky bedroom-punks TV Personalities. The first single on Creation was '73 in 83' by the Legend. The second was by Innes' Revolving Paint Dream.

'In an unconscious way, I was trying to merge psychedelia with punk rock,' recalled Alan in a February 2000 *Select* interview, which coincided with his closing down the label. 'I was obsessed with bands like the Creation and Syd Barrett, but I also loved Joy Division and PiL. And the music scene was dominated by shite, manufactured pop, like now. Me and Bobby Gillespie would sit saying how much we hated everything. We were full of pure fucking bile.'

Meanwhile, Bobby had left school at sixteen with four O-levels and started working in a printing factory. He hated the drudgery and the no-hope bigots he was surrounded by every day. Eventually he quit and stayed at home listening to his favourite records by the Velvet Underground, Love, George Clinton, Johnny Thunders, Dylan, Gram Parsons, Memphis soul singers and, of course, the punk bands. He lived for this, and would spend hours dreaming of doing it for himself one day. That's how he knows the words to every song that the Scream blast out at soundchecks. Bobby also had a short stint playing bass with Factory Records signing the Wake, appearing on two singles and their *Harmony* album, to which he contributed lyrics to a track called 'The Old Men'. The band also toured with New Order, opening up at Wembley Arena where a pissed-up Bobby managed to fall off the stage.

In 1982 Bobby started forming a band with another disenchanted youth he'd met called Jim Beattie. Rehearsing in a scout hut, they embarked on a mission to create as much noise as possible. The spirit of the Velvet Underground was never far away. The pair simply made 'a total racket' with two dustbin lids or the *Metal Box* case and a fuzz guitar, while screaming their lungs out over the top. Eventually the pair learned a few chords. The first song they played together was 'Heroin' by the Velvet Underground.

'It wasn't music, it was just smashing stuff up and screaming with guitars,' Bobby later told *Sounds*. 'We just used to make tapes of noises, then we found a few chords on the guitar and learned songs like "Mr Tambourine Man", "Waiting For The Man" and "Heroin". Then I thought I could do some songs myself . . . I started writing my own tunes and suddenly we had a pop group!'

They had the name Primal Scream before the music. It came from a 1970 book by Dr. Arthur Janov about the noises occasionally emitted from patients in psychotherapy clinics. 'Primal scream' was a term used for therapy designed to unleash childhood torments from within. John Lennon once used it to describe the unadulterated soul-baring of his first solo album. 'It's my primal scream,' he said in an interview. The same went for Yoko's accompanying effort, which is definitely a scream from somewhere. Both were letting loose everything that was eating away inside them and cleansing their spirits. When they recorded those first two solo albums both John and Yoko were undergoing therapy with Janov himself.

McGee says that Bobby and Beattie played the Living Room under the name Primal Scream sometime in 1983. They were backed by just a tape recorder and sounded like PiL, apparently. He also stuck the pair in the studio to record a single for the fledgling Creation. They came out with a track called 'The Orchard', which featured Judith Boyle of Spirea X on violin and vocals and Bobby on backing vocals. This was deemed too shite for release and got binned, but the North-South connection continued . . .

One of the venues favoured by Glasgow's punk aficionados was the Candy Club. In early 1984 owner Nick Low told Bobby about this mad band called the Daisy Chain – later to become the Jesus and Mary Chain – and gave him a tape containing songs like 'Upside Down', 'Inside Me' and 'In A Hole'. Apparently, Nick had deemed the band 'shite' but thought Bobby might like the Syd Barrett songs on the other side. Bobby loved the white-noise racket, rang the number on the cassette box and got bass player Douglas Hart. They got together and discovered a mutual love of books and records. Bobby passed on the tape to McGee, who promptly snarfed them up to record 'Upside Down' as a single.

It's generally assumed that Primal Scream's first proper gig was on 11 October 1984, supporting the Jesus And Mary Chain at Glasgow's Venue club. (The Scream returned to play there in April 2003.) The poster featured a still from the movie *If*, with Malcolm *Clockwork Orange* McDowell ready to lob a hand grenade, adorned with the slogan, 'Whose side are you on?' The set consisted of one song – a cover of Subway Sect's 'Nobody's Scared' – and a load of noise. Bobby also stood up and played a single snare drum for the JAMC's Jim and William Reid, who, during the 'Upside Down' sessions, had sacked their drummer because he wasn't on the same wavelength. One of Bobby's first gigs with the Mary Chain was alongside the Three Johns. They went bonkers and trashed their equipment. As a result they got half a page in *NME*, which said, 'This band are the new Sex Pistols.'

'I couldnae play the drums,' he later told the *Face*. 'I was just on the same level as them, I could understand. All of us had a romantic vision of rock 'n' roll, and we meant it. It was the best time of my fucking life.'

Primal Scream's first recorded material appeared on a cassette in the independent 'Pleasantly Surprised' series from Glasgow: two tracks called 'Intro' and 'Circumcision', which were basically in-yer-face white noise. Major influences were still the early Velvet Underground and PiL, but, eventually, they started easing into the West Coast pop sound of Love and the Byrds.

'We started off just making noise, a kind of release,' commented Bobby. 'It was very cathartic,' he told the *Face* in 1991. 'I was rolling around on the floor screaming, it was brilliant. Gradually we became more melodic.'

The influence of the Velvet Underground on both the Primals and the JAMC cannot be overestimated. Lou Reed's descriptive drug narratives like 'Heroin' and 'I'm Waiting For The Man' had materialised during the summer of love emanating from San Francisco. 'If you're going to

New York City, be sure to stick a needle in your arm,' was a top singalong retaliation to Scott McKenzie's hit of the time amongst the darker contingent. The hippies didn't like it, but the sheer impact of noise via electrical appliances, generated by the leather-and-shades cool Velvets, had to be felt to be believed, and that's what Bobby wanted. His band at the time couldn't quite cut it, but he found deafening salvation over in Camp Mary Chain.

The Velvet Underground: Black shades, white heat.

The Mary Chain sound was dissonant and brainsplitting, but carried undertows of surf music and classic pop. Bobby's first Primal Scream sessions were along the same lines, with those same heavy Velvets/Stooges influences. He later told me how this mentality got shaped, using the Velvets as an example: 'John Cale was hanging out with avant garde and jazz musicians and that influenced the Velvets, right? It brought that element of weirdness to it but maybe it was just a rock 'n' roll heart. In the end it made a great band. It's just things like that. That's where it came from. I remember with your Public Image interview and Rotten said, "I want our productions to sound like shit." That's saying something.'

This is all formative years stuff. Be inspired by a group, form a group, even if you can't play an instrument. Do a fanzine, start a club, fuck people up like the early Pistols, or even the Velvets back in 1967 or Suicide in 1977. Or stoke tears with the beauty and soulfulness of music itself. The Scream have always hated polite, complacent musical safety. Insurrectionism runs in the blood of Bobby Gillespie and his kindred souls. Or, as he put it in *Melody Maker*, 'I just want to prove how great music can be, how tragic it can be. Everything music does for me. I want to do it for other people.'

That ethic has stuck to this day. But if Bobby was fired up by punk in the late seventies, by the mid-eighties he was becoming increasingly smitten by American psychedelic rock and pop, in particular Love. Love's Arthur Lee remains one of his greatest inspirations and heroes. He was still checking him out in concert in 2003.

You could call Love a kind of proto-Scream blueprint. They dressed in the required psychedelic fashion of 1967-68 but, underneath the floral shirts and hipster strides, were more like a junked-up street gang. Look at their faces, scowling blankly behind shades on the first two albums. The popular saying at the time was that they should change their name to Hate. Into every drug under the sun, mysterious deaths surrounded them and Lee would eventually go down in the nineties for possessing a gun. One day in 1967, I was listening to pirate station Radio London. DJ John Peel said, 'This is the most beautiful record I've ever heard,' and lobbed on the ethereal Spanish delicacy of 'The Castle' from Love's second album *Da Capo*. One day on the tour bus nearly 30 years later, Bobby agreed that it's one of the most gorgeous things ever committed to tape. To my mind, it's the spiritual father of 'Higher Than The Sun'.

Love were punks before punk. You have to remember the musical terms 'punk' and 'garage' originally applied to disenfranchised kids emulating their musical heroes in both lifestyle and music. Punks were much-loathed street-gang leather boys, as in 'Hey boy, you a punk?' – bosh! – and 'garage' bands were so called because they normally got it together in their parents' garage. Names like the Shadows of Knight, the Cryin' Shames, the Standells, the Seeds, even Bob's beloved Thirteenth Floor Elevators, started in the garage.

Love were hoodlums with soul and genius, so Bobby had role models upon whom he could

Arthur Lee and Love: *The first album, bringing hate into the summer of love.*

weld his punk aesthetic. The Byrds were more of a melodic influence, with their jingle-jangle guitars and multi-tiered harmonies, which so influenced Bobby and Jim when they started taking songwriting seriously. You can still hear 'Eight Miles High' shining through on *Evil Heat*'s opening shot, 'Deep Hit Of Morning Sun'.

'When we started we wanted to make a record as good as the Byrds or the Beatles but our ambitions outweighed our ability. We always wanted to be a big group but we wanted to write beautiful songs. What other people were doing we considered grey. We wanted to do something like our heroes, not like indie music which I thought was stiff and grey. We wanted to do something uplifting. But when we started we just made a noise, we couldn't do anything else. Then we started learning to write songs properly.'

Meanwhile, Creation had been up and running properly since 1984. The label was based above a tiny club over the Roebuck pub in Tottenham Court Road. They hitched up with Rough Trade for distribution, got a grant from the Enterprise Allowance Scheme and stuck out singles by McGee's own band Biff Bang Pow, Revolving Paint Dream, Jasmine Minks and the Pastels.

Speaking to Keith Cameron in a major *NME* feature about the label in early 1994, McGee said, 'For the first six years I was a total chancer. I blagged it. All I did was keep choosing the right band and then try not to fuck it up too much, which I usually did . . . nobody taught me how to run a record company and I've made millions of mistakes. Luckily I've never got it wrong to the point of going out of business, but I've nearly been out of business three times in the last ten years.'

McGee's fearless attitude and knack of fingering what's cool rarely faltered in the early days. The first Creation masterstroke was signing the Mary Chain and putting out 'Upside Down', which sold 35,000 copies. Bobby was now their semi-permament drummer after the original one had left, standing up to play a single snare and cymbal like Mo Tucker in the Velvets amidst a wall of feedback. McGee was also their manager, so after 'Upside Down' he secured a nice deal for them with Warner Bros. offshoot Blanco Y Negro, giving them the budget to record the *Psychocandy* album.

In the same *NME* feature Bobby talked about how he'd introduced the JAMC to the guy he'd befriended ten years before the Scream existed: 'I remember no-one liked the Mary Chain, they sent demos to every fucking record label in England, to every promoter and no-one would give 'em a gig. I sent a tape to McGee and he loved it, he put out "Upside Down" and it went crazy from there. If it wasn't for "Upside Down" Creation wouldn't have existed. None of the other acts he had were good-looking enough, could write songs like that, or had that attitude. Those guys had vision, such intensity of focus – such a beautiful band, man.'

Primal Scream had made a four-track demo, including 'We Go Down Slowly Rising' and, unsurprisingly, signed to Creation too. After 'The Orchard' was aborted, their first single was 'All Fall Down' in May 1985.

Bobby was definitely leading a double life at this time. 'All Fall Down' was a jangly pop song, highly influenced by those West Coast Dylan-influenced folk-rockers the Byrds. Songs like 'Mr Tambourine Man' and 'All I Really Want To Do', and their distinctive twelve-string Rickenbacker sound, played a great role in shaping the early Scream sound. Obviously, Bobby and Jim had needed a rhythm section, so the band now also consisted of Robert Young on bass, Tom McGurk on drums and some bloke called Martin St John on, erm, tambourine. Bobby had grown a fringe and the band sported an array of polka dot shirts, leather and psychedelic finery in the fashion of the sixties West Coast bands – 'but I don't quite think we pulled it off,' he now admits in retrospect.

As he told *Melody Maker* at the time: 'We want to be seen as a really brilliant pop group that looks good as well as sounds good. We hated all the music around '83-'84. We thought it was stale and there was nobody you could admire. Look at this picture of Johnny Thunders. That was taken in 1973. He's dressed completely in leather and his hair's everywhere – he looks totally brilliant, like Keith Richards circa '66, or Johnny Rotten circa '77. It's not just the music. Certain people in pop music are inspirational. Y'know, they make you want to do something, they make you want to be in a band.'

And there was still the Mary Chain.

In 1985 I was deejaying at a London psychedelic club called Alice In Wonderland, along with Doctor of the Medics. We played pure, cranking garage psychedelia with smatterings of UK stuff and – my specialty – the Stooges/MC5, plus a bit of mad electro! One night we had the Jesus and Mary Chain playing. I'd heard stories about their gigs turning into riots, both onstage and off-stage, and, prepared for the worst/best, stuck on MC5's 'Starship' as they took the small stage.

It was instant carnage. Bobby smashed his snare under a total wall of feedback from guitarists who seemed hell-bent on inflicting as much brain damage as possible. The singer shouted and screamed and they seemed to be on the verge of an onstage ruck. The crowd – more used to beatific kaftan music – started heckling. A few things got thrown at them. The group had some kind of fight. Gear went toppling, the crowd were howling, 'Get off!' and it all screeched to a glorious, grinding halt about twelve minutes later. I thought it was the most exciting thing I'd encountered since Suicide got bottled off at the Music Machine in 1977. 'Oh my God,' said Christian, the normally tranquil promoter. Fantastic, I thought, as I regained my headphones and whacked on Alice Cooper before offering the drummer a line of speed. 'Just another gig,' seemed to be the band's response, as they continued bickering, but underneath they knew that their London debut had created the kind of impact we sorely needed back then. It was like 'LA Blues' – the last track on the Stooges' *Fun House* album – set in a Glasgow backstreet in a sea of broken bottles and transported onto a trendy London stage. And this happened at every gig.

'They used to fight on stage a lot,' recalls Bobby. 'I just used to stand back and watch.' But he was often at the centre of the action – not fighting with his fellow band members, just stirring things up and having fun. Like the time he kicked down the door of a crammed North London Poly to let in the kids who didn't have tickets. Everyone joined in the riot and it hit the headlines. At a Danish gig in 1985 William started screaming, 'You bacon-eating bastards!' and it all went off. 'I nipped away with some girls to take some more speed at that point,' elaborates Bobby.

Bobby miraculously also found time to run his Splash One club in Glasgow. It was named after a Thirteenth Floor Elevators

The limited edition JAMC 'riot single' package released in 1985. Syringe, piece of Bobby's shirt and bad jokes included.

1986 Primal Scream contract for Wendover's Division One club, near Aylesbury. Note modest rider consisting of lager and sandwiches.

song and ran from September 1985 until early 1986. Bob was trying to provide a good setting for bands, including Sonic Youth, the JAMC and 23 Skidoo, and also got to play his favourite records.

'We used to put bands on and held it in a discotheque because we hated universities and pubs and all those kind of adult establishments,' he told me a few years later. 'We just wanted to get away from that music biz type thing and do our own thing. It'd start at ten and we'd play our favourite records and have support bands and, at twelve, the band would come on and play for 40 minutes. Then we'd play records until about two o'clock. The kids used to stay and take acid, get drunk and take speed and stuff and have a good time. It was meant to turn a lot of kids on to a lot of music that they'd never heard before. It was good.'

The JAMC went on to gain further infamy by more riots, fights and pure noise assaults. When booked to play a five-date tour in January 1985, they only played one. Soon they were trashing the PA, and themselves, at every gig, with one at London's Electric Ballroom ending up as a proper riot involving Millwall and Chelsea fans. People were now getting hurt and the music was taking a backseat. That was how they 'unplanned' their initial impact – before they made classic pop records like 'Some Candy Talking' and gained a reputation as the UK's answer to the Velvet Underground. Their approach was pure V.U. – sonorous vocals and wistful pop melodies, enmeshed in the most calamitous sheet-metal guitar onslaughts since the finale to 'Heroin', all underpinned by Bobby's metronomic snare. They were lauded and written about by music papers who had nothing more exciting to write about than Yes reforming, or any number of simpering indie-shoegazers.

Towards the end of 1985 the group put out a very limited package in a polythene bag on Fierce Recordings, who'd already unleashed Charles Manson's *Love And Terror Cult* LP, a scorcher from my flatmate Youth, of ferocious funk punks Killing Joke, an EP by a group called Shame, 'the only band to have been kicked off Creation Records for misbehaviour,' a re-release of Warhol-proteges the Crash Action Winners' rare 'Two Trains' single, and some releases by Australian sonic terrorist Jim 'Foetus' Thirwell, who was mates with the likes of Nick Cave and Marc Almond.

The JAMC package contained a seven-inch recording of a riot scene at their infamous August 1985 London Polytechnic gig. No need to worry about musical copyright – it's just onstage chaos with lots of crashes and inter-band shouting. There's also a postcard containing 'Ten Whoppers From Jesus And Mary Chain,' like 'Stealing the wallet of a certain record company boss,' 'Not knowing the names of guitar parts,' 'Only having sex out of doors,' 'Heroin thrills – highly dubious!!!', 'Scratching your name on the R-Trade table,' 'Big riot, ah what a pity aye boys . . . ???' and 'Only taking speed and acid, pass me a joint man,,,??' There was also a syringe, a piece of Bobby's shirt, a 'Jesus Suck' badge and a JAMC 'LSD bar'. The accompanying press release, striking a punk rock stance, reads, 'So fuck 17 year old Alan McGhee [sic] up the fudge-tunnel with a big long stick – the ads are this moment in the music press and immortality/bankruptcy is just around the wee corner, laddie . . . also included in the new JAMC single will be Alan McGhee action man figures with full leather coatees – again the world waits with fevered excitement and come in its pants.'

Yes, we see. The label was based in Swansea, hell-bent on exaggerating punk attitude till it became an early embodiment of the 'aren't I shocking?' Marilyn Manson goth number.

So there's Bob in the most notorious group to hit this country since the Pistols, as well as continuing to pursue his own project. Alan McGee was venting his own passion by spurring on the Mary Chain as their manager and turning indie-dom into a viable enterprise without losing his buzz (or being shafted up the fudge-tunnel with a big long stick), while Innes was playing in Revolving Paint Dream.

'I was just young and didn't really know what I was doing,'

Beyond the fringe: a very early Primal Scream line-up consisted of (left to right) Jim Beattie, Bobby Gillespie, and Robert Young, aka Throb.

Bob told *NME* when the Mary Chain were placed at number 29 in the paper's Top 50 Artists of All Time chart in April 2002. 'You don't know anything when you're 24, you're just going along for the ride. It was meant to be a laugh but it got totally out of control. We did cap it in the end. We went to America, made *Psychocandy* and sold half a million albums. It was my first shot on goal and I scored.'

Bobby went on to play on classic JAMC material once they got past that riot stage: 'Some Candy Talking', the *Psychocandy* album and on into 1986, when they were really hitting it off. After the UK tour in February 1986, they asked Bobby to abandon Primal Scream and join them as a full-time drummer. But, despite what seemed like guaranteed stardom, Bobby felt compelled to leave for the sake of his own group, which had been lying dormant. He'd carried off the odd support slot with Primal Scream before leaping up to play that snare with the JAMC, but it was time to move on.

In August 2002, he told *Mojo*'s Keith Cameron, 'I had an amazing time. I loved those three guys. I loved the group, I loved the music. But they called us up and said, "we want you to be our full-time drummer and leave Primal Scream." And I was really broken up about it, because at that time I was having a better time with the Mary Chain than I was with our band, but I knew I could write songs, and I don't have the audacity to think I could've written songs for that band. I wouldn't have even tried, they were so incredible. I just thought, I love being in that band, but I think I'm a better songwriter than I am a drummer. It broke my heart but . . . it's worked out all right.'

The second Primal Scream single was 'Crystal Crescent', a year after the first. By now another school friend, Paul Harte, had joined the band on guitar. Away from the sonic assault of the JAMC, Bobby was still chilling to jangly West Coast nirvana around this time. These were good records which came over like a huge fan paying homage to his inspirations. Bobby later said he hated the A side – 'we were too fussy . . . and it had no spirit' – but Creation had paid good money for the recording and insisted it came out. It was the flip, 'Velocity Girl', which really pricked ears during its 90-second pop-punk rush. That track was also included on the *NME*'s now legendary *C86* cassette given away free with the paper, and John Peel made the tune number four in his celebrated 'Festive 50' for that year. Later, the Stone Roses' 'Made Of Stone' would almost play like a cover version.

Bobby stares down the camera on an early single, 'Sonic Flower Groove.', from 1987.

Primal Scream were now doing regular gigs – including a couple up the road from my home town of Aylesbury at the Wellhead Inn (later closed for putting on live sex shows during Saturday lunchtimes). According to promoter Robin Pike, the group flashed on, played for about 25 minutes and were gone. People at the bar were still asking when the band were coming on after they'd finished their high-velocity Byrds-blitz. The rider was a few cans of lager – a far cry from the several bottles of Jack Daniel's, vodka, wine and crates of beer demanded five years later. It was at this same spot that they'd debut *Screamadelica* live, at Jeff Barrett's birthday bash in mid-1991, between sets from Paul Oakenfold and Andrew Weatherall.

Around this time Bobby was getting worried that his band were being lumped in with the indie-wimp shoegazing trend – pure soppiness that was totally the opposite of punk, or even rock 'n' roll. Bobby was quick to distance himself in *Melody Maker*: 'We have nothing in common with all those bands [though Rickenbackers were a trademark of that sound]. We got a phone call asking us to be on an *NME* compilation and we said okay. That's all. If you look at my record collection you'll see I have no time for that sort of stuff. Independent music is pretty inferior. They can't play their instruments and they can't write songs. Independent music means anyone can make a record and that's a bad thing. There have been more crap records made in the last eight years than ever before.'

Hartie left in December 1986, to become the Electric Cowboy. After trying out another guitarist called Stuart May they were joined by Andrew Innes, who had been continuing to put out singles with Revolving Paint Dream on Creation and had also played with McGee's own group, Biff Bang Pow! Two more singles ensued when McGee started a new, ill-fated label called Elevation with the backing of Warner Bros. 'Gentle Tuesday' – released in June 1987 – was another Byrdsy one. The previous tracks had been produced by Creation man Joe Foster, but this one fell to Mayo Thompson, a semi-legend who used to put out deranged American pop music under the name Red Crayola. They also tackled a cover of 'I'm Gonna Make You Mine' by the Shadows of Knight, one of the best-known sixties American garage bands. 'Imperial' followed in September, notable for a languid b-side trawl through the Who's 'So Sad About Us'. It managed to scrape into the top 60.

And they were still trying to make their first album. The group had tried out Rockfield studios in Wales, birthplace of many a rock classic, and strained the Creation budget with producer Stephen Street. He might later produce Blur's studie-pop anthem 'Parklife', but the Scream were nonplussed with the results.

As Bobby told *Melody Maker*, 'We got too fucked, the musicians weren't good enough and Street couldn't really handle it.' They elected to start again with Mayo Thompson at the controls, but Bobby later reckoned they'd wrung out the record's soul in the re-recording. *Sonic Flower Groove* – released in September – was Byrdsy, psychedelic and poppy, all with good intentions. But the true spiritual power which infuses Primal Scream was buried or not nurtured to its full potential. The album got slagged off, and basically split the band. A disillusioned and burned-out Jim Beattie left to form Spirea X and realise his Byrds fantasies to the full with a couple of singles and the album *Fireblade Skies*.

At this point Primal Scream were down to the hardcore trio of Bob, Throb and Innes. Bobby had got fed up with all the commuting to Glasgow and crashing in London, so along with Innes and Throb – by now earning his nickname – he relocated to Brighton. They'd heard it was fun there.

Hair grew, light refreshments flowed, leather replaced lace and high-energy rock 'n' roll boot-

Kick out the jams: Innes and Bobby accelerating onstage around the time of the second album.

ed out aural prettiness. They also recruited a new rhythm section when former Nico back-up players Toby Tomanov and Henry Olsen joined on drums and bass, respectively. Now, this was a gang. Wasted, raunched-up and bent on sonic attack. Throb and Innes were fellow punks from the old days so, cheesed off with being jangly, they reinvented their sound.

'I was sick of the old style,' Bobby told *Melody Maker*. 'We'd taken it as far as we could. So we started to jam and write new material in Brighton and we became a rock 'n' roll band. To be honest, that's when I first started to really enjoy being in Primal Scream.

'We do what we fucking do and we like it. If you don't like it, fuck you. We know we're a great rock group. When we really hit we're the greatest group on the fucking planet . . . We've got more drive, now. Now Primal Scream can be anything from hard Les Paul rock to string quartets . . .'

Loaded with this fuck-you attitude, the group could fully vent their New York Dolls and Stooges obsessions – behaviour-wise as well as musically. Johnny Thunders from the Dolls was the band hero.

The New York Dolls had sprung out of the Big Apple like rampaging glam-maggots in the early seventies. They wore second-hand women's clothes while pumping out high-octane rock 'n' roll with a slash of glam. Johnny Thunders was the band's Keef Richards, its core and its heart, with black hair exploding everywhere as he lunged through Eddie Cochran riffs, and an amazing fallabout slide style he'd perfected. Thunders was also a heroin addict, along with drummer Jerry Nolan, who both went on to form the Heartbreakers. They were notorious for their excesses, and both died of them.

I spent several afternoons with Johnny and found him a lost soul with a true passion for music . . . and drugs. I saw him for the last time in the toilets at a New York club where he was playing around 1988. I was in worse shape than him, so, obviously, Johnny tried to borrow twenty dollars. A few years later I was mortified to read about his seedy death in a New Orleans hotel room. There were suggestions he'd taken – or been spiked with – acid, which he never touched normally, and had been robbed. The circumstances suggested he died from a methadone overdose but are still shrouded in mystery. But this man wrote 'Born To Lose' and 'You Can't Put Your Arms Around A Memory', which Bobby has often described as one of his favourite songs ever. I hear it in practically every Scream ballad. Sensitive, beautiful and emotional, with a subtle twist. And Thunders' sheer attitude spatters every Scream rocker.

The other side of Thunders was the rampant excess. This began to be mirrored in the Scream towards the end of 1987, when their reputation for certain refreshments started to blossom. Now black leather hoodlums, they were committing stun-guitar assaults and the Byrds were but a distant memory. Throb was growing his hair, strutting like a rock god, and it was getting loud out there. Bobby was howling at the moon or stroking the devil's erogenous zones. The group was firing up.

NME later got Bobby reflecting on this period: 'We just got on with living the same lifestyle even if we hadn't been in a band. I would, Robert would and Andrew would still have taken as many drugs and done the things we did. You should always be able to indulge yourself, you should always be free to do exactly what you want. It's just fucking England, it's too puritan, it's too uptight. It's not loose enough. It's much better to be loose. You can be loose but at the same time be moral. But British people are definitely too reserved. I think we're different from most British people.'

So the Primal Scream legend was under way and the band did nothing to stop it. Now they were like a proper gang, having the time of their lives, and the music was beginning to lead up to what was coming up. 'Ivy, Ivy, Ivy' was released as a single in September 1989, and uncorked a new high-energy rock 'n' roll guitar barrage, not unlike those MC5 boys. Unfortunately a confused music press didn't get it, and it didn't sell. *Melody Maker*'s Simon Price reckoned that 'all Primal Scream have actually done is ditch their crappy Byrds obsession and hit the fast forward from 1966 to 1969, through post-Altamont Stones and Detroit garage to electrified Bolan.' Undeterred, the band continued to gig relentlessly and became increasingly more wild.

Duffy has always been the joker in the pack since he joined Primal Scream.

The single trailered their second, eponymous album. It was a pure, raw rock 'n' roll affair which veered between high-octane asaults like 'Gimme Gimme Teenage Head' and 'She Power' to stoned ballads like 'Jesus Can't Save Me' and 'I'm Losing More Than I'll Ever Have'. The album was also met with little acclaim at the time but 'I'm Losing More Than I'll Ever Have' was to have a profound effect on the group's future. Credited on the sleeve: 'Piano by Martin Duffy.'

Enter Martin Duffois from Birmingham, who'd been in respected Creation band Felt and played on their acclaimed *Train Above The City* in 1988. The first Scream track he played on was 'I'm Losing More Than I'll Ever Have'. That piano figure was what beshaped the Weatherall-overhaul of imminent classic 'Loaded'. He didn't look back. What with his Aston Villa fixation, fascination with alcohol and extraterrestrial rants about the virtues of Mr Kipling's Bramley apple pies and brown corduroy underpants, Duffy was tailor-made for the new Scream team gestating beneath the gathering acid-house thunderstorm.

Words like 'glove' and 'fit' spring to mind. He can take it there, and he has the same fascination for music as the rest. You can always tell a Duff piano lick. He might look like he's going to keel over any second, but the magic stroked from those fingers has captivated and impressed everyone from Tom Dowd to George Clinton, not to mention the Scream. What more could

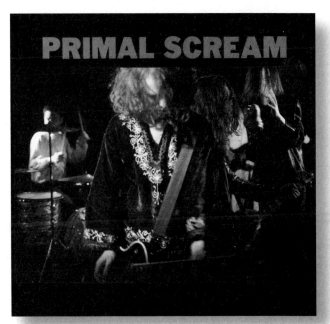

you want – a piano-sparking genius who lets loose an endless stream of verbal entertainment, and finds it perfectly natural to stick a fake pineapple on his head at the soundcheck? The man is hilarious, with more dodgy stories than *Roger Mellie's Profanosaurus*. It's my ambition to get Duff to write a film for which he does the music *and* the comedy sketches.

Duffy wasn't really *in* the group until he'd bashed some keyboard devastation into *Screamadelica*, after the success of 'Loaded'. That's him on 'Movin' On Up', caressing it like one of the Memphis guys on the ballads and filling Brian Wilson's surf-pants with soul on tracks like 'Inner Flight'.

Kings of speed: The second album.

Bobby whisked me aside when we were talking one day. 'We've got a guy called Martin Duffy, who plays with us and he's like a Nicky Hopkins for the nineties,' he told me. 'He's only 23 and he understands music.' Nicky fuckin' Hopkins. That's a tall order. He played all the great keyboards for the Stones in that *Beggars Banquet-Let It Bleed* era, including 'Sympathy For The Devil'.

Martin's style recalls the great New Orleans piano players. There's a book called *A Left Hand Like God* and it centres on the boogie-woogie style that first emerged in New Orleans in the early years of the last century. There were guys like Professor Longhair and Phineas Newborn, who blew apart their pianos and pioneered a technique which involved the left hand as much as the right. Duffy knew about all this, but also knew Willie Mitchell's Hi Recordings work with such soul saints as Al Green. Rampant funk attack and soft, silken keys in the same soul bag. .

By the time of *Screamadelica*, Duffy would be an integral part of Primal Scream. As Bobby describes, 'We were doing a track called "Shine Like Stars" and at the end we were putting on these star sounds. He was saying, "I'm in the stars and I'm looking down at New Orleans." We had him in that night and he was wasted and telling us about how in 1905 the Professor [Longhair] came to New Orleans. He started telling us about the left-handed piano player – Professor Longhair and guys like that. The way he did it was really good. Then he was talking about animals – "skunk? He got skink!" Total free association. But it was cool. It was poetic. That guy could play with Sun Ra's band. I believe he's that good and he's only 23, I think. He's steeped in it. He loves everything – rockabilly, jazz, blues, funk, disco, acid house, rock 'n' roll. He's cool.

'He could think of things to do that no-one else had ever done and then do them. He had, like another pianist observed, "a boogie-woogie left hand, a bebop right hand and this third hand."'

After that ballad on the second album turned into the supernova that was 'Loaded', Duffy eased his way into becoming the fourth core member of Primal Scream. 'Is William Burroughs still dead?' is a characteristic Duff-style comment.

But that second album was widely dismissed at the time as a turkey of the highest order. Apart from, that is, by an occasional *NME* contributor, *Boys Own* fanzine writer and budding DJ called Andrew Weatherall.

It was time to get Loaded. And have a good time.

Throb, Innes and Bobby behind the wheel in Brighton, 1990.

'Loaded' And The Making Of Screamadelica

'I think white rock music is in a slump. Most of the exciting things around seem to be happening in black dance music.' – *Bobby Gillespie, 1989*

By mid-1989 the Scream had been bitten by the smiley face of acid house, discovered ecstasy and realised that this was the most exciting musical movement to come along since their beloved punk rock. Of course it was quite the opposite of the high-energy rock 'n' roll and gentle ballads that made up the second album, but Bobby loved nothing better than excitement and innovation. Here was something he could really relate to.

Bobby already loved disco and Motown. Now, drugs went hand-in-hand with the pioneering efforts of producers in Chicago and Detroit to create a new strain of music that white kids could lose their melons to. There was the indie-dance thing, courtesy of great bands like Happy Mondays and the Stone Roses, but going to raves at Shoom nights and the Zap Club in Brighton was planting a seed in Bobby, Innes and Throb (who even played a few gigs as an Italian House DJ). Acid house was just what the band needed, but even they could never have predicted the eventual outcome.

Initially, the Scream found it difficult to wind down from speed-frazzled MC5-style high-energy rock 'n' roll to the blissed-up locations they would visit on *Screamadelica*. Just a little pill will go the longest, to quote a well-known reggae artist.

Jeff Barrett and Alan McGee were ecstasy missionaries. Wizards of the (as they were soon-to-be-known) 'little fellas' or 'Jeffs' – after Detroit techno masterblaster Jeff Mills, geddit? – who set about turning on the Scream, having been converted themselves at Paul Oakenfold's Ibiza-inspired Shoom and Future nights.

Nobody could have predicted the youth revolution which would be sparked by acid house. When the early anthems like Farley Jackmaster Funk's 'Love Can't Turn Around' and DJ Pierre's seminal 'Acid Tracks' appeared – and DJs started making an art of mixing them together – it turned everything upside down, like punk rock. Except this turned into a world movement which continues to grow and develop. Amidst the corporate world of mid-eighties American dance music, the wild new sounds lunging out of Chicago and Detroit had a seismic effect that soon spread across the water. The tunes got picked up by DJs like Danny Rampling, Pete Tong, Paul Oakenfold, Dr Alex Paterson and the aforementioned Andrew Weatherall, burst forth at London clubs like Heaven, Gossips and the Wag, and there was genuine excitement in the air.

All these stirrings were compounded and combusted by a drug called ecstasy.

The little fellas had first turned up in London around 1982 when a friend of Marc Almond's called Cindy, erm, Ecstasy brought some over from New York. My first encounter was at Steve Strange's night at the Camden Palace, from Cindy's batch. Expecting the usual speed pill, I was quite surprised to later find myself hugging people I usually avoided. But the stuff didn't really start filtering through in large quantities until a few years later, when places like Ibiza, swiftly followed by London, caught on. By 1987 – when the Scream were introduced to it via Alan McGee – a whole new drug-fuelled movement was raging, based around the inspiration of house music. However, the Balearic movement – which basically meant you could play anything and people would dance – was also coming up. This is what let the Scream in.

When they were touring for their second album, playing that high-energy rock 'n' roll in black leather, the tour bus listening was house and soul. Heavenly Records' Jeff Barrett is one of the longest-running friends of the Scream, has been their press officer, and their A&R manager, one of the most passionate people about music I've ever met. I don't see many record industry bosses getting raging bollocksed, leaping about to a record in the office if it curdles their custard, or racing around the world following a band purely for the reason that they love the music. And they're not even on his label! Jeff is the master of turning people on to new sounds and was seriously instrumental in getting the Scream into acid house. Along with the recently-converted Alan McGee, he'd send tapes of new tunes to the boys to play when they were on tour. He also took them to the hot clubs of the time.

'We were all bang on it,' McGee told *Uncut's* Michael Bonner at the end of 1999. 'We were all just E heads. I was phoning Bobby at four in the morning saying, "This is amazing! Shaun Ryder on stage in gold lamé punching the air!" Gillespie's going, "sounds amazing, McGee – what are the drugs like?" And I was going, "fucking awesome – you've got to get some of this!" So we took them along to thier first club.'

'We spent ages trying to get the band involved,' added Barrett. 'They were kind of sceptical at the time. It wasn't where their heads were at, or they just didn't get it at first. But they were aware something was happening because they'd seen a change in me and Alan. Then they started dipping their toes in, and it took them all five minutes to realise what joys could be had with ecstasy. Then I met Weatherall through Richard Norris [then one half of the Grid, now in the Droyds and running God Made Me Hardcore Records – the label I'm on!]. This became really important in the scheme of things.'

'McGee and Barrett were missionaries,' said Bobby to Paolo Hewitt in his *Positive Energy Of Madness* interview. 'We were touring the country, playing these high energy MC5 rock 'n' roll songs, but it was house tapes in the van and taking these E's and speed. We'd play some gig in Hull and drive back to London, long-haired, leathered-up and dancing away. That was a great time for us because we opened up to a lot of music. I used to go to these acid house clubs with long hair and I'd deliberately go in my leathers. It was good because people would look at you and think "what the fuck is that?" I used to sit in the club up on the railings, E'd up, getting ideas for lyrics and songs and people would be saying "who the fuck is that guy?" Really good time.'

'People aren't going to gigs any more,' he declared in *Melody Maker*. 'They're going to clubs. What I like about the dance thing is people want to participate. The heroes are the people on the floor, not the people onstage. For a long time I've found it really hard work going to rock concerts. It really pisses me off to walk into a venue to find there's no sense of excitement or danger and none of the atmosphere that I can remember from when I went to see bands like The Clash.

'A rave or a club is an entirely different matter. The music is energetic and people have an adventurous spirit. The whole house scene has the same kind of vibrancy that punk used to have. That's why so many young kids are into it. They wanna get loaded, get wasted and have a fuckin' good time. Generally, I walk down the street and want to kill myself. I don't wanna be part of the

Bright lights, bright eyes: Innes, Throb and Bobby on the rampage in Soho, London, 1990.

human race, but now there's a real buzz.'

That second album didn't exactly set the world on fire but, compared to the 1989 climate of soppy indie waftings, it stood as a piece of flawed rock 'n' roll honesty. On the other hand, next to the pulsating acid-house exploration erupting in the clubs, it was decidedly retro. By the time of the album's release the group were already getting raved up. When they toured Europe to promote it they felt like they'd left that sound behind. By now the group were so fucked anyway that different members of the band kept ending up in the wrong country, and the jaunt was scrapped.

Alan McGee still stuck by his old mates, as he recalled in the *NME* feature celebrating ten years of Creation in 1994: 'I've been friends with those three boys now for twenty years, ten years before their group. You've got to remember that when they came off Elevation, Primal Scream were fucking cold. I was probably the only person in the world that really loved them and so, whether we liked it or not, we were there for each other. From where they've come is pretty fascinating. The big thing for them and me was discovering acid house in 1988.'

Around this time, the sun began to poke a smiley face above the clouds for Primal Scream. A young DJ-journalist called Andrew Weatherall had appeared on the scene and liked their album.

Andrew grew up around Windsor. In May 1992, he told *Mixmag*'s Mandi James that he used to wander around with a hand-held cassette recorder playing David Bowie's 'Rock 'N' Roll Suicide' over and over again. 'Bowie really inspired me. It was like if you ever need evidence for not being normal then here it is, this is what it's all about. Then I saw the Sex Pistols and that was it. Punk was supposed to break down all the barriers and for a while it did, it really inspired me,

Andrew Weatherall wakes up in Birmingham on the Screamadelica *tour, '91.*

but eventually all it did was create a new set of rules. That's what has happened now.'

The young Weatherall was passionate about buying records, an enthusiasm that remains undimmed – 'I know that every day I can walk into a record shop and find a piece of music that's going to make the hairs on the back of my neck stand up. That's what I've done since I was about twelve.'

Andrew started off with the usual DJing at parties, met another DJ called Terry Farley and got some six-in-the-morning spots in London. He really got going when he discovered acid house at clubs like the Astoria and Danny Rampling's Shoom. Andrew was also part of the *Boys Own* crew with Farley, Steve Maize and Cymon Eccles, who put out an irreverent fanzine which centred on football and clubbing. They eventually started a record label and a musical collective called Bocca Juniors – whose 'Raise' and 'Substance' are rare classics.

One morning Andrew was playing at a party above a café in Islington and got chatting to Danny Rampling. Blown away by his selection, Danny gave Andrew a regular spot at Shoom – 'the club that started everything.' He never looked back, building a reputation as a brilliant mixer, and a DJ who always provided a fiercely unpredictable evening's entertainment. When 'Loaded' kicked off his remixing career he gained a similar reputation. Andrew sometimes didn't use any of the original track at all, but always seemed to retain the spirit of the song as his monstrously funky sonic tapestries were unfurled. He's continued to chart his own unique path, never compromising and always surprising. Andrew has never bowed to the obvious, if he had he'd be bigger than the likes of Paul Oakenfold. And it's why he got on so well with the Scream.

Late, lamented dance magazine *Seven* paid tribute to *Screamadelica* on the tenth anniversary of its release, even putting the Scream logo on the front cover. In the feature Helen Mead, who was *NME*'s live and dance reviews editor, told Anthony Teasdale how the Scream came to hitch up with Weatherall: 'I had three writers at the time who did various columns . . . Weatherall did the house. Andy came in one day and he was all pissed off because his column had been slashed in half . . . He said he wanted to do something really rock 'n' roll. At the time the Primals were doing the tour of their *Primal Scream* album and were having a tough time getting the press McGee expected them to get. They hadn't had a live review . . . and I had Barrett on the phone saying, "Alan's threatening to fire me if I don't get some press on the Primals." And I said, "well, look if I come up with the right person can we send someone down to do a couple of days on the road with them?" They were so desperate – that was the sort of thing no press officer would agree to do in a month of Sundays at the time – I sent Andrew down. That's how Weatherall and the Primals first met.'

The first time Andrew Weatherall met the Scream and Alan McGee was at a Shoom event in a field outside Brighton. At the time there was an evergrowing circle that took in Weatherall, The Orb, KLF, Youth, Richard Norris and now Barrett, McGee and future Heavenly artists like Flowered Up.

But the end result was that the band, by now firmly favouring 'the little fellas' over their traditional speed, asked Weatherall – who wrote the Exeter review under his Audrey Witherspoon pseudonym – to remix one of the tracks off the album. This was despite the fact that he'd never been in a studio before. He was particularly taken by the end section of a pleading soul ballad called 'I'm Losing More Than I'll Ever Have' and opted to do something with that.

'It was Andrew Innes who asked me one night at Spectrum,' recalled Andrew in *Seven*. '"Go in the studio with our engineer and do what you want." I was a bit scared at first 'cos I didn't know the rules. I didn't want to pull it apart. Innes came in and said, "that's not what you want to do is it?"'

So they went back in, threw the track out the window and grafted on a low-slung funk groove from Edie Brickell's 'I Am What I Am'. (This beat was also used by The Orb on the first demos for 'Little Fluffy Clouds' – coincidentally, Andrew was living in the flat above Alex Paterson's Battersea abode at the time!) He kept the Stax-like brass riff and extended everything to seven minutes, topped with dialogue by Peter Fonda from cult sixties film *The Wild Angels*: 'Just what is it that you wanna do?' They couldn't get hold of Peter Fonda to approve it, but someone at Warner Brothers persuaded his sister Jane to play it to him and he was cool. The only bit of Bobby left was a solitary 'oh yeah!' The result was called 'Loaded', and it was stunning.

'I start a remix bearing in mind that the band have already done what they think is the perfect mix so you don't need to touch that,' Andrew told Mandi James. 'I try to retain the spirit of the original and touch all the stuff that's imperfect which makes the remix more interesting.'

'The point is that, even though Andrew didn't know what the fuck he was doing, he had the attitude and enthusiasm to give it a go,' said Bob. 'That kind of spirit is what really matters and that's what's missing from so much of today's indie and rock music.'

'For ten years, I've never been able to make up my mind if I'm a punk rocker or a soul boy, so why not be both?' threw in Andrew.

'It didn't sound like anything I'd ever heard in my life before,' said then-Creation press officer Laurence Verfaillie. Jeff Barrett was bowled over as, in the space of a few weeks, this band that the music press had dismissed had come up with a cutting-edge monster that slayed anyone in its path, be they indie kid or dance loony.

'We did "Loaded" and it was fucking awesome,' recalled Jeff to *Seven*'s Anthony Teasdale. 'It was one of the best days of my fucking life when it got delivered. The day we heard that finished we were like, "fuck me, what's happened here?" Anything was possible.

'They really met a like mind in Andrew. I can't stress enough how much there's been psychedelia in that group. There's always been a rock 'n' roll element to Weatherall's music. It really was a meeting of minds that happened.'

'I see it as a dub record,' said Bobby. 'I think it's closer to the sort of radical reconstruction that Jamaican producers like Joe Gibbs used to do with reggae in '73 or '74 than anything else. "Loaded" taught us about rhythm and space. We've always been good at harmony, but learning how to use a sampler gave us a new palette of colours. The sampler opens up a whole new world of psychedelic possibilities.

'A record like "Loaded" could never have been made if there wasn't a vast chemical indulgence within this band. It's a celebration of getting loaded, isn't it?'

And so the die was cast, with everyone falling over 'Loaded', which was released in March 1990. The epitome of indie-dance, lauded by the media – apart from some quarters of a puzzled music press – it elevated the Scream to the status of coolest band in town. It became their first Top Twenty hit, reaching number sixteen. (Thirteen years later the full version was still playing in the bar of the Queen Vic in *Eastenders*.)

'In 1989 everybody hated our band,' Bobby told *Sky* magazine in 1992. 'No one came to see us. Not even the record company. I discard our first two albums. To get here we had to do what we did. Everyone starts out a bit weird.

'Our band has been truly touched by what's happened over the past couple of years: "Loaded" was a really honest statement.' As for the derision of the trad-rock press, he simply shrugged it off: 'they use the guitar as a symbol of goodness, like it's so much better than the fuckers making the dance records. Well no it isn't, a good record is a good record, however it's made. They have no feel for the music or the scene, no spirit for it. That record was a hit in an underground way; because what we did at the end of last year, Andy gave it to selected DJs so it was already creating a buzz. It had really big advance orders four weeks before it was released, so when it was released it went straight into the charts. It bypassed radio and the music press, just from people hearing it in the clubs, and saying, "what the fuck is this? I want to buy this record."'

Bobby revelled in finally giving vent to his passions and opinions in front of an attentive media. To the music press – some of whom had slagged off the by-now huge 'Loaded' – he came up with stuff like, 'Bands today aren't good enough. They're not beautiful enough. They're not sexy enough. They're not violent enough.'

Or, 'Releasing "Loaded" was a big risk for us. We could've alienated a lot of people who've supported us over the years but I don't think it matters when or how you make a record as long as it's good and means something to someone. All this is a big experiment for us. I think it's time to stop saying "this is a dance record" and "this is a rock record." If you can play music, you can do whatever you want. Just use your imagination . . .'

Fired up, they turned another track over to Andrew, who was now working with an engineer called Hugo Nicolson. Hugo hailed from Burnham Beeches near Slough and cut his studio teeth at West London's Townhouse Studios in the eighties, starting as teaboy and working up to engineering. Everyone used Townhouse, from Scritti Politti and Pepsi and Shirley to – 'there were some

good ones' – Bob Dylan, Ronnie Wood and Eric Clapton. His first major project was a Julian Cope album, which gave him a choice between working with Nick Cave/Birthday Party producer Flood on Depeche Mode or hitching up with this guy Weatherall for some remixes. Hugo was already getting severely into clubbing and chose the latter: 'I was working on a day to day engineering basis and heard that this DJ needed an engineer to work with him. The first track we worked on was "Abandon" but he'd already done stuff like "Only Love Can Break Your Heart" with St Etienne.'

Andrew and Hugo had worked on several groundbreaking remixes, which usually followed the approach of ditching most of the song, including vocals, and embarking on a remarkable musical journey into dubbed-out sonic skullduggery. This was the partnership which spawned *Screamadelica*, hatched it with the band and bolted out of the chickenhouse firing nuclear sonic eggs into the stratosphere. Basically, Andrew was the public face of the production team with brilliant ideas running around his brain. Hugo turned them into reality.

'Everything we ever did was always building to a crescendo at the end,' says Hugo now, as he fits in

Hugh Nicolson, Weatherall's right-hand man circa Screamadelica.

recording his own album with work for David Holmes. 'Andrew would bring in a bunch of ingredients and we'd put them together. A lot of people around me felt that I didn't get the credit but he was the person with the fun-bus who had all these ideas. I was the one who helped him put it together. It didn't really bother me. If he'd have worked with anyone else he still would have gone on. It is a funny one but Andy's a genius. People would say, "how does Andy do that stuff? It must be that bloke Hugo," but I really respect Andy for everything he does in the studio. It's confidence and taste in music and ability to understand music. He was always so positive.'

Their first Primals teamwork set the benchmark for *Screamadelica*. 'Come Together' had started life as a gorgeous Velvets-style pop ballad riding an acoustic guitar riff out of Elvis' 'Suspicious Minds' with loved-up lyrics and a rousing gospelly chorus. Our knob-twiddling heroes seized the chorus and planted it over a thudding acid house beat. The ever-growing groove reached a celebratory peak enhanced by a fiery plea for unity from Jesse Jackson: 'Today is a beautiful day / It is a new day / we are together/ 'Cos together we got power.'

If anything, the effect was even more earth-shattering than 'Loaded'. Weatherall unveiled it on acetate at his gigs – the first time Hugo experienced its effect in a club was at Dingwalls – and the crowds simply went apeshit. Just about the all-time-great loved-up anthem or end-of-nighter. The atmosphere that tune could stir was incredible, and being in a room full of saucer-eyed smiles as dawn rode in and the first strains of Andrew's slate boomed out remains one of my greatest ever clubbing moments. Perhaps because of the furore following 'Loaded' and the fact that it was included on *Screamadelica*, two accompanying versions of both tunes have been somewhat overshadowed. Another rising DJ from the *Boys Own* crew, Terry Farley, tackled both songs, his 'Come Together' focusing on Bobby's lovely vocal, which is totally absent on the Weatherall version, and the addition of the Tabernacle Choir. Keeping it in the family, it stoked the fires of the eclectic movement known as Balearic.

Bobby described the track at the time as 'a modern-day "Street Fighting Man"', referring to the Stones 1968 rabble-rouser. 'It's certainly not a statement of vapid New Age optimism. Rather, I see Weatherall's side as tragic – like, "if only the world could be as one but I know it never will be . . . You've just got to look at the country we're living in. Thatcher's policies are the policies of division and isolation. If someone stands up and says they believe in love and freedom, I think that's a strong thing.'

Turning their preferences from speed to ecstasy also made the band aware of the need for decent comedown music. Stones ballads, Southern soul, Brian Wilson's more beatific visions and spaced jazz were perfect Sunday evening chill-out balm.

The band started playing live again with a Japanese tour during the 1990 World Cup. Programmer Tony Hypnotone, merchandise man Grant Fleming and DJ Tim Tooher had joined the squad. It was the first time the band had swapped greasy rock for loved-up celebration.

Back in the UK the band were easing into *Screamadelica*, having bought an eight-track mixing desk and built a basic studio in Hackney. Much of what became *Screamadelica* was demoed there. One brain-watering taster was the cathartic solar orgasm that was 'Higher Than The Sun'. Enter Dr Alex Paterson, aka the linchpin and mad mind behind The Orb. The song had already been demoed in Hackney and Dr Paterson came in to steer it to the heavens.

The Orb – aka Dr Alex Paterson and friends – has been a unique force in music since its inception at the dawn of acid house. Alex has always had a special relationship with Primal Scream.

I first encountered Alex in the late seventies when he was a roadie for Killing Joke. By the early eighties I was sharing a flat with bass player Youth and Alex was a regular visitor. Amidst many hazy frolics, we'd play records ranging from sizzling dub plates to the blatantly stupid or classy disco tapes from New York's pioneering KISS FM radio station. You could say those tapes changed our lives, and those of several others on the London underground.

The station invented the 'Mastermix' technique, which involved cutting, splicing and sampling

Dr Alex Paterson takes time off from The Orb to warm up for the Scream, Cambridge, '91.

top tunes of the day to create epic new mutations. This set a kind of benchmark for the upcoming house-DJ explosion, and eventually Alex and Youth – plus another mate called Jimi Cauty – started making their own dance-based sound paintings as The Orb.

When I moved out in 1985, Alex moved in. A short time later, gripped by the new acid house explosion, they started turning out singles like 'Kiss' and 'Tripping On Sunshine', before Jimi left to form KLF. After the epic 'A Huge Ever Growing Pulsating Brain That Rules From The Centre Of The Ultraworld', The Orb went sky high and were credited with defining chillout – some called it ambient – music. But they also rocked the party and their 1991 debut album, *The Orb's Adventures Beyond The Ultraworld*, cemented it, paving the way for the chart success of 'Little Fluffy Clouds' and their second album, *UFOrb*, which reached number one. Youth went on to become a top producer/remixer and in came manic studio wiz Kris 'Thrash' Weston.

Alex met the Scream when he was spinning in the chill-out room at clubs like Shoom and Land of Oz. Weatherall lived upstairs, so he was soon in the camp. But the main bridge between the two camps came via Alex Nightingale, who acted as agent for both bands.

'That's the connection there,' recalls the good Doctor. 'Alex just said to them, "look, give 'em a chance. Give 'em a track to plink plonk upon." So we came out with "Higher Than The Sun". One of the singles of the nineties, really.'

The song was already a beatific drugs anthem. Alex and Thrash simply wrapped it in Technicolor gossamer and booted it into orbit, shimmering and reeling in a hallucinogenic mind-warp. The result was one of the greatest Scream songs ever, released in June 1991. It cemented the fact that this was now one of the greatest groups on the planet, even though it wasn't a hit. Bobby said later that he knew it probably wouldn't chart, but had to release it as 'a declaration of intent, a manifesto.'

'This is the best record we've ever made,' he enthused to the papers. 'It's as good as anything I've ever heard – as good as T. Rex, the Temptations or the Rolling Stones. We've actually made a classic record, a record that people will be able to listen to in 40 years time – and it will still be as relevant as it is now. It's got more in common with free jazz, John Coltrane and Ornette Coleman, than anything that's gone down in contemporary rock music in 1991. I'm happy about that. It's like a massive jump onto another planet . . . it sounds like the music of the future . . .

Bobby in flight at Tokyo's Club Quattro, during the 1990 Japanese tour.

Jah Wobble, shaking the foundations of Aylesbury's Reaction club, '92.

it's like a spaceman floating off into space. He's disconnected himself from the spaceship because he's looked at it and thought, "I ain't going back there." He's just expounding his philosophy and feeling about himself as he heads off into oblivion. As long as man exists and people listen to music, whoever finds "Higher Than The Sun", I know they'll be digging it.'

The Scream had already reckoned that Alex would make the perfect warm-up DJ for the *Screamadelica* gigs and he ended up spinning for them on all the tours.

'I had this fuckin' brilliant relationship with them for about eighteen months or something but I had to get on with The Orb. I couldn't just be DJing. The thing with "Higher" was it was an exceptional record and an exceptional moment for all of us. At that point they were like another project that was equally as good and me, Weatherall and Wobble were like the three corners, the axis of this and it worked.'

When Andrew Weatherall and Hugo came in to do their 'American Spring Mix – A Dub Symphony In Two Parts', they called in the mighty Jah Wobble to supply one of his trademark earth-shattering basslines. Wobble had also been a member of the original Public Image Ltd line-up which recorded *Metal Box*. A prime Scream influence playing on a Scream record. Proper.

'We needed a bassline, well there's only one man for the job,' recalls Weatherall, who went on to remix two singles by the bassman's Invaders of the Heart, 'Bomba' and 'Visions Of You', shortly afterwards. Wobble's theories about the bass at the time explain why he fit 'Higher' like a glove: 'I use a lot of sub lows. You can't hear it but you can feel it. Like 30 hertz causes difficulty in breathing. Low frequencies I find more comforting. Some people find them disturbing. Certain parts of the body resonate at different pitches. You can kill people with sonic attack. If you can find the resonation for the liver, for example, you can disintegrate it.' Not that the Scream needed any help in that department!

Wobble had his 'wild man of Borneo few years – I behaved like Keith Moon. Mental. Real rock 'n' roll.' But he gave up drink and drugs completely in the eighties. He later told me he thought the Scream were 'nutters' but rated them and Andrew as major talents he was happy to play with. 'Like John Lydon is a real character. They're bread and butter to me and they're few and far between in the music scene. Most people are so transparent.'

The single was also notable in that, for the first time, it boasted sleeve artwork by artist Paul Cannell. Cannell went for the abstract, splash-image approach and – with his paintings photographed by Grant Fleming – provided memorable images for all the *Screamadelica* singles. He also came up with the enduring Scream sun logo which graced the album sleeve, and still pops up today in various places.

Screamadelica

Around the 'Higher' time, the group took their show around the UK. They'd added Hugo Nicolson on programming, Martin Duffy and singer Denise Johnson to the line up with Alex Paterson and Andrew Weatherall on the decks. Denise was already an accomplished session singer, having sung with A Certain Ratio, Electronic and Hypnotone, as well as fronting Manchester indie band The Joy. She says she got into the Scream after hearing 'Loaded' but turned them down six times when asked to sing with them. But then she contacted them at Creation and ended up on tour, doing 'Don't Fight It'. She stayed with the group until early 1995 before embarking on a solo career, working with ex-Smith Johnny Marr on her first single, 'Rays Of The Rising Sun'. 'People said to me I'm like an act within an act,' said Denise in 1994 when she was essentially a member of Primal Scream. 'I'm not prepared to go and sing backing vocals and then go home. I want to feel a part of it. With Primal Scream I definitely feel like part of the group . . . I'm not saying I'm the best singer in the world. I'm not. But there's something I've got that people want and if I like what they're doing I'll give it.'

The tour climaxed at the now-legendary gig at the Empire in London's Leicester Square, which showed a band just getting better all the time. It was an awesomely messy affair, some of which is captured on Douglas Hart's *Screamadelica* video. They encored with John Lennon's 'Cold Turkey' and added snatches of John Coltrane's 'A Love Supreme' and Sly Stone's 'Don't Call Me Nigger, Whitey' to 'Higher Than The Sun'.

At this point, the upcoming album was just about finished, with the tracks that hadn't been singles completed in under two months. *Screamadelica* contained the previous three singles with both original and 'American Spring' versions of 'Higher', plus the upcoming 'Don't Fight It Feel It' and six other tracks. The sleeve would be a small detail, a big smiley sun, which Grant Fleming had plucked from the 'Higher' sleeve and blown up.

'I wish we were a lot more prolific than we are but we never have been . . . We work in our own time-scale,' said Bobby to *NME*'s James Brown. 'Working in our own time scale has, on occasion, meant checking into an expensive recording studio and then over-indulging on prescribed

Manchester's supreme diva Denise Johnson, who sang with the band through the first half of the nineties.

Denise joins Throb, Bobby and Innes for a gentle stroll around Soho, 1990.

medication that's left the band comatose, the engineer frantic and the record company bewildered.

'I was pretty addled at the time but I remember being in some expensive studios and having some fun,' Weatherall told *Seven*. 'I do remember the album because we were in an expensive studio costing thousands of pounds a day [Often Jam Studios in Finsbury Park, London]. I decided to stay in Rimini for an extra week when I was supposed to be producing *Screamadelica*. But "Shine Like Stars", my favourite track, wouldn't have sounded like that if I hadn't had that extra week in Rimini.

'I'm very cynical, but once I get enthusiastic about something I have to go for it hell for leather. I'm like that with music.'

Even the singles couldn't have prepared anyone – including the band – for the end result. 'Loaded' opened the door, 'Come Together' roused the troops, 'Higher Than The Sun' took modern music to an impossibly beautiful plane and 'Don't Fight It Feel It' became the hedonist soundtrack of the year. But *Screamadelica* was simply one of the most groundbreaking team efforts of all time. The group's creative butterfly had finally exploded into full Technicolor bloom. A consummation of the Scream's transition from rock band to all-encompassing force – a stunning, delirious milestone which effortlessly charted the opiated realms of the stoned soul picnic and made their other indie contemporaries at the time sound extinct. Listened to in its 63-minute entirety – the way it was meant to be appreciated – the record was up there with *Pet Sounds*, *Exile On Main Street*, even *Sergeant Pepper*, as the new soundtrack for a generation. A perfect reflection of the times.

But *Screamadelica* doesn't start with one of the Weatherall-Nicolson tracks. 'Movin' On Up' is pure gospel-driven rock 'n' roll, co-produced and mixed by none other than Jimmy Miller, the man behind the desk on a slew of classic Rolling Stones records. His dense, magical touch is prevalent on the song, which remains another of the best things the Scream have done. Later on in the track listing, Miller also produced what could be the best ballad the group have ever recorded – the ultimate comedown classic, 'Damaged'. Spaced, stoned and stroked with a delicate, heart-stopping beauty, 'Damaged' could only have been produced by the man who did 'Wild Horses'.

New York-born Jimmy Miller sprang to prominence in the mid-sixties when he produced the Spencer Davis Group, co-writing 'Gimme Some Lovin''. He moved on to Stevie Winwood's Traffic and then hitched up with the Stones. The first tracks he did with them were 'Jumpin' Jack Flash' and 'Honky Tonk Women' before he moved on to the classic albums *Beggars Banquet, Let It Bleed, Sticky Fingers* and *Exile On Main Street*.

'You get someone like Jimmy, who can turn the whole band on, make a nondescript song into something, which is what happened on *Beggars Banquet*,' said Keith Richards to *Crawdaddy* magazine in 1975. 'We were just coming out of *Satanic Majesties* . . . Mick was making movies, everything was on the point of dispersal. I had nicked Brian's old lady. It was a mess. And Jimmy pulled *Beggars Banquet* out of all that.'

Rumours say Jimmy became another Stones casualty and he didn't do much after leaving the group before *Goat's Head Soup* in 1973. But here he was doing the Scream! Another hero, who was initially going to be involved in the next album but had kind of lost it. That would have been great but someone said he just spent his time carving swastikas into the mixing desk. Other reports have him running around drunk and naked in his New York apartment building, shooting up the ceiling with a machine gun. Unfortunately, Jimmy Miller died in October 1994. I dedicated the winter 1994 UK tour programme to him because the last group he produced was Primal Scream.

Jimmy tapping a wine bottle is one of the first sounds you hear on *Screamadelica*, along with the abrasive mix of acoustic and electric guitars. Then it's an ebullient Bobby: 'I was blind / But I can see / You made a believer / Out of me' is his opening salvo, before the whole band steam in with a glorious celebration of optimisim, hope and defiance. The song could have come off *Exile On Main Street*, but the vibe and sentiments are pure gospel, with a full-on female choir to back

'I-fang-ew!' Bobby and Throb, London gig, 1990.

A still from the 'Higher Than The Sun' video.

it up. The tune soars, lifts the heart and goes pure rock 'n' roll when Throb weighs in with his sleazed-up solo. By the time of the 'My light shines on' coda you feel like you've died and gone to heaven. In fact, the song has been played at more than one funeral. Even the Labour Party and New York Stock Exchange have wanted to use it for promotional purposes. And been instantly turned down. It's that kind of anthem, but it belongs to Primal Scream.

'Slip Inside This House' is a throbbing cover of the Thirteenth Floor Elevators tune original-ly planned for a tribute compilation. The Elevators are one of the legendary sixties psychedelic groups, most famous for 'You're Gonna Miss Me' on the *Nuggets* compilation. Originating from Texas, they were fronted by an acid-fried fruitcake called Roky Erickson, whose lyrics and antics made him the American Syd Barrett. Obviously a Scream hero then. The track was produced by Innes and Manchester's Tony Martin, aka fellow Creation signing Hypnotone, with additional production by Weatherall. Bobby credits it with introducing the Scream to recording with sam-plers. The treatment is throbbing, psychedelic and bass-heavy.

Next up is the huge, slamming call-to-arms of 'Don't Fight It Feel It' and its 'Rama lama lama / Fa fa fa / Gonna get high till the day I die' hook. The group wanted it out as the follow-up to 'Come Together' but, according to Bobby, 'Creation went "nah, you can't, it's too freaky, too disco." And we're going nah, this is where we're at, this is what we're listening to.' Riding a sinister, bullfrog-whistle disco vamp, the tune marked the recorded Scream debut of Denise Johnson. Bobby had a couple of goes, but decided a female vocal would suit the song better, so they called up Denise.

Bobby had no qualms about not appearing on one his band's singles. As he told *Melody Maker*, 'We consider it to be a soul song. Something like Chairmen of the Board with a Northern Soul feel-ing. I knew my vocal wouldn't fit in because I can't sing in that style, much as I'd love to. So we asked Denise to sing my vocal ideas and she did them perfectly. To me, it's great that the group can do that – nobody's got an ego about it. All we want is to make good records, but I know people are gonna freak because it's not me singing on the record. But it's simple really, like the Velvet Underground. Lou Reed got Nico to sing some of his songs because he thought she could do a better job.'

'Don't Fight It' – which was originally entitled 'Scat' and ran for seventeen minutes – was unleashed as a single in August and proceeded to demolish dancefloors everywhere, after the tra-ditional buzz-building by Weatherall playing the only available copy. There was also a remix by 808 State's Graham Massey. When the first promos came out I took one over to New York. While I was there, Puerto Rican house music sleazestress A Bitch Called Johanna took me to an underground dance club where I persuaded the DJ to stick it in amongst the deep house he was pumping the floor with. 'What the fuck's this crazy shit?' was the general comment as the room erupted.

The original mix of 'Higher Than The Sun' follows before a truly gorgeous instrumental called 'Inner Flight'. Here the band employ deep sax, flutes, bells, harpsichord and a heavenly choir which Andrew and Hugo sculpt into a majestic aural massage. It could have come from the Beach Boys' *Pet Sounds*. The ten-minute Weatherall mix of 'Come Together' follows before 'Loaded', then the aforementioned 'Damaged'. Then it's another Weatherall/Nicolson expedition with the self-explanatory 'I'm Comin' Down', a doleful, hallucinogenic ballad with tablas, jazzy sax solo and a pained vocal from Bobby: 'I'm comin' down / I can't face the dawn.'

Next, another visit to 'Higher Than The Sun' – this time Weatherall's 'Dub Symphony In Two Parts' – before the album winds up with 'Shine Like Stars'. The track that Weatherall later cited as his favourite, it coasts plaintively along on a harmonium splattered with dub effects. A gentle and beautiful lullaby that perfectly closes an amazing album.

Journalist Andrew Perry summed it up in *Seven*: 'The whole album is constructed like an ecstasy trip. You've got the initial euphoria of "Movin' On Up" then you've got an incredible psychedelic dance experience for a few tracks. Then you get to the end of "Loaded" and you get a washed up chill-out lovely thing for another 25 minutes. It's the ecstasy experience . . . a little pocket trip.'

Added Jeff Barrett in the same feature: 'They're one of the greatest groups of all time and that is one of the greatest albums of all time, without a doubt. "Higher Than The Sun" – beat that. I remember when Andrew had the first slates of "Don't Fight It Feel It" and I remember that caused chaos. Then when it all came together as an album . . .'

Screamadelica – about to change the world.

Exotic noodling during the 'Don't Fight It Feel It' video shoot, '91.

Three

The Scream Unlimited Arkestra

'We just want to make beautiful music. Whatever it takes to do that we'll do it, by any means necessary.' – *Bobby Gillespie, 1991*

The spectacular chain reaction started by 'Loaded' meant that anticipation was high for the new Primal Scream album. But few could have foreseen the mindblowing impact when the *Screamadelica* mothership finally touched down in September, or the shockwaves which would resonate for years to come. Apart from, maybe, the band and their associates.

The album reached number eight in the charts. Over six years later it would be voted number 27 in *Q*'s 'Hundred Greatest Albums Ever' roundup.

Reviewers fell over themselves with comments like 'a landmark in rock history' and 'not so much an album, more an event'. Bobby responded with a batch of articulate interviews which invariably gave the music press good copy. Laurence Verfaille talked about the incredible reaction to the album in *Seven*: 'To be honest, people were just queuing up wanting to do things. It was very much a take your pick situation because we had so much support. *NME, Select, Melody Maker*, all did covers.'

One of the best was the *NME* interview with James Brown, who called the album 'sexy, dangerous and definitive,' continuing, 'You now have this choice: Do You Want Tomorrow Today Or Yesterday Forever?' Over two days, he got 'the eclectic warrior' Bobby to open up in some depth: 'To a lot of people I think music is a commodity, not spiritual, it's something you put on the mantelpiece and it's there, like a set of golf clubs or an ironing board, whereas to us it's a holy thing, and none of us are religious.'

He is indeed a master of the Quote, with declarations like, 'Most bands today deal in black and white, Primal Scream deal in glorious Technicolor.' Or this one in *Melody Maker* – who went as far as to give away a free Scream booklet that week: 'All these bands saying they want to be in complete control. Who wants to be in control? The best times in my life have been when I've been completely out of control, when I've not known what the fuck was happening, when you forget you're on Planet Earth. It's happened with drugs, it's happened with sex and it happens all the time with music. I love it . . . I live for it . . . being completely abandoned, it's spiritual orgasm. It's good to get lost from time to time. It's good to let yourself go and not be under control all the time. It's good to wander . . . it's certainly been good for me, letting myself go, getting lost – in sex and drugs. You can only find things out about yourself if you open yourself to experience.'

Bobby at Osaka station during the 1990 Japanese tour.

He also spoke about drugs and, unlike many music biz flannellers, didn't shirk, instead reiter-ating the Keith Richards philosophy that drugs should be treated like a gun and it depends on what you do when your finger's on the trigger: 'I actually think drugs are a good thing . . . peo-ple who use drugs wrongly, y'know, that's their problem. If you've got a brain then you're okay with drugs really. It's like a motor car, you can kill yourself if you drive wrongly. Give people the choice, that's what I say.

'We're a pretty sleazy group. I think, with the drug thing, people think it's hype – but it's not. It's just the way it is. We don't glorify drugs and I don't think it's anything to be proud of, either. But I'm not gonna judge anybody by what they do to themselves.'

So that's the drugs bit done then. One of that year's interviews was to be with myself in August. I'd never met Bobby before and the last thing I wanted to do was the same old prying into the band's personal 'hobbies', although I did intend to home in on Bobby Gillespie's biggest obses-sion of all – music.

I suppose I was nervous, but more likely excited at the prospect of meeting the man partly responsible for the best album I'd heard from a British band in around a decade.

It was my first time at the Creation offices in Hackney. And they were tiny! Situated above a dry cleaners was a main office where promotion and general business – as well as some top partying, by all accounts – went on. There were a couple of smaller rooms, plus a broom cupboard, which apparently doubled as a crash-hole on more excessive occasions. The biggest room at the end served as HQ for Alan McGee and partner Dick Green.

Bobby came bounding out of the bathroom, hand outstretched, sporting a Generation X t-shirt, jeans and massive grin. Black, semi-Keefed thatch, pencil thin and emanating a kind of wasted charisma. Next door was a greasy spoon cafe, which Bob opted for instead of the boozer. It imme-diately became apparent that he'd known about me for the previous fifteen years, citing various fea-tures I'd written when I edited *Zigzag*. In fact, he later confessed that he'd been nervous about meet-ing me. With no ice to be broken, our encounter soon became a house-on-fire scenario as I trotted out Clash tour tales and we enthused over records we both loved. If I mentioned an album or group Bob hadn't encountered, he scrawled down the name on a napkin. One was Count Ossie and the Mystic Revelation of Rastafari, the Jamaican drum-chant collective who I'd got into through the praisings of Mr Richards. Bob was happy that I regarded *Screamadelica* so highly and, with mutu-al respect duly established, the interview became more like two music fiends gushing at each other.

But I was here to talk about the album that I knew would change the face of British music forev-er. Funnily enough, the interview was for conservative soul weekly *Echoes*, bastion of reactionary Luther Vandross blandness. Maybe they let me do the Scream 'cos they had a black girl singer. I was just pushing them as the best soul band in the country.

When in full flow Bobby Gillespie is articulate, blazingly passionate and up there with Rotten and Strummer when it comes to the put-down. His comments during our first interview turned out to be a blueprint for Primal Scream's existence since day one – or his own *raison d'etre* since childhood. The ever-recurring theme was how much great music had been made over the years, and how stupid it was for people to bracket themselves inside just one genre. How one gold peb-ble could start a trail to a whole gleaming mine. Bob and his group were indeed on a mission to educate, but were only doing what came naturally, and if people picked up on it and it led 'em on to seek out those initial influences then it was a bonus. They didn't hop over musical barriers because they simply didn't see any in the first place.

We kept coming back to the fact that it was sad, partly thanks to blinkered elements of the media, that many kids just getting into music didn't know of anything further back than last week's *NME* front cover. As mutual hero Joe Strummer put it in 'White Man In Hammersmith Palais', 'new groups are not concerned, with what there is to be learned.'

Even listening to the tape of that interview over ten years later made me want to dig out the entire

Scream guffaws while waiting for the Bullet Train at Osaka station, Japan, '90.

contents of my record collection. Bob's passion is that contagious, and this belief in music has always been his essence. His comments that day still stand and, I believe, are the closest you'll get to the heart and soul of Primal Scream. What makes them tick.

Bob?

'When I was young my parents would play the Stones, Beatles, soul, Motown. Even if you're only seven years of age and hearing Martha Reeves, the Temptations and the Four Tops at the same time as the Beatles, Stones and Dylan, you can't help but soak it up. They used to play a lot of Ray Charles. In the seventies when I was growing up on the radio you'd hear T.Rex, the O'Jays, Thin Lizzy but also something like Ann Peebles' "I Can't Stand The Rain". All these records were hits. I never differentiated. I'd never think "that's rock" or "that's soul" or "that's disco." They were just good records to me. I've never tried to box music. It's crazy. It's taken us a while to use our reggae and soul influences but we are doing that and we are doing it very well.

'People limit themselves to listening to a certain style of music at the expense of others. We do have a lot of influences and we use them in making different styles of records. Not conscious. These things are subconscious. That's the thing. I just don't believe in limiting yourself.

'It's taken us three years to get here [with this album]. You look at the Stones, Beatles, Bolan and Bowie. They made great records but it took 'em a long time to get there. Bowie was doing "The Laughing Gnome", wasn't he? The first Stones album sounds like Arthur Alexander, Chuck [Berry] all the way, Howlin' Wolf and Muddy Waters. These bands took years to develop their own style and create their own vision. It's the same for us but you find in this country people get reviewed in the music press before they've made a record. A lot of the time too much is expected of young bands. There's very few bands that really do it on their first two albums. The New York Dolls, Stooges, Pistols, Clash . . . somehow they managed to do it. The first Ramones album. Wherever did it come from? It's mad!'

I mentioned the fact that I was doing this interview for a soul publication. Of course, this launched a frantic rattling off of great names like O. V. Wright and James Carr, who could well be Bobby's favourite singer of all time. Carr is described in Peter Guralnik's definitive soul bible *Sweet Soul Music* as 'a simple, uneducated man, with a "church-wrecking" voice' who 'couldn't handle it all and ended up disoriented, confused and eventually in and out of mental institutions.' His best known song is the heart-breakingly desolate love ballad 'Dark End Of The Street' from 1966, which Bobby numbers as one of his favourite songs ever. It's been covered by everyone from Aretha to Gram Parsons with aching beauty, but the version I have on tape of Bobby doing it unaccompanied has made people cry. And that's soul music.

'One thing that separates our band from the other bands is that we do listen to a lot of soul music. Black music. There's a blues inflection in our music which is missing in most of the white bands. We use blues notes and feelings. It's just a natural thing. We're not gonna sit down and try and sound like John Lee Hooker, because we can never be that. We've got to be ourselves. You listen to a track like "I'm Coming Down" and it's a blues track. "Damaged" is a blues track. I think that "Higher Than The Sun" is a blues track as well but it's a different kind of blues. It's our blues. It's a funny thing to say but it's an important fact that we're willing to experiment. Most journalists who write about rock – or Primal Scream – don't know much about anything else except indie rock music. When I think indie rock music I think badly played, badly written, badly produced, badly arranged rock music. It sounds fuckin' terrible! If I want to listen to rock music I listen to good rock music.

'The term "soul music" often means Otis Redding but Otis Redding was not that good a singer anyway. James Carr is a much better singer, I think. To me I've always felt that Iggy and the Stooges were soulful as anybody. I think applying terms to music's a mad thing anyway because certain records leave you speechless and you just look at each other and it gives you a great rush. You [pointing at me] have got a hard job because you've got to write about the music, but certain records go beyond words and leave you speechless. You can't even speak about them because it gives you such a great rush.'

Bobby and I share the same theory that musical appreciation is a linear progression. When I got into the Rolling Stones at the age of nine I read that they'd come together through Mick, Keith and Brian sharing a love of Bo Diddley, Chuck Berry and the American blues greats. So I checked out the blues and still love it now. I likewise loved The Clash and through them got into the dance sounds coming out of New York in the late seventies. Bobby has always hoped that punters will find a springboard in the Scream and bounce into the endless garden of unearthly delights which have galvanised them over the years. That really can mean anything from the symphonic visions of Brian Wilson and insane dub of Lee Perry to the incendiary politicising of the MC5 and freeform space-jazz of Sun Ra and his Solar Arkestra. Plus, of course, The Clash. All music from the soul.

'I had to do a list in *Melody Maker* of my top ten records. I had Augustus Pablo, *The World Is A Ghetto* by War, *There's No Place Like America Today* by Curtis Mayfield, *Africa* by John Coltrane . . . so there's four great albums that someone who's eighteen that likes Primal Scream might come across one day and think they're worth checking out. If they dig the Scream stuff they might get into that stuff. That's how I got into it – through reading interviews with bands that I liked. I got into reggae through the Pistols and The Clash. Lydon would mention people like Dr Alimantado, Tim Buckley, Can and Captain Beefheart and me and my mates would go out and search for those people, buy something like *Best Dressed Chicken In Town* by Dr Alimantado or *African Dub Chapter Three* by Joe Gibbs and the Professionals. We started to freak out because there's so much music and no fuckin' time to listen to it. Your collection getting massive, then listening to someone like you and you're talking about this stuff and you think, "I've got to go and get this." Then you've got all the dance stuff. It's overload!

'You could only take the punk thing so far. You had to try and listen to new things. You're talking about the influence of PiL. "Death Disco" had a reggae bassline, disco drumming, "Swan Lake" on the guitar then Lydon singing lyrics about his mother dying. When was "Swan Lake"? About the sixteenth or seventeenth century. It's the most bizarre mix up. It's quite inspirational really.

'Me and my friend used to play along to PiL records. Wobble would sit and listen to reggae basslines and that's how he learned to play bass and we would learn by listening to Wobble basslines, which in turn got us into reggae. The first couple of bass lines I learned were *Metal Box* basslines: "Albatross", "Public Image", "Death Disco" and then some Joy Division ones – Peter Hook. They were inspirational as well. And then "Good Times" by Chic. We were in this guy's bedroom and we recorded a version of "Good Times". So he was playing the bass and tried to get a Jah Wobble sound and we had the "Metal Box" [the album came packaged in a round aluminium tin] and used it as a drum.'

Bob starts intoning Chic's classic like a cross between Lydon and Kraftwerk. As Chic are one of my all-time favourite groups, I have to ask him about this one.

'Yeah, Chic were great. Even stuff with Sister Sledge – "Thinking Of You", "We Are Family".'

Primal Scream do an immaculate soundcheck cover of 'Thinking Of You' which, with the band's syncopated guitars and Bob's yearning vocal, would be an instant hit if they wanted the easy option. It's just a rare thing I've heard only a few times but which will live with me forever. He continues.

'There's another version of "Come Together" that's on the album. The first half

Bobby in Manchester, '91.

sounds like the Velvet Underground's "Sunday Morning" type sound but for the last part we got all the gospel singers to come in and went wild with soaring strings, brass and a lot of vocal overdubs. We never set out to do this but looking back at it I know I was totally influenced by the end section of "We Are Family". Just the way it builds.'

Back in 1991 modern music was totally compartmentalised. The dreaded purist would only listen to one style of music and sneer at anything that dared to be different. It was almost a missionary crusade with Bobby to change all that. At that time kindred spirits like the Scream, The Orb, Jah Wobble and Andrew Weatherall had no conception of or time for musical fences. They did, indeed, come together and forge the most formidably healthy nucleus of creative talent in music at that time. They were all on *Screamadelica*.

'There's a lot of good ideas and a lot of good attitudes,' enthused Bob. 'The main thing with the people involved is the fact that they don't see any barriers. People talk about breaking down barriers but us and Wobble and The Orb don't see any. We're digging everything. It's really mixed. It's just other people who limit themselves to listening to a certain style of music. Sometimes we think we're wrong but we do have a lot of influences and we're not afraid to show them and make different styles of records. I think listening to just one type of music is the pits. You get people like jazz snobs who listen to nothing but jazz. There's jazz influences on this LP, gospel influences, R&B influences, reggae influences, psychedelic influences, but I think we've retained our identity throughout the whole album. It's very melodic.

'All musical forms are interrelated. Take Bob Marley, for instance. When he started he was influenced by Curtis Mayfield and the Impressions. Rock 'n' roll has influenced a lot of reggae music with cover versions and all that. Reggae has influenced us and definitely Weatherall. There's a lot of reggae basslines. But we prefer to call it Space Blues. That's the best way to describe it. We've got a song, "Step Inside This House", which is the second track on the album, and the piano break on that is not a house break, it's a reggae break. There's a speeded-up reggae bassline, house kind of drum break and space noises on there as well.'

'Movin' On Up' has always been compared to *Beggars Banquet*-era Stones, probably an easy reference point down to the fact that it was part-produced and mixed by Jimmy Miller. But the celebratory chorus is more akin to a classic Stax track by the Staples Singers or a full-flight gospel tune. Bob lights up when I say that as he had been listening to a lot of gospel at the time. In fact, a certain spirituality imbues the whole album.

'Totally! That's the thing. People don't realise that when they say it's Stonesy but "Movin' On Up" is a great gospel song. It's totally influenced by listening to gospel music. Do you know "Am I Groovin' You?" by Freddie Scott? Ronnie Wood done it, but not a very good version. If you listen to Freddie Scott's you know that the Stones have listened to that record so many times. To me that's on *Exile On Main Street*. It sounds like "Ventilator Blues" or something.'

Then 'Don't Fight it Feel It' has to be the best hedonist dance party anthem of that year – though so-called 'dance music' station KISS FM wouldn't play it because it was by a so-called 'rock group'.

'Oh aye,' said Bob, visibly relaxing and warming up. 'It's a classic record, I think. It says "Rama Lama Lama, Fi Fi Fi / Gonna get high till the day I die."'

That call-to-arms hook is derived from a track on *Kick Out The Jams*, the incendiary live debut album from Detroit's legendary MC5. The Scream had already included their live version of 'Ramblin' Rose' from the same album on the B side of 'Loaded'. The two groups had a lot of common and still do. The MC5 released *Kick Out The Jams* in 1969, choosing to do it live as it was the only way they could capture their explosive, dual-guitar politicising. The Five preached revolution, being affiliated to the White Panther group, and full-on high-energy rock 'n' roll. This greatly influenced later Scream albums like *Xtrmntr* and their stage shows from 2000 onwards. In fact, the Scream's favourite encore seems to be their juggernaut assault on 'Kick Out The Jams' itself. Bobby also does a mean rendition of 'Sister Anne' from the Five's third album, this being the name the Scream collectively adopted for their production on the *Primal Scream* album.

'"Don't Fight It" takes that influence from the MC5, whose whole live thing was taken from James Brown's show. James Brown was the main man. We're taking that influence from the MC5 and then making it Chairmen of the Board style. It's a Space Disco record . . . I don't know how else you'd describe it. We're just mixing it up and putting dub effects on there as well.'

Bobby also talked about the fact that it's Denise Johnson's voice you hear on the record instead of his. How many other singers would relax their egos sufficiently to do that? Even Keith Richards is lucky to get one vocal on a Stones album. Several times Bobby has heard a new Scream track and decided that he simply doesn't need to be on it. The otherworldly 'Inner Flight' is another *Screamadelica* track without his lead vocal.

'Aye, our whole thing is we just want to make beautiful music. Whatever it takes to do that, we'll do it, by any means necessary. We're not like other bands. We don't just play guitars. We play keyboards, vibes, tablas, piano, synths. We can do all sorts of stuff but if we think someone can do a great piece of work for us then we'll do it. Wherever an instrument sounds good for a song then we'll use it, whether it be harmonium or harpsichord or vibes or whatever. If we can play it, we'll play it or we'll get somebody who's good at that instrument to do it. The great bands have always done that. The Stones have always done it. It's just like, we have to make great records.

'Listen to the Philadelphia stuff Gamble and Huff did. They could write a song, produce and orchestrate it as well. They just got the best musicians available, got the feel right, got the right singer for the right song. That's how they made records. We're trying to do that kind of thing but in the framework of a band, keeping the essential core musicians but working with a lot of different people, whether it be Weatherall, Wobble, Denise . . .

'We've got a real clear vision of what we want to do and we don't want anything to distract it, especially egos. We don't have that kind of problem in the band where some guy who plays guitar has do a guitar solo in every song. That's silly. It's annoying when people say you don't play on your records. Just because there's not a guitar on the record it doesn't mean to say we haven't played on it. Also you can make guitar sounds with other instruments due to studio techniques. "Don't Fight It" has got guitars all over it, so's "Higher Than The Sun", but it doesn't sound like guitars. It's a Les Paul guitar through Marshall amps on those records but we've made it stranger and I ain't gonna let anybody's lack of imagination bother me. We're a group. This is the way it's gonna be.'

I mentioned Dr Alex Paterson, a key player during the whole *Screamadelica* period.

'Alex did a mix of "Shine Like Stars" too but we haven't used it yet. We did "Shine Like Stars" with Andrew Weatherall and did two takes. One was pretty fast and I never really liked it. The rest of the band thought it was fine but it never really worked out that well. I wanted to re-record it and we did, just slowed it down. We only used vocals, harmonium and some bells and things. That's the way it appears on the album, as a lullaby kind of thing. You know like "Goodnight" on [the Beatles'] "White Album". We're not copying that but it's a good album closer.'

We talked about the Scream's gigs of the time and the DJ sandwich surrounding their set. In 1991 rock concerts consisted of a dodgy support band, roadie's tape, headliner, then home to bed. DJs were confined to all-night raves. Another barrier stormed then.

'Yeah, that's what we did,' agreed Bob. 'When people came in Alex would play records for about two hours and the audience would be vibed up and we'd come on and play for about 45 minutes. We don't like long sets, just to give the maximum impact. Total energy. Then Andy would come on for an hour and a half, maybe two hours, until two or three in the morning. Every gig we do we manage to get a late licence, so it's different for a night out for people.

'I've always felt that I'd go and see bands and if I liked them I'd be really pissed off when it finished with all this adrenalin and there'd be nowhere to go. The audience would be kicked out into the street. Sometimes I think that's why kids smash windows and stuff. You've got to release that energy after gigs. You're looking at this massive vacuum of energy for some rock 'n' roll bands – the last thing you want to do is go home and sit in your bedroom. You've got to get rid of that energy and we just felt like now was the perfect time to try something like that.'

Around this period, the group started gathering an ever-changing entourage which has become part of Scream life. Alex Nightingale – son of Radio One DJ Annie – came in as their agent and eventual manager. He was the perfect choice, being a wild card totally in tune with the Scream line of thinking, which included imbibing large quantities of everything. He also lived in Brighton, then home to both Throb and Bob. By *Screamadelica* Alex was almost like a member of the band. His partner was another mate called Simon Stephens, who acted as tour manager.

As the Scream have moved on through their different phases their gigs have veered back more

Kick Out The Jams, *the classic first MC5 album from 1969. A lifelong Scream manifesto.*

toward conventional hours – though, following their lead, every other band since has had to have their own DJ. But they still make sure there's someone on board to warm up the crowd and let 'em down gently afterwards. And no UK tour is ever complete without a mad late one at Brixton Academy.

The thing about Primal Scream, and Bob's next comment backed this up, is the sky's too restrictive to be the limit for this group. Maybe space is the place. A few nights earlier, he'd been to see Sun Ra and his Arkestra in concert. Sun Ra is another hero of his. Now dead, since the fifties he was a fearless, groundbreaking prophet in the often-reactionary jazz world as he started pushing the boundaries of bebop past Charlie Parker, Coltrane, and even Miles Davis, to end up orbiting Saturn, the place where he claimed to have been born. This isn't entirely true, but the man certainly looked the part, in his flowing robes and golden head-dresses, as he conducted his awesome, ever-shifting Arkestra through the outer perimeters of freeform jazz and beyond.

There were core members like hornplayer John Gilmore, but the rest of the ensemble ebbed and flowed depending on Sun Ra's current direction of choice. He traversed the spaceways with unearthly walls of sound, released scores of albums, and by the sixties was light years ahead of any of the emerging psychedelic bands. Bob and the boys have been inspired in several ways by Sun Ra, noticeably in the flexibility of line ups around the core musicians, and also the urge to fearlessly step into the sonic unknown. But, just like Sun Ra could propel his band back into familiar bebop at the drop of a bejewelled finger, so the Scream can vault from the outer limits of 'Higher Than The Sun' into the gospel uplift of 'Movin' On Up'.

'I went to see Sun Ra and I was sitting there thinking, "I'd love to do a piece of music using these musicians." His band were really good and I'd love to do something really strange and beautiful with them but there's no reason it still can't be Primal Scream. It is still Primal Scream. That's good because it means you can go and see a gig like that and suddenly think, "This is amazing, I wish I could do something like this."'

The Scream actually got to fulfil part of this wish when horn duo Jim and Duncan joined up for some of the *Vanishing Point* tracks and ensuing tours, introducing a definite space jazz feel for a while. But back then I didn't have a clue exactly as to how many members were in the group.

'Oh, I think there's about . . . eight or nine or seven. I don't know! If you include Weatherall, Hugo Nicolson as well. Hugo plays onstage with us and is Andrew's engineer and co-producer. He's doing live samples and beats. He's got two eight-track mixers on stage and dubs stuff up spontaneously.'

Dance music made it possible for anybody to become a record producer. Like Andrew Weatherall, who had never been in a studio before he tackled 'Loaded'. You went in with an idea – there's the key – and got someone technical to translate it into sound for you. That's how Andrew started, with Hugo twiddling the knobs before he hitched up with Sabres of Paradise cohorts Jagz Kooner and Gary Burns and, later, Two Lone Swordsmen compadre Keith Tenniswood. Alex Paterson bounced his wild visions off Thrash when 'Higher Than The Sun' was born, as well as albums like *U.F.Orb*.

I was inspired by Weatherall to do it myself and ended up on his Sabres of Paradise label with Secret Knowledge.

Phil 'Trigger' Hamilton [left], the only man who can tour manage the Scream, with Alex Nightingale [right], former manager and partner-in-crime.

Bobby didn't know how to work a computer but he sure had ideas, as did Innes and Throb which, mated with Weatherall's fervent imagination, got translated by the underrated Nicolson.

'Andrew's some guy that just likes playing music. Producers are basically jumped-up engineers. A producer should be a man of vision. A soulful person, not somebody who's technical. A producer should have vision and soul. How did you get dub? People like King Tubby could rock the mixing desk but they had ideas and vision in their heads. Thanks to guys like that we've got dub. They had that vision.'

The band jumped at the chance to work with legends like Jimmy Miller, Tom Dowd and George Clinton. But highly-paid, bog-standard 'professional' producers get short shrift from Bob: 'Those cunts don't have any vision.'

As my first afternoon with Bobby Gillespie drew to a close, he let loose his final volley and the final piece of the Primal Scream attitude plopped into place. He'd been talking about Keith Richards, a somewhat obvious but mutual influence of the highest order.

Bobby at Club Citta, Kawasaki, during the '91 Japanese tour.

'Keith's a blues singer, isn't he? He's got a lovely voice, really soulful. I've always thought with the old guys there was a nice style that went with being a musician.' He'd be referring to Love's Arthur Lee or the MC5's Wayne Kramer here, rather than muso wash-ups like Phil Collins. 'You take a band like INXS, who I think are terrible. There's no danger. It's just like . . . dead clean. I don't think they look dangerous.'

This attitude was given voice in James Brown's aforementioned *NME* piece: 'Melody, sex and violence. That's what I'm interested in, bands being totally into what they do, being on the verge of exploding. These are the things I'm into . . . I like wild stories. I'd rather read the interview with a band who're full of crazy stories than an interview with a band explaining a guitar sound. Although there's always been inevitable journalistic embellishment, most of the Primal Scream stories are true.'

After the Summer of Love ecstasy spirit that imbued the *Screamadelica* period, Bob was starting to sow the seeds of the attitude the group would adopt as the nineties wore on, climaxing with the ultraviolent sonic assaults of *Xtrmntr* at the end of the decade.

'I've got this theory about groups being gangs,' was his parting shot as I got ready to leave. 'I think that's part of what appeals about our band. Some kid going, "I wish I could be up with them, they're having such a good time." None of those groups seem to be like that. They're not the groups I'd like to hang out with. They ain't got the balls. They don't rock and they don't feel rock either. They're not degenerate, basically. Bands should be degenerate. It's like The Clash were a gang, or Motorhead. We need that. "Speed isn't a drug. Speed's food." That's the attitude. I love that.'

At that point I knew that Primal Scream were indeed the proverbial Last Gang in Town, and that I'd be seeing a lot more of them and this degenerately beautiful outlaw called Bobby Gillespie.

Four

Higher Than The Sun

'I can't remember taking anything but I ended up looking for the steering wheel of the Sydney Opera house so I could drive it to Atlantis. I checked into hospital . . . '
– Hugo Nicolson, 2003

he *Screamadelica* shockwaves ran riot after the album's release and so did the band, as they interrupted the 24-hour party to set off on the road again in October. Japan saw their profile boosted even higher, with teeny-Scream fever and the usual chaos this country brings out in their ranks. It seemed like they'd really started something as top local music biz chaps called one gig the country's first proper rave!

Then it was the UK again. It was the first tour since the album came out so proceedings were madder than ever, with the band attracting all sorts of 'new mates' and hangers-on. Consequently, they were partying even harder.

The tour climaxed with a rammed and raucous knees-up at London's Hammersmith Palais. According to legend, Kylie Minogue was in attendance and dived enthusiastically into the Scream spirit of things. Around this time there was also a photo session with Bobby for *Select*, where the band admitted trying to get her to imbibe an L.D.C. (lethal drug cocktail) of ecstasy, speed, cocaine, methadone and valium, all put in the blender. The pop princess politely declined as Innes bowled up and tripped right over her.

In December 1991, the *Face* published its now infamous account of the Scream on the road at that time. It came complete with photos of Bob looking totally off his face, a headline listing the band's supposed drugs menu, and writer Miranda Sawyer looking on in awe at the band's excesses. It's been often repeated that the incoming refreshments consisted of methadone, ecstasy, speed, mushrooms, bugle and hash. But it was when she quoted Bobby that the Scream's infamous reputation for excessive intake was established: 'You know, it was a love of music that brought us all together and that's what we get really excited about. But we also get excited when the drugs turn up . . . really excited.'

Bobby made no bones about drug use in interviews. He is one of the few who doesn't resort to saying 'never touch the stuff' before leaping off to the bathroom for a livener. 'I think if you're allowed to speak about drugs and give your ideas clearly and independently and within context it's fair enough . . .' Fundamentally, he was saying that people should be allowed to make up their own minds.

'I do believe that. But if you look at our band and you look at the drug usage involved it's not just as simple as ecstasy. It's basically everything you can think of. How could I put it? A lot of

Another rare sighting of the Mercury Music Prize! Innes at the Savoy Hotel in London, '92.

Take me away. Bobby in the limo outside the Savoy hotel on the night of the Mercury Music Awards.

what we do is quite hallucinatory. A lot of what we do is quite . . . quite . . . quite strung-out and quite heroin-y. And the group does love amphetamines as well.

'It's part of a life experience thing that the drugs are influential and that can go into your song-writing because . . . I don't think excessive drug usage is going to lead anybody to a place of enlightenment. It might in the sense that they might meet situations they can learn something about themselves through . . . But that can't happen on alcohol. It can happen by just meeting somebody and going home with them and three days later you're involved in some mess or some-thing. It can happen in a lot of ways. But I'm not one of those people that thinks if you take acid it's going to make you more spiritual than somebody who doesn't.'

He then expounds on the *Screamadelica* tour and its revolutionary (for then) programme: 'We give energy to the audience and they give it us back but more and the energy builds and . . . it's like sex!

'See the whole point of Primal Scream is that we want everybody in the audience to get their rocks off. And for us to get our own rocks off in the process. So everybody gets their rocks off and feels high. That's an important thing to say. That's the whole point of it. To get your rocks off. We wanna get our rocks off and we want the audience to get their rocks off.'

I think there's a song in there somewhere . . .

The tour over, it was time to think of the next record. The single was going to be 'Movin' On Up' from *Screamadelica*, but it would eventually front the *Dixie-Narco* EP. The Scream had already recorded an epic track called 'Screamadelica' with Andrew and Hugo. Confusingly, it was not on the album of the same name. This track was Bobby's dream of a 'Goin' Back To My Roots'-style dance music journey bought to life, with its hallucinogenic disco groove rippling with flutes, lazy brass and unearthly atmospherics. It always makes me think of Norman Whitfield, the frighteningly-innovative sonic mastermind behind the Temptations. Anyway, it's a Weatherall/Nicolson masterwork, as Denise takes lead vocals again and the title chant makes its point, while the track rolls blissfully along for over ten minutes. Weatherall said at the time it would be good theme music for a Scream cartoon show. This was borne out when it was used with the opening credits for the upcoming *Screamadelica* video compilation. The Scream Theme indeed.

The other two cuts would be ballads. All this berserk behaviour in dance music situations was fine fun, but the band had been immersed in that kind of E-culture for the best part of three years and anyway, who wants to go home and whack on bangin' techno after several hours cavorting sweatily to that brain-pummelling four-four beat? A bit of soothing soul massage was in order, and when Bob was asked to compile a giveaway cassette for *Select* magazine in December the mood was distinctly balladic: Dion's Phil Spector-produced 'Born To Be With You', Mott the Hoople's 'Trudi's Song', which Ian Hunter had written about his wife, 'Debris' by the Faces, Crazy Horse's 'I Don't Want To Talk About It' and Marianne Faithfull's chilling rendition of the Stones' 'Sister Morphine'.

In late October the band convened to Memphis, Tennessee, with Andrew, Hugo and video director Douglas Hart – Bob's old mucker from the JAMC who'd directed the videos for 'Loaded', 'Don't Fight It' and 'Movin' On Up'. The band loved Memphis. Apart from the King, the place had seen more blues and soul than probably any other city in the world, and given birth to much of their favourite music. They had a blast soaking up the ambience, checking out the history and enjoying the local hospitality. And Douglas filmed much of it for the upcoming *Screamadelica* video. That's Bob there by the freeway leaping up and down on the spot in sheer joy during the opening credits. Throb's in Rocky's Tattoo Parlour having his black panther done. Weatherall went for a rather painful design on his inner forearm the same day.

The group moved into the famous Ardent Studios, where Alex Chilton and his legendary Big Star had recorded their three classic albums in the early 1970s. Big Star were a major influence on the early Scream with their Byrdsy pop jangle and the suicidal ballads on their heartbreaking third album. With those ghosts still hovering around, the group laid down two haunting ballads: the fragile, broken 'Stone My Soul' – which, even seven years later, Weatherall said was his favourite out of everything he'd ever done – and a desolate cover of the late Beach Boy Dennis Wilson's 'Carry Me Home'. The tracks, somewhat similar in mood to 'I'm Comin' Down', pointed to a Screamic sonic shift which would only become apparent two years later when the next album finally got released. It would also be several years before Primal Scream worked with Andrew Weatherall again.

Dixie-Narco – so titled because in Bobby's words, 'music's a narcotic, it relieves the pain' – came out in January 1992 and entered the UK charts at number twelve on the first week of release. Douglas's video for 'Movin' On Up' was a black-and-white gospel celebration with Bobby in white satin shirt, Innes leaping up and down and a female choir soaring through heavenly beams. The video helped the single on Saturday morning's *The Chart Show*. Despite the escalating chaos which surrounded them, there was no getting away from the sheer power, glory and purpose enveloping this band now.

There were more gigs to start the New Year. Firstly Europe, a tour which Alex Nightingale

The Dixie-Narco EP *('92). The little girl came from Memphis. The photo was taken by William Eggleston, who would later supply the cover shot for* Give Out But Don't Give Up.

53

organised for his debut as the band's agent. He started in style with Amsterdam's lovely Paradiso, followed by Germany, Switzerland and France. Then there was a little stint in Ireland before Primal Scream embarked on their first American tour.

The Scream obviously rose to the occasion, despite the fact they had little more than an underground following in America and were lumped in with the 'alternative' college radio audience, who 'lerved you crazy British people.' Even though America was repeatedly throwing up dance classics from Chicago, Detroit and New York, musical segregation was rife. White bands simply made dowdy, grungy pub-rock or went the other way with poodle-haired metal mania. There had not yet been an acid-house explosion in the States, even though the muthas invented it. That was strictly confined to the underground clubs of the aforementioned cities, which were often gay, booze-free and fuelled by cocaine. But producers like Lil' Louis, Marshall Jefferson and DJ Pierre carried on the hedonistic abandon of disco and loved to see what those synthesisers could do when abused. Hip hop was huge but a whole culture to itself, unless you counted the loud punk wannabes who'd copped off on the Beastie Boys and welded beats to guitars.

The Scream weren't like that in 1992. They had the beats and they had the guitars – plus more than enough attitude – but they also had open minds, a love of classic soul and could appreciate the Velvet Underground on ecstasy. Radio-ruled America might have created some of the finest music in history, but always had to have a handy category to shove it into. It took events like the late Larry Levan playing The Clash at NY's legendary dance joint Paradise Garage or Run DMC touring with the Beastie Boys to start breaking down these barriers.

The Primals were riding in from their E-fuelled UK holocaust with the *Screamadelica* experience and playing to conservative, beered-up white audiences, a few punks and some of the trainspottery kids who avidly scanned the UK press and were curious, but also yellow. They needed to be told. Their party fuel was beer, not drugs. They needed a decent pill to catch onto this new, multi-hued warhead from over the water. Ironically, by the time the Scream toured America again with the rock-oriented *Give Out But Don't Give Up* album, the pills had arrived, kicked in and dance music was starting to blow up big-style. If it had only been two years earlier . . .

Melody Maker carried a review of the gig at The Ritz in New York in February. Simon Reynolds described the looming backdrops of Scream inspirations like Elvis, Little Richard, Johnny Thunders and, erm, Noddy Holder and wrote, 'I wasn't prepared for just how literally iconographic the Primal Scream live experience is.' The set now consisted of most of the album, plus *Screamadelica* itself, and a blistering rendition of the Stooges' 'No Fun' for the encore. In Detroit they'd paid tribute to the MC5 with a version of 'Ramblin' Rose'. It's ironic that many of the crowd must've thought those two were Scream songs. I know a few writers who did.

Incidentally, probably the most famous and arresting Scream photo of all time hails from that gig. Grant Fleming was with the group, as ever, and, knowing a good shot when he sees one, automatically snapped the band as they staggered off the stage, exhausted and definitely the worse for wear. You can see it on the inside of the *Give Out But Don't Give Up* gatefold and on the front of the 'Rocks' single, plus of course, on the cover of this book! It wasn't posed, it's the real thing and counts for more than a million studied studio stares. It also looks like the cover of the MC5's second album, *Back In The USA*. The band must have known that one.

Back in the UK it was another all-night Brixton Academy landmark, with Portsmouth and Birmingham keeping it company. This tourette bore the title 'STP'. The Stones had used it before, ostensibly for 'Stones Touring Party', even though it was inspired by a mind-bending big brother of LSD that was around at the time. The Scream had all this in mind as well as 'Scream Touring Party'. It also stood for Shot to Pieces. And quite rightly so.

The Brixton show was utter lunacy. In March 1992, ketamine had made its entry onto the London club scene in a big way. Obviously the Scream and their compatriots put on their Columbo macs for some investigation. Ketamine and ecstasy ruled that night, and tales abound

Chicago, '92.

Grant Fleming's classic shot taken after their gig at New York's Ritz. Recalling the MC5's Back In The USA, *it popped up on the cover of 'Rocks' and gatefold of* Give Out But Don't Give Up.

Bobby, with co-manager Simon Stephens, on their way to make a bit of history at Glastonbury in 1992.

Waiting to go on at Brixton Academy, March '92.

about the warped-out psycho-planet state of the participants, the crowd included. Youth and Alex Paterson, who were DJing in one of the rooms, thought their heads were glued to the wall at one point. The band, meanwhile, rode it out with customary gusto, and probably invented a new cocktail in the process. Despite the fall-of-ancient-Rome braincell-holocaust going on that night, *Melody Maker*'s Simon Price still reckoned, 'maybe Primal Scream can be called the ultimate band. They make dance music but Primal Scream are as perfectly rock 'n' roll as it's possible to be.'

That year also saw Alan McGee – still smarting financially from the Elevation disaster – sell 49 per cent of his share in Creation to Sony. At the time much of the blame was laid at the feet of Kevin Shields and My Bloody Valentine, and the amount of time and money it took to record the *Loveless* album. McGee said it was a quarter of a million, but Kevin put the figure at £140,000. Whatever, the company was on the verge of bankruptcy and needed the three and a half million they were paid. My Bloody Valentine went off to Island shortly afterwards. 'It nearly drove me insane,' said McGee later, while Kevin finally found a more productive home in the ranks of the Scream.

April saw the release of *Screamadelica – The Video*, which took the old concept of promo-compilation to new heights. It was ten tracks roped together by Douglas and turned into a musical reflection of the group on tour. This started with the Memphis footage and was linked with stuff like Throb having his black panther done at Rocky's Tattoo Parlour, Bobby in a guitar shop, or the group just chilling out. There were also segments filmed at soundchecks and gigs, where he sometimes slowed down the footage and added effects. There's a rather disquieting sequence of 'bad trip' noise and distorted visuals filmed in the foyer at the Leicester Square gig, where I'm sure Led Zep's 'Stairway To Heaven' is playing in the background. And doesn't that sign outside the gig say, with some foresight, 'Get Your Rocks Off'?

Featured songs were 'Screamadelica', 'Movin' On Up', 'Slip Inside This House', 'Don't Fight It Feel It', 'Higher Than The Sun', 'Come Together', 'Damaged' (filmed in a Memphis bar and

Primal Scream touch down at Brixton Academy for a night of insanity, March '92.

Not a dry high in the house. Crowd shot at Brixton Academy, March '92.

where *did* Duff get that hat?), 'Loaded', 'Shine Like Stars', featuring beautiful footage of Bobby's girlfriend Emily, who he'd started seeing in 1990, dancing in slow-motion wearing a Sex Pistols t-shirt, and 'Inner Flight', over the closing credits. The video was a groundbreaking achievement in itself, fantastic to stick on at six in the morning when you'd just got back from a club. Or indeed a Scream gig.

Would this tidal wave of drug-crazed euphoria and mayhem ever stop? Next up was their spectacular show at the Glastonbury Festival, where the Scream followed The Orb's mesmerising performance and simply blew the mind of everyone on the site. Right band, right place, right time – total history. Glastonbury '92 is cited as one of the great Scream gigs of all time. Organiser Michael Eavis still remembers it as one of the best sets his festival has ever seen.

After some summer festivals, a sort of crowning glory was the infamous Mercury Music Prize incident. The Scream scooped the Best Album at the first ever awards ceremony at the Savoy, and

'Yes!' Smiles all round as Throb and Duffy hear they have won the Mercury Music Prize for best album. They will then send the Archbishop up to collect it. Then lose it, along with the £25,000 cheque.

were duly handed a trophy plus a cheque for 25 grand. Not to Bobby though – he'd turned up briefly in a Davy Crockett hat and shades, before commandeering the limo to go round to partner-in-crime Tim Tooher's place.

But not before he'd been cornered by a nice lady from the BBC World Service. 'How do you feel?' she asked, innocently.

'Fucked,' replied Bob.

Then she asked what the group intended to do with the prize money.

'We're gonna spend it all on drugs.'

The rest of the band steamed into the celebrations with gusto. When it came to presentation time they sent up the Archbishop, a lovely, loony mate from Brighton, prone to dressing up as the Archbishop of Canterbury. His day job was as a London tour bus guide. On returning to the now raucously celebrating Scream table he handed the cheque to Nightingale, who put it in his briefcase. Festivities continued and ended up in a club off Tottenham Court Road called the Milk Bar. Next morning the cheque was nowhere to be found so they had to get another one, which they did indeed spend on drugs. They also lost the award.

After that it was a benefit for miners' families on 28 September at Sheffield Arena. The band had always had a political conscience. Bobby's dad's Labour background had installed similar feelings in his son. He and the band had been further stoked by the way Thatcher's Britain had screwed people up. The concert was designed to raise cash for the families of miners affected by all the pit closures at the time. (Ten years later, Joe Strummer would do the same thing for striking firemen.) The Scream and The Orb played what were probably their biggest indoor shows to date with DJ backup from Paul Oakenfold, Justin Robertson and long-time Orb decksman Lewis Keogh.

The Orb came first and were in their fired-up *U.F.Orb*-period: stretches of swelling ambience, Dr Paterson dropping mad samples and roof-raising, kick-propelled dancefloor mayhem. The Scream simply consolidated the glory of their *Screamadelica* set and by the time they hit 'Movin'

Throb holding the Mercury Music Award before it disappeared.

On Up' it was a standing-on-seats blinder. More to the point, they raised £30,000 for miners' support groups. As the flyer said, 'No guest list. All proceeds to miners' families.' The Archbishop even turned up in the full regalia of his namesake.

After the gig I played my first ever DJ set for the band at the aftershow party. I'd done an Orb aftershow earlier, and for some reason ended up sporting black miniskirt, fishnets and lace bra. Maybe they were expecting a repeat performance, but it didn't matter. Bobby and a few of the crew came and hung out in the booth of the small Sheffield club and we had a bit of a blast. I'd gone with some mates who became known to the Scream as the Aylesbury Posse, notorious party animals in their own right. One of them – Bern 'the Gurn' – woke up on the toilet and found the club had been locked up, so he had to break out, setting off all the fire alarms in the process. It was that kind of night.

Hanging out at the hotel afterwards, it was fairly obvious that not all the band were in good shape. I only spotted the ghost of Bobby Gillespie once, as he drifted through the lobby and gave a distant smile.

This must have been what Bob later cited as the 'difficult' period. Even if they were now one of the biggest groups in the country, nobody can keep up that level of craziness and emerge like a Saturday morning TV host. This was the success the band had always wanted, but they loved the excess too, and it seemed to be creeping up on them like all great comedowns inevitably do. But the touring continued as they hit Australia first, followed by Japan.

In early 1992 I had formed my own band with an American soul songstress called Wonder and we'd put out a primitive deep house tune called 'Make Me Scream' on our own label. Weatherall picked up on it and started playing it at his gigs. That would have been enough for me already. But Andrew, who was still in demand as a remixer post-*Screamadelica* and acclaimed in his own right, was in the process of starting his own record label, Sabres of Paradise. After Wonder contributed vocals to 'Wilmot' – a single by his group, who were also called Sabres of Paradise – he asked if we'd like to do something for the new label. We came up with a sexy dub-house trancer called 'Ooh Baby', brought Wobble in on bass and it became the second single on the label. As a result I was hanging out a lot with Andrew and his management, Jeff Barrett's Heavenly operation. Situated in Covent Garden, it was a hive of activity, both musical and hedonistic. The Scream, and similarly-inclined mates like Flowered Up, were about quite a lot as Jeff had worked with them in various capacities for years, so I started seeing more of them.

Duffy and the Archbishop, Sheffield Arena, '92.

Around this time the group were attempting to start the follow-up to *Screamadelica* at Roundhouse Studios in Chalk Farm. Talk about 'follow that'! It was a slow start, and what might have been slowing things up a tad more was the fact that some of the band seemed to have done another drug switch – from ecstasy to heroin, which could have explained the disquieting Sheffield encounters. After the party and euphoria of the 1990-1992 period it was back to reality. Back to work, in a way. A bit of a comedown from a three-year high, and they were dealing with it by simply getting comfortably numb.

My next encounter with Bob and the rest of the band was in December when Keith Richards and his X-pensive Winos were playing a secret gig at the Marquee Club, then in Charing Cross Road. I'd met Barrett and co in the pub and the first people we saw when we walked in were the Scream, taking a little break from the studio to check Keef. It was a great gig, which ended up with me and Bobby charging up the front and howling like teenagers as he ploughed through his new stuff and classics like 'Time Is On My Side', with Bobby Keyes – the man who played sax on 'Brown Sugar' – at his side.

Afterwards there was to be a little bash for Keith in the bar upstairs. Me and the band grabbed the table next to Keith's dad Bert, wife Patti and son Marlon, and waited for the Man. I'd got to know him during several interviews and hotel room sessions some years before, but hadn't seen him since 1984. Therefore I was quite surprised when he staggered into the room, clutching a pint of vodka and orange, swayed through the horde of pestering music biz types, nodded at his family – and made straight for our table! 'How ya doin', man?' he chuckled after a Keef-hug, but only stayed for about a minute before being dragged off by his entourage, waving at the rest of the Scream as he went. Made my night, if only for the looks on the Scream's faces.

After the party we duly repaired to Roundhouse Studios which, for some reason, had been rechristened the Brownhouse. There was no Weatherall about as he'd decided not to do the project, being too busy and heading in different musical directions anyway. But Hugo was there, trying to grab something out of the chaos surrounding him.

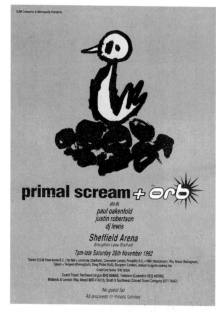

The flyer for the monumental miners' benefit at Sheffield Arena.

Throb armed himself with a bottle of red wine and spent some time laying down the solo on a ballad called 'Everybody Needs Somebody'. The mood was celebratory after the Keith buzz but much of the night's activity centred around the foyer. The Jack Daniel's was in abundance, not to mention a whole load of tin foil being used in pursuit of a mythical flame-breathing monster.

Bobby was fired up to talk about music, Duffy was spouting his surreal theories, Nightingale vigorously attacked the JD and Innes careered about in one of his many drug-slogan t-shirts. It was fairly crazed and the work process slow, but my first taste of a proper Scream-style hoot which didn't end until the sun was up and the cleaners were in. Me and Bob were the last to leave and felt so guilty about the mess that we helped them clean it up, before going back to Bob's Camden abode to play records and carry on. I think we called it a day around one in the afternoon.

It was all great fun but, having been on smack for the best part of the previous decade, a little worrying. Not for myself – I hadn't touched it for three years and wouldn't again – but for some of the group and their poor album.

It later became obvious that it wasn't working out too well for Hugo either, who'd seemingly become another 'Scream casualty' and dropped out of the picture completely. He got a thanks on the album sleeve.

Hugo recalls that those Brownhouse sessions did 'dissolve into chaos', although they'd started work on tracks which later became *Give Out But Don't Give Up*, the aforementioned 'Everybody' and 'Star', which eventually showed up on *Vanishing Point* a few years later. 'It was a bit weird because everyone was a bit strung out on various things so nothing much got done. It was hard. We'd been trying for ages and done nothing for ages.

'What happened was we went to Australia to do a couple of dates before Christmas and that's when I lost it. I was in Melbourne and lost it completely. I can't remember taking anything but I ended up looking for the steering wheel of the Sydney Opera House so I could drive it to Atlantis. I checked into hospital so I could sort myself out. I just wasn't trusting anyone. They wanted me to go back in the studio but I just couldn't.'

Checking in for Cokenhagen – Mr G and Lord Sabre.

Hugo adds that the new direction of the band can partly be attributed to the fact that, when he was doing the programming live, the computers would often crash, leaving the band to jam away on old rock and soul faves during soundchecks while they were fixed.

'That was when we had a hint of what was going to happen next. Then they were given the chance to make the record they always wanted to make and that's what they did in the end, but at the time I was with them everyone was higher than the sun.'

I saw the band again the following month when Alex's mum, Annie, held a huge party in her large Brighton house to celebrate her son's birthday. Alex traditionally had a belter of a knees-up and this one went on for three days. My longest DJing stint ever! It was fairly obvious that the Scream were still totally out of it, but weren't we all at that one? Andrew Weatherall walked in on the Saturday night, shook his head and strolled out again. There was a madness surrounding this band to which few others came close, but drew like-frazzled minds like magnets. Andrew Innes famously branded River Phoenix a 'lightweight' when the actor collapsed and died outside LA's Viper Room club.

Alan McGee calls 1993 his 'lost year'. His intake of drugs and booze had spiralled considerably after *Screamadelica* and after he'd been forced to sell the massive share of Creation to Sony. The tales of McGee's pre-sober years are rife, especially as his partners-in-crime were often his old mates the Scream. According to those who were there, he'd sometimes close the office early, dumping a bowl of cocaine and a handful of pills onto the Jack Daniel's-strewn coffee table and invite the assembled to tuck in. He was partial to LA and spent a lot of time there. Once, lying wasted and wired in his hotel room there was an earthquake. McGee just thought it was the drugs.

'By that time I was completely out of control. I nearly lost it completely in August '93. I was at a party in LA with the Primals and Evan Dando, and I ran back to the hotel with fucking shit-loads of drugs, and I mean fucking shitloads. I locked my door and started doing all of them and

Evan Dando is knocking on my door, and I'm saying, "Fuck off, I'm in bed!" I was a total fucking drug addict . . . I was running away from meetings about finances because I'd rather get pissed or do drugs. But I was still amazing at getting money out of people.' He does stress, however, that he never fancied heroin – 'it's a dirty drug . . . because it was brown.'

Alan totally lost it on a flight to LA after a night with Throb and the boys. 'So I'd had no sleep and about four hours into a twelve-hour flight to LA I got the most almighty panic attack. I'd had them before but this was off the scale. It was so scary, like I was on acid or something, just pure psychosis.'

When he reached LA, Alan was diagnosed as suffering from nervous exhaustion and put to bed. But he was out again later that night and got totally pissed on Jack Daniel's. Lying in bed he woke up around four in the morning.

'Now everything is getting really fucking bizarre. I think that the blinds are moving and I'm getting utterly freaked out. I'm not in control of my body and I'm certainly not in control of my mind and I feel like I've got a metal pole in the back of my neck, which I realise now is hypertension.' Paramedics came, Alan was whisked into hospital and pumped full of valium before going into rehab.

Around that time I went to see Alan with a view to signing Secret Knowledge to Creation. He was into the idea and showed definite interest. Unfortunately, Alan suffered a complete breakdown shortly afterwards so the deal fell through. To this day he doesn't remember a thing about that meeting. He spent most of 1994 getting back on his feet and, when he emerged clean and sober later that year, thought he'd better give the Scream a wide berth. He wasn't quite ready yet to face a Scream tour and hardly showed at any of the gigs.

Primal Scream's own focus seemed to be getting clearer as 1993 progressed. In February 1994 Bobby cryptically explained to Cliff Jones of the *Face*: 'We just got sidetracked. For a year we were disabled. Things weren't going too good for a while. We were doing nothing . . . I would do nothing but walk around my house just thinking.' He later told David Cavanagh of *Select*: 'We came through a really bad period in our lives, a really bad period, but somehow we got it together. We went too far . . . got a bit ill.'

Primal Scream have a knack of getting out of tricky situations and emerging from difficult periods, in a way that makes the phoenix look like a ragged black crow. 'We refused to let ourselves fall apart,' says Bobby in reflection. 'Music always gets us through. It's like a religious experience.'

So the group ended up getting round it as only they can. But they were about to embark on a different kind of trip altogether.

It had all started with that pilgrimage to Memphis almost eighteen months before. Since then they'd got higher than the sun then lower than a worm's arse. As 1993 started easing in, that sun started rising again – from America's Deep South.

The Scream were going to Memphis to work with gods.

Bobby G, '92.

Give Out But Don't Give Up

'Behold a pale horse.' – *Book of Revelations, quoted by George Clinton*

So why did Primal Scream decide to record their next album in America's Deep South? Why not a sky-high studio paradise which their new-found success could afford them, in New York, Los Angeles, Miami, or even Jamaica? Why not their own country?

The reasons were basically two-fold. Firstly, in any of these places there would simply be too many distractions in the form of mates, hangers-on and those anxious to grab a piece of Scream action by bearing dangerous-but-fun gifts. They would hardly do any work, as had been proved by the Brownhouse experience. Bobby later told the *Face*, 'put them in the wrong place and the studio becomes a cross between *Carry On Screaming* and *Fellini's Satyricon.*'

It was time to get back to what should be the band's main and most important motivation, the music. The group wanted to go to a main source of inspiration for much of their music and work with the men responsible for many of its golden moments. So, to quote Chuck Berry, it was 'long distance information, give me Memphis, Tennessee.' Revered veteran soul producer Tom Dowd, who died in 2003, agreed to produce the album after being sent four Brownhouse demos and a copy of *Screamadelica*. That clinched it. He was on. According to Hugo Nicolson, he had a quite a 'rare deal' where he got paid according to how the record sold.

The vibe the Scream had got during the *Dixie-Narco* sessions was a big reason, along with Stanley Booth's brilliant 1991 book *Rhythm Oil.* I first heard of it through Jeff Barrett – the sort of bloke who lovingly makes tapes for his regular pub just to add to the vibe – and lapped up its soul roots tales. Booth had previously written *The True Adventures of the Rolling Stones*, itself a bit of a Scream bible with its colourful accounts of their US tours, which greatly contributed to the mythologising of Keef. *Rhythm Oil* had rapidly become Essential Scream Reading. The stories, characters and glorious music pulsating out of its pages made Memphis a mighty magnet to sheer fanatics of the Real Thing.

Legendary Memphis pianist and Big Star producer Jim Dickinson, who ended up playing on the Scream album, summed it up when interviewed in Peter Guralnik's equally vital *Sweet Soul Music*: 'Memphis is an ugly place but I love it. People have traditionally been drawn here because, I guess, it's always been a centre for crazy people. This says an awful lot about the thing that happens in Memphis musically. You can't reject it. You have to either learn to live with it on one level or another or admire it. I, frankly, admire it.'

And so did Primal Scream.

Memphis – once cited as the murder capital of the world, the place where Martin Luther King was assassinated in 1968 – was a hotbed of jazz and blues from the turn of the century, throwing

Funky dollar bill in Chicago, '92.

The empties line up at Alex Nightingale's office, London, '92. Jack Daniel was an old mate from the Deep South who made quite an impression on the Scream.

up such giants as W. C. Handy, Phineas Newborn, Furry Lewis (who in 1991 was working as a street sweeper), Howlin' Wolf, Fred McDowell, Charlie Freeman and Sleepy John Estes. It was all happening around the lowdown bars and jukejoints around Beale Street, and by the 1950s little studios and independent labels were springing up.

One such label was Sam Phillips' Sun Records, which rode the first true wave of rock 'n' roll via artists like Carl Perkins, Johnny Cash and Jerry Lee Lewis. Sam also gave a young local boy called Elvis Presley his first recording session, and changed the face of music forever. This has always been the city's main claim to fame, but things really exploded in the early sixties when Stax Records opened shop with their own label and recording studios, followed by Fame, Willie Mitchell's Hi set-up, which launched the supernova talent of Al Green, and Goldwax – home of Bob's beloved James Carr – plus Sonic, Ardent and American. But it was Stax, who were taken over by the New York-based Atlantic in 1959, who bust Memphis soul wide open by pebble-dashing both pop and R&B charts with such names as Otis Redding, Carla Thomas, Sam and Dave, Booker T and the MGs, the Mar/Bar-Kays, Aretha Franklin, Arthur Conley, Rufus Thomas and Isaac Hayes.

Tom Dowd was often behind the mixing desk at these sessions. He joined Atlantic's New York studio as a 22-year-old engineer in the early fifties and by the sixties had set precedents in recording standards, with innovations like multi-tracking. He worked with John Coltrane and harnessed soul power from the likes of Wilson Pickett. Atlantic big cheese Jerry Wexler sent Tom down to Memphis to oversee the modernisation of the Stax studios and work a bit of magic. His first session was the one which produced Otis Redding's heart-stopping 'I've Been Lovin' You Too Long'. He never looked back. To quote Peter Guralnik in his book, 'As far as clarity of recording, trueness of pitch and engineering balance were concerned, there was little comparison with other independent labels, and that was mostly attributable to Tom Dowd.'

In the mid-sixties Dowd was brought down to Muscle Shoals, Alabama, to perform a similar task. This was the place where Dan Penn and Chips Moman created some of their finest works, like James Carr's 'Dark End Of The Street' and Percy Sledge's 'Out Of Left Field', while Arthur Alexander had earlier recorded 'You Better Move On', which had been covered by the Stones in

1963. The first major tune here was Percy Sledge's 'When A Man Loves A Woman', the first soul song to top the US charts and reach the top five in the UK in 1966.

Other essential players on board the Scream's Memphis bell-end included bassist David Hood and drummer Roger Hawkins, who'd been with Dowd from virtually the start and eventually became known as the Muscle Shoals Rhythm Section, along with Barry Beckett and Jimmy Johnson. That's them you can hear on Aretha's 'Respect' and Wilson Pickett's 'In The Midnight Hour'. In 1967 Hawkins co-wrote and played on 'I Can't Stop (No, No, No)' with Dan Penn for Arthur Conley's *Sweet Soul Music* album. It was produced by Otis Redding with Tom Dowd at the controls. This is the kind of pedigree we're talking about here.

Muscle Shoals rapidly became the place to be, with its hipness factor rising sky-high when the Stones came in during their ill-fated 1969 tour, recording 'Brown Sugar', 'Wild Horses' and 'You Gotta Move' for their *Sticky Fingers* album with Jimmy Miller. Jim Dickinson, who'd played piano for nearly every independent soul label coming out of Memphis, was on those sessions. He also produced Big Star's devastatingly heart-wrenching third album in 1978. Another big name from the soul hall of fame was the Memphis Horns – trumpeter Wayne Jackson and saxman Andrew Love played on many of the classics and also supplied brass for the Stones on their 1972 US tour. Scream credentials or what?

The whole Memphis 'soul stew' business is steeped in history, greatness and the kind of spontaneous combustion and wildness which few bands other than the Scream can grasp. Guralnik's book tells of the rampant use of amphetamines at those old round-the-clock conveyor-belt sessions, and cites a favourite studio saying which was later adopted by the Scream: 'Behind every great song is a great pill.' The book goes on, with uncanny future relevance: 'For many it was virtually impossible to separate a chemically-induced exhilaration from the sheer exhilaration of the times, and the discovery of a new high could be almost as exciting as the creation of a new song.' So the guys back then were actually worse than the Scream!

Bobby later told Ian Gittins, of Tower Records' in-house *TOP* magazine, 'Tom Dowd is an inspirational man. He helped us make exactly the sort of record we wanted. It may be a different kind of record to *Screamadelica* but it still has the same spirit.'

Pre-production for the album actually began in London in April, when Dowd sent over Hood and Hawkins to test the water with the Scream in a North London studio. A week later, the 67-year-old Dowd arrived and started putting the group through their paces and working up the new songs. The band thought they'd died and gone to heaven. Bob would later say that working with these legends remains one of the best memories of his life. He wouldn't necessarily cite the album as their best ever in later years. In fact he would slag it off as 'a smack album'. But it was enough to have worked with the greats, and it spurred the group into some kind of action.

Armed with some songs and ideas, the Scream relocated. First they went to Muscle Shoals to get settled in and write some more, before proper recording started the following month at Ardent, another history-drenched haunt. Here B. B. King had cut his early stuff, Phineas Newborn – the boogie man who could 'reduce a 3,000 pound piano to smouldering ashes', according to a fellow musician – played his last. Most importantly for the Scream, those immortal Big Star albums had been recorded here. That's the tip of a formidable iceberg.

Muscle Shoals no longer houses the original studio. That's the one in the Stones' *Gimme Shelter* movie where the band are shown listening to the playback of 'Wild Horses': Keith zoned out, eyes closed, with just a tapping snakeskin boot to show he's still alive. Now the building, which started life as a coffin factory, is disused, with the new one situated up the road overlooking the Tennessee river, where some of the Scream actually indulged in a spot of fishing!

It was there that they managed to cook up a couple of new items – a loose semi-instrumental, aptly called 'Funky Jam', and – possibly affected by the calm and vibe – a pure soul ballad called 'Sad And Blue'.

'I'm yours! You're mine!' Throb, Bob, Denise and Innes in the 'Jailbird' video.

Then it was time to go to Memphis. This is where they opened the first ever Holiday Inn, where the band were staying, although it had now become more like a block of flats. Our assembled crew consisted of Innes, Bob, Throb, Duff, Henry the bassman and the mighty Muzza. Add to that Hood and Hawkins and then, for good measure, Andrew Love and Wayne Jackson, aka the Memphis Horns, plus Tom Dowd in the producer's chair, and things were looking promising.

The group duly set about recording the two new Muscle Shoals tunes, two rockers, 'Rocks' and 'Jailbird', and the soul-massaging ballads '(I'm Gonna) Cry Myself Blind', 'Big Jet Plane' and 'I'll Be There For You'. Then there were a further three tracks which came to a similar roadblock as 'Don't Fight It Feel It': 'Free', 'Give Out But Don't Give Up' and 'Funky Jam'. As we've already heard with *Screamadelica*, Bobby ain't too proud to hand over the mike when it's necessary.

So who you gonna call? Denise Johnson came to Ardent in July and sang lead on those three songs, as well as doing some backing vocals. 'Free' was an impassioned ballad, 'Give Out' a crawling funk snake and that mischievous thang called 'Funky Jam' simply needed her belting tones in its bubbling groove-stew. Basic recording was just about finished.

Now it was on to the next stage. Tom had directed and extracted sublime and incendiary performances from all concerned and recorded a masterful album. While the band took a short break, he got down to mixing it. The plan was for them to come back in a few days and hear the results.

Ah, but this is Primal Scream . . .

While Innes, Bobby, Henry and Muzz checked out New Orleans, Throb and Duff popped up to New York for the annual New Music Seminar. It's one of the biggest gatherings in the American music calendar: a top excuse for loads of music biz types to schmooze-booze about town on their expense accounts and maybe cut a few deals into the bargain. Some take it seriously, others simply have a free laugh. The thought of our dynamic duo let loose here, representing the band Sire were bigging up as soon-to-be-huge, is hilarious.

Around this time, Duffy was formulating a plan to market a line in brown corduroy under-pants called W-Pants. 'With caramel-coloured piping,' he would always stress. That must have confused the execs when they were trying to talk about the forthcoming album over drinks. Nightingale flew over to join them, which would've made it even more interesting as, at

Brown corduroy W-pants. One of Duffy's greatest inventions is unveiled on my birthday card.

that time, he'd traded in hard drugs for hard liquor and loved his Jack 'n' Cokes. Confronted with either media or mogul type, he would launch into his passion for the group, take no shit from no-one, and revel in the chaos which ultimately knit together the world's greatest band. As the long-suffering Creation press office often said, 'he's the only bloke who can manage that lot.'

Alex was going to pick up Throb and Duff from NY, and fly down with them to Memphis, and join the rest of the band to hear what Dowd had come up with. He arrived to find more chaos than he'd bargained for. The previous night, Duffy and Throb had been touring the New York bars. A brilliant way to spend an evening – depending on what neighbourhood you're cavorting in. Somewhere along the crawl Duffy had got himself stabbed in the side, but the pair had become so pissed by this time that it took the barman to point out there was blood seeping through the piano-man's clothes. Alex arrived in time to collect Duff from hospital, but they wouldn't let him on the plane, so they didn't make the playback party. Nobody at the time – least of all Duff – knew how, where or when the incident had occurred. It later transpired that Duff and Throb had been at a party where Martin had climbed up a bookcase and fallen onto a table of glasses, managing to stab himself in the process. The shard of glass had missed his kidney by an inch. He spent some time in hospital and flew back to London for further treatment and recovery. In January the following year he would also have an operation to correct a damaged throat, and it would take a couple of months for his surreal rants to return to full flow.

Meanwhile, back at the ranch, the band weren't entirely happy with Dowd's mix. They loved most of the ballads, but plans were made for a second pass, and the band would return to hear it at the end of August. So they promptly bowled over to Los Angeles, and booked in at the infamous Chateau Marmont Hotel off Sunset Boulevard. That's the place where John Belushi fatally OD'd. Ostensibly to hitch up with McGee, they had time to kill, and commenced partying in the grand Scream tradition.

One of these knees-ups resulted in them meeting George Drakoulias, the man renowned for producing the first two Black Crowes albums, who is also top dog at Rick Rubin's American Records. Rubin himself made his name producing hip hop tunes by LL Cool J and early Beastie Boys stuff for Def Jam – the label he started with Russell Simmons in his New York college dorm. When I was spending a lot of time at Rick's apartment around 1987 to 1988, while working in a

More New York dressing room madness from the Ritz.

local record shop, rock was his main agenda: dirty biker rock and even speed-metal like Slayer, who he gleefully signed up to Def Jam. This may have had something to do with him breaking away from Russell and starting Def American. Rock central, sure, but also home to the sublime quartet of Johnny Cash albums he's produced.

When George learned at the party that the Scream weren't too happy with their new album's twin rockers, he asked for a blast, and got an earful of 'Jailbird' off Bob's Walkman. Another new convert. This was compounded when the band returned to Memphis and heard Tom Dowd's second attempt. They agreed that he'd worked his magic on the ballads, without question, but they needed some extra sauce on the rock 'n' roll, not to mention 'Funky Jam'. They ended up using his finished versions of 'Sad And Blue' and 'I'll Be There For You' – a ballad, originally called 'Jesus' which started life in the Brownhouse and later popped up in its early form on the *Star* EP.

Dowd also brought home another ballad called 'Big Jet Plane' – eventually. The group hadn't been too happy with the first version and felt it needed re-recording. 'We felt it needed something else, a deeper soul,' reckoned Bobby. The only problem was that the vital ingredient, Duffy, was back in London recuperating from the stabbing incident. Dowd's answer was simple – he brought in Scream idol Jim Dickinson to add swirling organ. The results were transcendental, and it was another memory for the band to cherish.

This particular Memphis jaunt is also notable for the well-told story of the Scream doing the obligatory Graceland visit: Innes threw up in the grounds and, as he was unceremoniously escorted away, bellowed, 'first guy to do it since the King!'

Back in London, the group were still mulling over the question of the final mixes. An excellent piece on the group by Cliff Jones in the February 1994 issue of the *Face* – which boasted Bobby on the front cover with the banner 'The Last True Great British Rock Star?' – brought up Mr Weatherall's distance from the new record.

'No disrespect to them, because I love them, but this is just too rock 'n' roll for me,' said Andrew. 'It's a sidestep compared to *Screamadelica* . . . get wasted on Jack Daniel's and understand it totally. Maybe I will! Besides, if it pays for the continuation of their ridiculous lifestyle, then good luck to them . . . They went off to be rock stars.' Andrew had been confronted with remixing the album's title track, but couldn't wreak his creative juices on 'a 68bpm funeral-pace jam', although he later went to town for the 'Jailbird' single release.

There was also the question of what to do about that 'Funky Jam'. After a bit of communal head-scratching Chris Abbott, who ran Creation's techno offshoot Infonet, suggested P-Funk legend George Clinton. Thoughtful frowns turned into grinning raised thumbs all round, including Dowd's.

Uberfunkmeister George Clinton is one of the largest living legends in music. Now in his mid-sixties, he's had as much impact on the course of black music as James Brown, and has certainly been sampled as much. He started off in a barber's shop quartet in the fifties doing doowop songs at the hairdressers he ran in his native Newark, New Jersey. This evolved into the Parliaments, a fiery soul ensemble most noted for their 1967 hit '(I Wanna) Testify' – another Scream soundcheck favourite. When Newark was rioting, they moved to Detroit, and evolved into Parliament, along with Funkadelic.

As the seventies dawned, the Funk Monster was being unleashed from James Brown's strict blueprint, and snapped its chains from the straitjacket of the soul tuxedo. Sly Stone growled, 'there's a riot goin' on,' but George looked through acid-dipped glasses at the untamed holocaust of Jimi Hendrix and white rock bands like the MC5, and decided that cabaret dinner suits were not where it was at. Funkadelic were the experimental, psychedelicised side of George's schizo-being. Their first albums were all recorded in one day on strong LSD, but works like *Maggot Brain* and *Free Your Mind And Your Ass Will Follow* remain insane, dirty, supremely funky and ahead of their time. *America Eats Its Young* saw them off acid and formidably politicised for the times. In 1971 they brought their mad stage show to the UK for the first time, which caused a sensation with its drugged-up rudeness.

Parliament were the cleaner, stadium-friendly alternative who would eventually take the stage in their own flashing-light behemoth 'mothership', with George in waist-length wig accompanied by around 40 band members, some wearing nappies, some occasionally naked. If he didn't have a costume, George would simply take a sheet off the hotel bed, cut a hole for his head and wear that – with nothing underneath. It was the wildest stage show around. They scored massive hits with songs like 'Knee Deep' and 'Flashlight'.

Throughout the seventies the Parliafunkadelicment Thang was responsible for some of the most wildly creative music ever committed to vinyl, along with Hendrix. Their albums are the pinnacle of whacked-out, lysergic heavy metal funk in a sci-fi twilight zone. No group has ever sounded like them or ever will, and Clinton's influence on today's dance music – whether it be hip hop or funky house – is immeasurable. He's also the most sampled artist in the world, apart from James Brown.

Like the Scream, the ever-growing Parliafunkadelicment Thang revolved around core members, such as Fuzzy Haskins, Bernie Worrell, Eddie Hazell, Cordell Mosson, Gary Shider and Bootsy Collins, the awesome bass player who had turned James Brown's band into a funked-up sex machine when he was only seventeen. When JB's band got pissed off with being fined for having a stain on their shirt, quite a few headed for the Mothership, including the incredible J.B.s brass section of Fred Wesley and Maceo Parker.

As the cash flowed in, the P-Funk empire grew and grew, with George scoring deals and producing a string of offshoots like Bootsy's Rubber Band, the Horny Horns (J.B.s) with Parlet, and Brides of Funkenstein for the ladies. Of course it would burn itself – and some of the members – out, but George continued making his funky-dog mark through the eighties, and by the nineties was continuing to spread his funk gospel with the P-Funk Allstars. Disco and electro-tinged classics like *Loopzilla* and *Atomic Dog* showed there was still life on Mars.

'I use all the styles,' he told Big Apple punk fanzine *New York Rocker* – kind of a sister paper to my own *Zigzag* – in 1979. 'I ain't impartial to nothing. If I do disco, it would still be funk because it's that attitude, not the music. I don't dig one-dimensional funk or one-dimensional disco. You've got to keep coming up with new concepts, keep yourself interesting, because if you don't the novelty wears off. You have to be aware of being caught up in your own thing and get stuck with that because you know it works. Then you take that step and change it again. You know it's going to alienate some people, but you have to do that, every time their attention span catches up to you. And the more drastic the move the better, as long as you can define it. You can't make a move just to make a move, as long as you've got a pattern to what you're doing.

'My concept is that all different rhythms have to get together. It will be a long time evolving, they will have to work together a little bit at a time and feed that out. All different grooves have to work together, and when the combination is felt to be safe and comfortable, that will be a deep music.'

I interviewed George myself in 1989, when I lived in New York and edited a magazine called *Dance Music Report*. We met at the huge Warner Bros. building – at the time he was signed to Prince's Paisley Park label – and the conversation was fascinating. It was obvious this man had few limits, whether it be in personal behaviour or musical boundaries, but he was certainly no superfry. He was most hospitable, signing all my albums, and emptying half of Colombia onto the coffee table with instructions to dive in. Afterwards I wrote, 'He can take your technology, eat it and it comes out of his funky butt as prime groove material. Hall of fame? Put him in the rock one and he'll escape. Try the dog-pound for geniuses, but there's never been an enclosure that can contain George Clinton.'

I also asked him what defined a P-Funker?

He always giggles a bit when he speaks to you, but this was as direct as he gets, looking at me through those shades and multi-hued dreads: 'Someone with the groove, attitude, craziness and funk devotion.'

Shit, goddamn! That P could also stand for Primal, I thought when I first heard 'Loaded'. The next person I had interviewed with this uncannily-similar attitude was Bobby Gillespie at that Hackney cafe in 1991.

I thought then that the combination of George and the Scream – apart from being quite frightening in the mutual hobby department – might be amazing music-wise. It was all pointing to a link-up: one little-known coincidence is that when Funkadelic were recording some of *America Eats Its Young* at London's Olympic Studios – round about the time the Stones must've been using it – the man behind the desk on some cuts was Jimmy Miller. When I heard Clinton was being called in to help stir the Scream's own funk 'n' soul melting pot, I nearly shagged the nearest pooch.

Computer game on! George ended up doing three: 'Funky Jam', 'Give Out But Don't Give Up' and 'Free'. With 'Funky Jam' he was smitten by the Scream's funk, and felt compelled to add his own vocals to Denise's lead and they ended up with an air-punching Stax-on-the-Mothership war cry. Vocally, the same thing happened with the title track, a hallucinogenic nightcrawling slinker with distinct P-elements afoot. Denise found herself duetting with George, although the two wouldn't actually meet until the following January! With Denise's solo vehicle, the aching 'Free', he simply upped the stripped-down soul power and recalled his early work with the Parliaments. 'First time I ever remixed a ballad!' was his comment.

'Man, they pulled it off real good,' was George's final verdict on the team-up. 'I can tell the difference between some oldie-but-goldie vibe and something that's new. It's like what the Stones or Clapton did with the blues or what Funkadelic and Parliament did with gospel or doowop. Those boys are just picking up on the same vibe and doing their own thing.' As we watched the group from the wings at Brixton Academy, he beamed and declared, 'That's the damn funkiest shit I've seen for years!'

'Primal Scream, I had a ball,' George would later tell *Mojo*. 'I guess you could tell by the record I joined in a lot. It was really hard keeping myself off the record. When they say remix it, usually I just go in there and remix it, but they were reminding me of a lot of stuff we used to do in the sixties so I had a hard time keeping myself and the group off. Love 'em. It's hard remixing a ballad. Come off pretty good.

'There's so much soul on that record. Not only funk and rock, but R&B, straight-out blues. Rock and funk, rap – all of it to me is the same, but this is really bluesy funk: to be a rock group, they're very funky.'

More mysterious was his comment during a 1995 Q&A session in *Melody Maker*, when George was asked his fave Scream story. 'Behold a pale horse,' came his reply.

Years later, Bobby was asked about George Clinton in *Q* magazine's reader's questions column. He was on the button with his reply: 'George Clinton is not mad, he's one of the most intelligent, aware, funny people I have ever met. We did a lot of talking and he turned me on to a lot of good tapes. He hides his message in humour because when people are laughing, they're very open to suggestion. It's a good way of getting your message across. Pretty subversive.'

George and the band finally did hook up and together provided an American TV highlight and a UK gig of the year. They also collaborated on a track called 'Lost Dog' for George's *Dope Dogs* album, which was inspired by customs sniffer hounds. Bobby was bubbling over when he told me about

George Clinton. The funky dog who let the Scream pee on his tree.

George and Bobby doggin' out in the dressing room at Brixton Academy.

the recording session. George had told Throb to miss out notes, bass player Henry to play just one, and placed his hand on Duff's shoulder and said, 'go to church.' The band still tell this story with pride.

The 'Funky Jam' saga continued when Brendan Lynch got hold of it. Brendan had made his mark with the acid jazz/Paul Weller cool-and-funky brigade, twiddling knobs for the former Jammer on his recent solo stuff. You wouldn't really have expected someone associated with the traditionally-inclined Weller to go for anything as out there and debauched as Primal Scream, but he'd done a Weller mix called 'Kosmos'. There were only about a hundred promos about, and Weatherall was playing it all the time at Sabresonic. It was a funk odyssey dub explosion, which came as a blast up the strides in those fledgling big-beat days, where clichés were already urging students to rock the house (and don't stop rockin'). Brendan simply laid into the weighty dub-funk groove with the wobbliest, don't-give-a-shit aural acrobatics around. On a big sound system, your brain went off for a picnic with a posse of radioactive goats and, after imbibing some recently-unearthed original California Sunshine acid, got regally shafted up the tradesman's entrance by a man in a mod suit. Blimey.

It turned out to be Brendan's foot in a door marked 'future', as he gave 'Funky Jam' a 'Kosmos'-style fucking-over which was renamed 'Struttin'. Brendan has worked with the Scream ever since, slaving vitally on *Vanishing Point*, *Xtrmntr* and *Evil Heat*. This quiet, pleasant man with golden fingers sums up his involvement simply: 'I knew the band were in love with the whole spirit and soul of live music . . . feel is everything. Primal Scream seem to be about getting people who love music the way they do to work with them.'

November saw Innes making the trip out to LA to rework 'Rocks' and 'Jailbird' with George Drakoulias. They had given the former to Jimmy Miller, but reckoned there was too much harmonica on it. Then the whole band trooped out to record another rocker, the Faces-ish 'Call On

Me'. The outcome was an expected triumph. No-holds-barred anthemic rock 'n' roll dripping with attitude. George ended up playing some drums to add extra punch, and the guitars were like razors. Bob sounded like he was waving one.

Give Out But Don't Give Up was done . . . almost. There was one track to go, and I got a call one day from Mr Nightingale asking if I'd like to remix 'Everybody'. This was that drifting love ballad I'd first heard at the Brownhouse, as Throb wrestled with that beautiful – and fairly complicated – guitar solo. It had since been worked on with Tom Dowd and the boys but Innes – masterminding final mixes and track listings as usual – thought he might it throw it my way to see what happened. In the eleven months since those Chalk Farm sessions, I'd had success with Secret Knowledge and embarked on the remix treadmill. This has always been a dance music thing: you get a hot track and suddenly everyone wants to grab a bit of that magic. It happened to Weatherall, The Orb, the Chemical Brothers, loads of us. Of course, it was great getting paid tons of wedge for a couple of days messing about with someone else's track – I ended up doing mid-nineties boy band North and South once! But you're only as hot as your last remix, and that trend seems to have eased off a bit now.

But this was the Scream! We were mates, sure, but not as close as we would be a few months later. All I knew was that I was excited and flattered as hell to be asked because they were my favourite group. The problem was it was like being asked to paint a biblical mural in the Devil's front room. What the hell do you do? I remember getting the cassette through the letterbox one morning and hearing that rough mix for the first time. I swooned at the tranquil soul within before hopping about the room like a demented rabbit. Then I sat down, scratched my head and thought, 'What the fuck am I gonna do with this?'

The group had booked me into London's flash and highly-expensive Metropolis Studios for two days in November. At the time I did all my stuff in a tiny studio situated under London's Westway called Millennium, which was packed with old synths, samplers and the usual dance music essentials. Metropolis, on the other hand, was made for the likes of Elton John. So-called 'real' music played by 'real' musicians, who had no room for this new-fangled, computer-planned shit.

Luckily, I'd brought in Ben Recknagel, my studio partner-in-crime and computer wizard, expecting an upmarket version of Millennium. We'd manhandled the likes of the Boo Radleys and St Etienne with some success and were hoping to have some fun with the wildest group on the planet. We got there and found a multi-track, state of-the-art desk and a nice canteen. There was bugger-all kit suited to what I wanted to do, though. I think a computer got unearthed eventually. I was immediately out of my depth. I'm no Pete Waterman. All I could do was call in Secret Knowledge's Wonder to overdub mass gospel backing vocals and mess about a bit with the percussion.

One bonus at Metropolis was Innes and Duffy turning up to see how things were going, taking over the table football for some fierce tournament action. I'd never really hung out with them in a non-gig/unbollocksed situation before and it was very pleasant. At the end of the two days I was fairly happy with what we'd done, but knew I hadn't pushed out any sonic boundaries like the Weatherall-Nicolson axis.

Andrew Innes was tactful a few days later when he told me they'd decided the song had simply needed to be stripped down. I felt like an asshole, 'cos all I'd done was dress it in some clothes which didn't necessarily flatter the form. I think the technical term is 'overcooked'. I simply didn't know how to extend a section or anything like that, never having worked with master tapes in a 'proper' studio before. Maybe, in retrospect, I should've done a 'Loaded' and binned half the backing tracks, then grafted on my Ken Dodd album or something. I just thought it was a beautiful song and tried to bolster things up a bit. Maybe, not really knowing them that well yet, I was a bit scared of messing with the Scream.

Only a few months later, it would be a different story altogether when I realised I preferred working with knackered – but essential – equipment in a sub-Westway dive with a lunatic engineering genius. And by then I wasn't scared of messing about with the Scream. Strictly musically, of course.

Round about Christmas time in LA – meaning blazing sunshine and blue skies – Innes was back with George D. and his engineer Dave Bianco, remixing the rousing 'Call On Me', another beautiful soul ballad called 'Cry Myself Blind', and 'Everybody Needs Somebody', which simply got stripped back down to the bare style of my original cassette, and still sounded angelic. It wound up as an unlisted track at the end of the album, after 'I'll Be There For You'. This album may have been derided at the time, but these are two true soul outings on a level with anything the band have ever done. How silly does the term 'dance traitors' sound in this bright, heart-dredging light?

David Cavanagh was the one journalist allowed to be not only a fly-on-the-wall for the whole project, but a man on a mission, in the fashion that allowed Stanley Booth to pen *The True Adventures of the Rolling Stones* – and get the nod from Keith. His definitive *Select* account reports that Oakenfold did a mix of 'Call On Me', with McGee's instruction to make it a number one record. Alan deemed the result 'too polite'.

But the album was now under the Scream's waistband, and straining like a plutonium hard-on. Bobby was starting to come out loud and proud with descriptions like this one to Tower Records' *TOP*: 'It's heartbreakers, hipshakers and space odysseys. It's also a great rock 'n' roll album.'

Or on the Heavenly press release: 'It's the record we've always wanted to make but never had the opportunity or the money. By the way, it's rock 'n' roll, not rock. There's a big difference. Rock don't swing.'

Keith Richards has often voiced the same theory: 'You can't have the rock without the roll.'

Exactly. Rock on its own is overblown, pompous and self-consciously ROCK. Rock 'n' roll can be made on acoustic instruments like standup bass, two-piece drum-suit and a whacked acoustic guitar. Elvis Presley's original line-up proved that.

The Scream had been riding a white bicycle around the outer limits of sonic soul experimentation when they created *Screamadelica*. But it was still rock 'n' roll, in the true sense. Using an electric harpsichord they could create a groin-flash neutron bomb on 'Higher Than The Sun'. All the same, with Primal Scream, the guitars never went home. Innes and the Throb got theirs out in Memphis – guitars, that is – and seduced and caressed pure soul with the Horns before whacking the living shit out of the poor fuckers to get 'Rocks' off into anthemic orbit. If Throb can play 'Movin' On Up' laying on his back in Sweden . . . well, Johnny Thunders did the same thing with 'Do You Love Me?' at CBGBs with the Heartbreakers in 1978. Both not on purpose, I might add. But there is a similar spirit. Maybe something akin to Keef sliding across the stage on a tossed-up frankfurter, and not missing a beat, in Frankfurt.

So, with the onset of 'Rocks' and Bobby's first press appearances, we knew we were into another Scream strain of rock 'n' roll. Throb added ham to the roll: 'Never cheese . . . maybe pork though.'

The long piece by Cliff Jones in the *Face* was an excellent summation of Primal Scream rounding the bend, overcoming odds, and popping up with the record dreams are made of . . . and not every mutha's gonna get it. Did they care? The inside pics of Bob and Throb sprawled comatose in a hotel room surrounded by bodies, some not wearing very much, kind of said, 'We're back, on our own terms.'

'Seeing him aching, wasted and hopelessly lost in music, you begin to describe what drives Bobby Gillespie. The essence of Primal Scream and, by implication, the essence of rock 'n' roll is right here in this crumpled, wraith-like figure. Good times, bad times, love and loss, fuckedupness, elation, celebration, sin and redemption, passion and soul. Either that or he's the best faker in the business.'

I truly think that's a shit-hot piece of music writing, and totally sums up Mr Gillespie. Apart from the last sentence. There ya go.

THE FACE

No 65 FEBRUARY 1994 £1.80 • US $4.95
ITALY L7900 • GERMANY 11.90DM • NETHERLANDS 9.50HFL
JAPAN ¥1300 • BELG 166BFR • SPAIN 500PTAS • FRANCE 28FR

THE LAST GREAT BRITISH ROCK STAR?
Bobby's Primal Scream

Snowboarding

Tarantino's Pulp Fiction

Ren and Stimpy

Virtual nightclubbing

Amerika's most wanted
ICE CUBE, SNOOP DOGGY DOGG

Bobby Gillespie
photographed by Glen Luchford

tomorrow's people
Model Jenny Shimizu, comedian Dorian Crook and 25 more faces for 1994

Bobby makes the cover of UK 'style bible' the Face *in February 1994.*

The ultimate black box commentary on Scream Flight Number 666 – destination Pure Soul Unlimited Airport – came from Tim Tooher. Tim was a longtime gatherer of soul tunes and Bobby's high-street confidential during the making of *Screamadelica*. He entered into the Screamadelic burn-out with Technicolor honours, writing about the spirit of the thing without a single mention of a 'drug hell' in the whole piece. Being a mate, he got some unique stuff out of Bobby like this, from a simple comment about George Clinton being the kind of guy who could make you happy. Springboard time:

Bob: 'I think he has. There's so much shit people have got to contend with every day of their lives. Why add to the misery? Someone like Clinton, he's saved my life, man. Rock 'n' roll's saved my life. Jazz has saved my life. Music has saved my life. What would I be if I didn't have music? I've met all my best friends through music, a lot of beautiful cats. It's a great form of communication. It's a great way of getting in touch with other people. It's great to go on stage and see the joy on people's faces and watch them dancing and getting down. Just getting off on it and losing themselves in the whole fucking experience. It's a beautiful thing. I love it, man. It's sexy. Rock 'n' roll and sex.

'We need people to play music to. It's like if you're laying in bed, you need a lady, or you might need a man. To make love you need someone to make love to. And it's the same with

Innes, Dublin, '92.

music. It's great to play music to people. The energy thing is reciprocal. You need the energy thing from the audience to give the energy out. Music's one of the last things that can make you feel. If you sit and watch TV all day, all it does is nullify you, numb you out . . . But at a gig you're surrounded by people, and there's this energy from everybody in the room. There's electric energy coming from the stage, coming from the amplifiers. It's a real sexy thing at its best. It's like total communication.

'Sometimes if I'm alone I can put on a record like "Wait And See" by Lee Hazelwood, or "Please Forgive Me" by O. V. Wright and it makes me feel less alone. In fact, it makes me feel, which is important. The way the world is you can get numbed up and you can be cynical and you can be inward to the point of killing yourself, but music makes you feel. It can make you cry or dance. It can let loose emotions which sometimes you forget you've got, and that's the power of rock 'n' roll or soul or funk.'

Unfortunately, Tim took more of a back seat in Screamworld as some of the band's personal preoccupations took hold. They came through it all and moved on, but Mr Tooher, an inspirational figure, simply melted into the shadows. I've seen him a couple of times since, but an abiding memory is of one of Nightingale's birthday bashes when we were both DJing. He was curled up in a cupboard. I think I was in the next one.

Back then though, he got Bobby to open up about the way 'the music helps people to get in touch with things inside themselves'.

'Yes, it puts you back in touch with emotions you forget you had,' said Bob. 'Sometimes I get so introverted I think I'm never coming back, and that I'm going to be depressed for the rest of my life. When I feel like that I could go to sleep and never wake up, but you can play these beautiful records and they can speak to you. This may be a sad thing to say but sometimes I feel like music can speak to me more than most people can. I don't know if that says a bad thing about me or if that says a bad thing about other people. Maybe it says that I'm fucked up and I can't communicate properly with people. Maybe I can't open myself up. Perhaps the records help me open up to myself, to have a conversation with myself.'

Just to wind up, Tim guides Bobby through a beautiful finishing quote about the transcendent joy of great music, his life's mission and the pure Scream essence: 'It's got soul, it's got the feeling. It'll touch people's hearts and make them move at the same time. As long as the guitar plays, it'll steal your heart away. As long as Mr Young and Mr Innes and Mr Richards and Mr Berry and Mr Fuckin' Elmore James and Mr Slim Harpo keep on playing.'

In his own Scream diary section, Mr Tooher closed on this note: 'Primal Scream make music that they hope will touch people's lives like so much other music has touched theirs. They make music that celebrates feeling. Feeling good, feeling bad. Music that will stand by your side. That's all.'

Amen to that too, Tim. Hope you're okay, baby.

Tim's feature also carried some interviews conducted by Annie Nightingale with the group's accomplices on the album. Here's some highlights, including reflections from the late Tom Dowd. Where did he feel the band was coming from?

'I realised they were more deeply rooted in blues and American folk music than *Screamadelica* had revealed. They aspired to it, they were learned and they knew names of musicians, studios and so forth. They had teethed on these certain records that were familiar to me. So we had a common denominator . . .

'In fact, in the tradition of Ray Charles and Stevie Wonder, once or twice in the studio I made them all close their eyes so their hearing actually went up. And I knew when they were in clubs or sat in the studio listening they would have their eyes closed. Looking into what was going on with their ears. Becoming more and more aural-sensitive, heart-sensitive, an emotional group. They began to realise how simple and secure soul really is and they have the sincerity.'

Memphis Horn Wayne Jackson said, 'We're proud to have Primal Scream on our list of greats. Proud to have them on the list of people we've worked with. Primal Scream are like Aerosmith or something. They make you wanna dance.

'They came to Memphis for the ambience of the town and I think they absorbed a lot of good beer.'

Muscle Shoals rhythm section bassist David Hood said, 'I think they're really soulful, but I don't think they know it . . . When we weren't with them, we missed them.'

Drummer Roger Hawkins added, 'The way I missed them was they made me feel young again. It was almost like I was their age and I really liked that. And the fact that they were searching for a feeling. It was like I was reliving some things that I'd gone through before. When we were Primal Scream's age we were playing with people like Aretha Franklin and Wilson Pickett. And we were just trying to soak everything up from them. More than just the music, also the feeling . . . And I felt that's what these guys were doing with us.'

Jeff Powell, Ardent's in-house engineer, commented, 'They're very talented. They can evoke more emotion out of the way they play than most bands I've worked with. There were times when I would have a lump in my throat it was so pretty.'

Explosive Scream Moment in Tokyo, '92.

And the great Jim Dickinson himself was prodded to remark, 'I just think they're some very smart boys . . . I was aware of them but I wasn't really around the session until the end. The thing I record-ed with them was on the last night. In fact, I think it was after the last night. The end of the end.

'"Big Jet Plane". I told Bobby that night the song was like the Box Tops playing "No Expectations" and he said, "Finally, somebody gets it." That night was great. It was sheer chaos, which is my favourite thing.'

What was his overall impression of them?

'They were obviously very serious about what they were doing. To be that into the American music that they're doing, which is not mainstream American pop music by any stretch of the imag-ination. They touched my heart. Because that's what I've spent my life doing, playing this obscure, redneck southern music that they're obviously way off into.

'Rock 'n' roll is something you're mama's not supposed to like. If your mama likes it, it ain't rock 'n' roll enough. I'm an enemy of institutional order and corporate structure, at least artisti-cally. I think good music comes up from the street and it's harder and harder to get in the door. So when a band like Primal Scream comes along and makes an artistic statement, as this record obviously is, it's good for everybody.'

Annie also spoke to George Drakoulias – the last man on board the album, but first out of the gate with his mix of 'Rocks'.

'Well, at first they said just make it regular American rock 'n' roll and I said, "Andrew [Innes], if you want me to do that I will, but it's not gonna sound a lot different. But if you want I can make it sound really stupid and ruin it." And he said, "Go ahead." So I just made it more stupid. I played it to a friend and he said it sounded like a cross between the Archies and T.Rex. So I knew I was on the right track.'

How do they compare to other bands?

'I think they're the most enthusiastic. They just came in the studio and they were ready to go. They live hard, drink fast and do what they have to do, they don't really do anything lightly or slowly.'

Well, that was the album done then. Innes stayed on at the Chateau Marmont for a couple of weeks to celebrate its completion and get away from London berserkness for the festive season with girlfriend Alison. There was one music paper gossip item about our man falling for a story from the assembled company, relating to what was supposedly a hotel tradition: as the New Year comes in there you get naked and run around sweeping the corridors with a broom. This he supposedly did, and ended up being locked out of the room. It might've had something to do with top madame and party animal Heidi Fleiss allegedly being one of the revellers.

Meanwhile, back in London, they had to have a title for the album. I remember the panic over this one. Pressing plant, printers and record company were all Primal-ed up with hopefully somewhere to go. While Innes was doing his job of editing and mastering, Bob came up with final track names and eventually lifted the title from one of the Clinton tunes: *Give Out But Don't Give Up*.

The front cover is a large photo of the Confederate flag, the reason being that they recorded most of it in America's Deep South and that's the vibe. The band simply liked the image and how it corresponded with the recording location. But it did lead to an outcry, as some saw it as a symbol of redneck racism and slavery. Bobby would simply retort that the neoned-up flag was actually a work by a black American artist entitled *Troubled Waters*, and was used as an anti-racism statement. And anyway, this from a band with a black singer, producer Tom Dowd, who'd discovered many of the biggest soul stars ever, and an alliance with prime funk mover George Clinton? There was another black man on the back cover too: original Funkadelic guitarist Eddie Hazell had recently died, so in tribute they used a lovely, grainy photo of him flashing a huge grin.

The Scream were confronted with this overblown issue on a few occasions. Dele Fadele – one of the better *NME* writers, who happens to be black – cornered Nightingale in a cab the three of

The controversial artwork for Give Out But Don't Give Up *which – somewhat ironically – was based on a work called* Troubled Waters *by William Eggleston. A black photographer.*

Bobby learns the drill during the recording of 'Call On Me', at Ocean Wave Studios, Hollywood, '93.

us were sharing one night. Secret Knowledge's Wonder – a black soul singer from West Virginia – had also reacted to that flag and sided with Dele. Sure, its image can inspire fear and loathing, but why leave it hanging in redneck bars? Alex could only say it was a great sleeve, a striking image meant with respect.

That flag was not entirely irrelevant to one of the album's main missions – the pursuit of soul's Holy Grail. Soul came from the South to give black people a world platform and some cash. It inspired many people, including Primal Scream. How many cornball Yankee outfits have used the Stars and Stripes and got a Budweiser raised in their direction? Sly Stone used the flag of the North to ram home the point of *There's A Riot Goin' On*. What about the Jam using the Union Jack? Did that make them NF advocates? George Clinton used a funky dollar bill for *America Eats Its Young*. It's all about images, statements and communal nerve-tapping. Striking images that also strike nerves have been used for decades by people who make music all over the world. Tellingly, the Scream had not been vetoed by their US record company, Sire.

Bobby later said, when quizzed about it by *Trainspotting* author Irvine Welsh for *i-D* magazine, 'We used that image because it was a beautiful picture, and our album was recorded in the

South and a lot of the musicians who influenced us were born there: Muddy Waters, Robert Johnson, Elvis, Lee Dorsey, Jerry Lee Lewis. One thing I would really baulk at would be using the Union Jack or the Stars and Stripes as imagery. To me, that's racist.'

Ultimately it was water off a duck's back, even if the Black Crowes – ironically, the band who George Drakoulias had made his name with – slagged off the Scream's adoption of their beloved flag. The Crowes weren't too impressed with the Scream's decision to marry Deep South soul spirit with classic rock 'n' roll and their other musical strains. Plus, they were from across the water. Bobby and I went to check out the Black Crowes at a 'secret' London gig in late 1994, after we'd done the Criminal Justice Bill protest cover for *Melody Maker*. We lurked subtly at the bar. The looks we exchanged after a few Crowe-Quo pub-plodders couldn't have been called smug but, in the light of their comments, might have been called big grins.

Anyway, Grant Fleming's immortal backstage-at-the-Ritz shot graced the inside gatefold. It was the best backstage visual encapsulation since Annie Liebowitz's *Rolling Stone* photo of Keef passed-out on an early seventies Stones tour. Nobody can argue with that.

So everything was sorted, all systems go, and the first taster – 'Rocks' – was a total killer. Big sighs of relief all round.

The album kicks off with the false-start/tune-up power-chord sleaze 'n' roll of 'Jailbird'. Bobby's in there immediately, no messing: 'Scratchin' like a tom cat / Got a monkey on my back / I'm gonna push and pull / And howl like a wolf / And drive my cadillac.' The momentum is continued with the monster-stomp party anthem that is 'Rocks.': 'Dealers keep dealin' / Thieves keep thievin' / Whores keep whorin' / Junkies keep scorin'.' Oh yes. These two tracks put the Scream's cards firmly on the table, even if they alone were enough to get the band branded 'dance traitors' by those nerdier elements who liked their music predictable. The dance mob can be the snobbiest, most up-rectum bores in the world. I know, 'cos I got stick for years for following the Scream/ Clinton attitude.

'That's just nonsense,' retorted Bobby. 'Great music is great music.' He told me that 'Rocks' made him laugh. Look at the videos and he's smiling. Not that he didn't take that roistering call-to-arms dead seriously. Every time I played it at gigs the place would erupt, whether it be a pub, an aftershow party or a Heavenly Social-style club. In other words, it detonated people who knew how to party.

'Humour is important,' cackled Bob. 'We had to make a record that people can relate to. The bluesy, dark, really hurting songs are important, sure, but so are the songs that make you want to smile and dance and jump around! . . . It all just sounds like Primal Scream to me.'

Then comes '(I'm Gonna) Cry Myself Blind', which ranks as probably the saddest song the band have ever done. Bobby comes up with probably his most soulful vocal since 'I'm Losing More': 'I been crazy since you left me / I'm so sorry for what I've done / Why did you go? Why did you go? / I'm so lonely.' The chorus simply repeats the title. It was a masterpiece of melancholic soul and became the album's third single.

'A lot of girls like our band because a lot of the songs are about emotions and being vulnerable,' said Bobby. 'I'm not afraid to say I cry . . . but there's humour too. I can be campy, wear makeup, wiggle my arse and it's funny. It's just a question of mixing it right and letting it go.'

Next is the perfect pick-me-up in the shape of George's whooping mix of 'Funky Jam', which is simply a brilliant affirmation of everything Bobby and himself had been saying for years about the meeting of musical styles. 'Big Jet Plane' soars majestically overhead but hits to the heart and gut: 'My heart feels like a stone / I'm payin' the price of a drunken night / I'm wastin' in the twilight zone.' Then it's 'Free', Denise's George-mixed *tour de force* ballad, before 'Call On Me', that last-minute rocker given a raunch injection from the other George. 'Struttin'' is Brendan Lynch's wigged-out 'Kosmos'-style take on 'Funky Jam'. 'Sad And Blue' is probably the track which most shows those ageless Memphis soul roots – hearing Bobby singing in this context is startling, while

Watching the world go by in West Hollywood, '93

hearing the Scream boys bouncing off the seasoned session vets is quite sublime.

Like *Screamadelica*, this album makes its point on a loud and speedy level early on, and is content to take the listener out on a chilled but inspirational sequence of slower tunes: the title track is the aforementioned Clinton-Denise duet and pure P-Funk spine-crawling. "I'll Be There For You' and 'Everybody Needs Somebody' are just beautiful love ballads.

Three years after *Screamadelica*, Primal Scream had finished their new album. Now a new rollercoaster ride was about to begin . . .

Bobby, Los Angeles, '93.

Pennie Smith captured Bobby, Innes and yours truly after the Tokyo gig in August, '94. The lovely Pennie wrote, 'Wahey!' on the back, which about sums it up, really.

Carry On Screaming
A Year On The Road With
Primal Scream

'Dance music is whatever makes you dance.' – *Bobby Gillespie*

After the endless pregnancy, problems and prolonged labour which eventually gave birth to the *Give Out But Don't Give Up* album, it was time to promote and revel in it. And so the monstrous Scream gig machine started cranking into full-blown life at the start of 1994 and would carve a trail of rock 'n' roll carnage around the world for over a year.

I got a call from Alex Nightingale's office one day saying the band wanted me to DJ on the UK leg of a world tour which would eventually take them around Europe, Japan, America and then the UK again at the end of the year. Although I'd hung out with the band in the past, I had a couple of warm-ups to test the water and it snowballed from there. After the first jaunt I ended up going on all of them, apart from the States. And lived to tell the tale.

Going on the road with Primal Scream is like a trial by fire. You either swim, flap around madly or sink. I probably went for the middle route, but it wasn't that hard amidst the hilarious chaos which imbues the Primal Scream rock 'n' roll circus. When mates or business acquaintances found out I was going on tour with the Primals they'd either laugh, give knowing warnings or sadly shake their heads. Or more often than not go, 'Lucky fucker.' It seems like the only people who get scared of the band are those who don't know them, mainly because the group – quite an insular family – won't let them. They don't trust people or suffer fools that gladly.

'Rocks' was the first single to be released from the upcoming album, on 28 February. An immediate winner. The low-life lyrics like 'he's always got a line for the ladies,' that defiant run-up of 'ain't no use in praying, that's the way I'm staying, baby' exploding into the chorus of 'get yer rocks off, get yer rocks off, honey' added up to the ultimate definition of Screamworld. The defiant vocal, and music which hitched belting Memphis brass with buzzsaw guitar action and a thunderous beat seemingly derived from a classic soul stomper, made for a Scream classic. Even Rod Stewart covered it four years later. It would be paired up with 'Funky Jam', the track George Clinton had come in to funk up and Brendan Lynch took out to the kosmos.

First of all 'Funky Jam' was leaked out to dance DJs as a plain white label sealed at the top with a sticker boasting the Scream logo and title. One side contained two George mixes, while the other

'Rocks' video shoot at the YMCA, January '94.

featured Brendan's dubbed-up sonic barrage, which was first called 'Funky Strut' before appearing on the album as 'Struttin''. Reviewing it as my Single of the Week in *NME*'s dance column, 'Vibes', I said, 'This is how you deal with the past and seminal influences – with love, respect and desire to springboard into your own vision and orbit.' *Select* made it Single of the Month and called it 'a work of utter genius', adding 'this is the purest form of rock 'n' roll to shimmer and sashay among the singles releases for ages.'

The group now looked quite different from the *Screamadelica* period's psychedelic collision with acid house. Maybe it was all the hard partying of the previous few years, but rock 'n' roll had never left the building, and they'd mutated and glammed up the black-leather-'n'-long-hair sleazy glamour of the second album. They now looked like a proper gang of hoodlums straight out of MC5 Detroit circa the early seventies. After the ups and downs of the previous three years they meant business.

The 'Rocks' video would be shot at a live, invite-only gig at the YMCA off Tottenham Court Road in London's West End. The group had commandeered a regular glam-dance knees-up called Billion Dollar Babes to play the single and generally mess around. Myself and Alex Paterson were hauled in to DJ in the bar for a specially-invited posse of freaks, glamorous hooligans and party babes. Sticks of rock appeared with 'Primal Scream' running through.

Back in the dressing room Bobby had put on his new cream-coloured shirt and plastered his face in pale panstick and lipgloss. Scream-style backstage mayhem was in the air as Throb strutted about with a bottle of Jack Daniel's, Duffy spouted and guffawed and Innes chuckled at all the lunacy while a stream of well-wishers, mates like Weatherall and assorted nose-hopers trooped by.

It was my first time spinning for the Scream since the miners' benefit aftershow, so I'd thought long and hard about the selection. It was all dance music, but in the true sense of the word. No house or bangin' techno. Punk rock from The Clash, the Pistols and Thunders, the Funk from Sir George Clinton, disco from Donna Summer, soul and reggae, the Rolling Stones, Prince, the MC5, some hip hop classics. Anything but bangin' house and techno really, which had kind of been my brief. It's no coincidence that my t-shirt said, 'Suck My Deck.' But it seemed to do the trick and also served to vibe up the band, who piled onstage to warm up and swoop into 'Rocks'. As the crowd cavorted to its bludgeoning, two-fingered celebration it became fully apparent for the first time that this song was a total Scream roof-raiser. They furthered the party with an impromptu stroll through the Rolling Stones' back catalogue, with Secret Knowledge's Wonder getting up to wail with Denise on 'Honky Tonk Women' and 'Start Me Up', as well as Iggy's 'No Fun' and the Who's 'So Sad About Us'.

A rather cynical gossip column entry in *Melody Maker* laid into their party set and described the 'ongoing party situation' as getting out of hand. All good fun, succinctly summed up by 'a statement from the band's publicist': 'Plenty of broken camera equipment, several black eyes and some imaginative sexual couplings . . . you'd grab hold of a girl and then find out it was a boy.'

At that time the core-band consisted of Bobby, Innes, Throb and Duffy. Denise was still Bobby's vocal sparring partner and Henry Olsen supplied his inscrutable bass. Session man and former Style Council drummer Steve Sydelnick had come in on drums at the last minute after Toby Tobanov had, apparently, become the most recent Scream casualty. This was indeed a firing live unit, and one which would be together for many months to come.

Later that month I happened to be in New York. So, coincidentally, were Primal Scream, recording a special live spot for MTV with George Clinton. Even though the two parties had a record out it would be the first time they'd ever met him. US label Sire had big hopes for the album because of the classic American flavours in the music. I'd already established contact, so I duly turned up at MTV's Manhattan studio.

I walked straight into Mr Clinton, who recalled the interview and massive coverage I'd done

'Rocks' video still, from the Japanese tour programme.

for him a couple of years earlier. He was on fine form, rolling up lethal weed and expounding on the glory days of P-Funk. He obviously knew he'd found some kindred spirits with these crazy white dudes, and started playing tapes of unreleased P-Funk. The one which most blew us away was a doo-wop album he'd done with some of the original guys, which must have harked back to those barbershop quintet days. The band played three songs: 'Jailbird', 'Funky Jam' and 'Rocks', with George joining in when he felt like it. Despite being in his late fifties the man bounced around the set, not to mention the walls, with the best of 'em. He doesn't even appear on 'Rocks' but, fired up by the incendiary version of 'Funky Jam' they'd just done together, joined in anyway. It was simply one of those classic television moments.

Celebrations were in order, and the long day turned into a long night as we repaired to a Lower East Side Indian restaurant, a few bars, and then made a swift trip to the liquor store to load up on bourbon before we hit the apartment where I was staying.

That was one of the first times I'd got to talk to Throb properly, as I showed him sights dating from the time I lived in the city and we swapped notes about the Rolling Stones. By 'sights', I mean assorted bars and corners where I used to wait for the proverbial man. Throb is a bit of a legend, with a fearsome reputation. I think it was round about this time that *NME* described him as the most frightening man in Britain. I never found this at all. He's been through the whole rock 'n' roll mill sure, and the acid house one to boot, but he's never been less than the real thing, a true giggle and a law unto himself. Nobody else could have got away with those Keef-in-'69 snakeskin boots! He turned into my partner-in-crime on the road, and might occasionally end up howling at the moon on a New York tenement rooftop, but was never less than a true gent.

By the time we reached the apartment on Avenue B the refreshments were starting to take their toll. The place belonged to a dear old writer mate of mine called Steve Mirkin. We all piled round, Throb strolled in, plonked himself down in a little straw chair – and promptly went right through! Then it was on to a swanky music biz type's luxury apartment on Broadway, and by this time we

George and yours truly hanging in the MTV dressing room, New York City. A personal Magic Moment.

I vent some Scream spleen in the tour programme.

were all a bit messy. Bobby fell straight through the CD cabinet before deciding to go back to the hotel and trying to hail a police car. Some of us, like Grant Fleming, went to legendary dance club Sound Factory to check it out and ended up watching then-hot DJ Junior Vasquez lord it over a load of naked gay guys towel-dancing. But it's all a bit of a haze.

In social situations the lunatic core of Bobby, Throb, Innes and Duffy never stop enthusing passionately about anything from music to football, laughing their bollocks off at the unlikely situations that always seem to present themselves and continuing an eternal quest to get gloriously pissed. Well, at this time anyway – nowadays they're more selective. By the time I staggered out of the hotel a couple of mornings after the first night's cavorting, I'd done my first stretch of brilliant madness with Primal Scream up close and made some friends for life. This also went a long way in explaining just what makes them laugh and tick.

The next task was to write programme notes for the upcoming tour and I attacked it with relish, describing the band as 'a beautiful monster devouring what lies in its ravenous path'. Referring to the classic soul influences coursing through the new album, I gibbered thus: 'The Scream gorge on inspirational diamonds from the past, letting them mate with their own unique soul as another stimulus to be pursued, hued and spewed back into the maelstrom. Primal Scream not only walk it like they talk it but enter the pole-vault and limbo championships to boot.'

If *Screamadelica* had been the group's exploratory mission into the unknown then the new album burned a swathe through the garden of earthly delights which has yielded some of the greatest music ever, while dropkicking it into Primal orbit. As ultimate music fans, the Scream finally had the means and opportunity to revel in a lifetime of passion. . . In moving on Primal Scream looked back, captured the essence of something that was nearly lost forever and propelled it into the nineties. It was a marriage made in Heaven, Hell and the soul.

The album did spark confusion and abuse – and not a small amount of praise – from a music media who wanted, or expected, *Screamadelica Part Two*. There were snide jibes in the gossip columns and always references to the Rolling Stones.

Select might have headed their review 'On A Jagger Tip!', but Adam Higginbotham gave it five

primal scream
tour 1994/95

Euro '94 tour action, from the Japanese tour programme.

stars, writing, 'It is uniquely, tremendously, fabulously derivative – in the best possible way,' adding, 'It's the kind of attitude that makes them real-life, gold seal, Olympic-length rock stars. And, incredibly, very, very cool indeed.' He also said it was 'as good as *Screamadelica.*' Traditionalists *Q* said, 'You won't hear a better Rolling Stones album this year, or perhaps ever again,' while giving it four. *NME*'s Max Bell said 'the record succeeds on its own stop-the-world-I-want-to-get-off-in-1974 terms' and deemed it a seven.

'Rocks' had been a hit, entering the UK ckarts at number eight, the album buzz was gearing up well, and the upcoming UK tour in March sold out well in advance. They appeared on *Top of the Pops* on 9 March with Bob in impenetrable shades. The band were still operating higher than the sun, having a whale of a time and couldn't wait to get back on the road. They knew it would get a bit *Apocalypse Now* as they stayed on tour for a year. For the first UK leg poster they'd selected a classic shot of Keith Moon perched proudly next to a champagne bottle he'd inserted into a wall, which he'd taken the trouble to frame.

Undoubtedly the best, most incisive feature to appear about the Scream around this time was *Trainspotting* author Irvine Welsh's contribution to style mag *i-D*'s Drugs Issue. Irv gets off to a flying start by boarding the Edinburgh to London train, somewhat bollocksed after a chemical weekend, coming down the day before a reading tour to interview the Scream. Irv admits at the start of the feature that he didn't care much for the new album at first, preferring the dance moves of its predecessor. But after a few plays he's warmed to it and can't stop singing 'Rocks'.

Kicking off with his rock vs dance theories, Irv is soon steered into open musical pastures by Bobby, who outlines his blowing-up-boxes philosophy and says that rock 'n' roll has always been dance music: 'It's the feel of the music that's the thing. It's nothing to do with the head, it's to do with the heart.'

It's obvious that Irv and the Scream hit it off immediately. He writes, 'The Scream are a good posse of punters who don't like anyone to be excluded from the gang. Meeting them for the first time feels like teaming up with old pals. All my cynical wee notions . . . seem pretty ludicrous in response to the openness and straightforwardness of the band.'

He continues, 'Primal Scream have to feel the music for it to work. They're probably the furthest possible thing from the outfit who try to predict cultural trends and fire out a product to flog to the style androids of the grave new world. Whether they are innovative, as in *Screamadelica*, or paying tribute to their own heroes, as in *Give Out*, the process is an organic one from people who just want to make music.'

Irv describes Robert Young as 'the antithesis of the traditional, defensive musical luddite that rock 'n' roll guitarists are often portrayed as. Says Throb, when asked if the Scream are making a statement against the dull grunge that rock has become, 'No, it's not a reaction against anything. The only statement that we're making is that this is ours, this is what we're doing. We're not

stone me

Bob in his Keef t-shirt with subtle Japanese heading. Japanese tour programme, '94.

analysing what's going on around us . . . It doesn't matter what it is, if you can use it to make music, it's just another instrument.' Making the point that now the Scream are using their new-found studio confidence to make music with any instruments they feel like, Robert adds, 'We didn't really know how to make an album before Andrew Weatherall.'

Bobby becomes animated: 'Nae rules, nae boundaries . . . that's no realistic. There can't be boundaries to the expression of emotion.'

Throb: 'Music's about breaking down boundaries. You can look at that anyway you like, but that's an essential basic fact.'

By this time Irv's 'intentions of staying straight until my reading promotions have well and truly gone out of the window.' He quotes Denise Johnson as saying, 'Primal Scream is a party you can leave at any time,' adding, 'I'll just stick around a bit longer. I'm enjoying the vibes.'

Obviously the two parties talk about drugs, and Irv asks if Bobby ever worried about the rock 'n' roll casualty thing. He replies, 'Well, this band was in a mess about a year ago, but it's good to go through that. It's just that sometimes you maybe almost have to lose something, like destroy it, before you find out how much you love it.'

Irvine rounds off in spot-on fashion, prodding the inevitable thought that if he ever decided to pursue a career as a music writer he'd be up there with the greats like Lester Bangs, Nick Kent and myself. (Only joking.) 'Primal Scream are good people who deserve good times. These rock 'n' roll ravers have stayed true to their roots, while simultaneously embracing the house culture. They are emphatic, honest, open-minded and easy-going, dedicated to what they want to do: these qualities are infectious, and as I've said, they make you look at your own musical hangups. I've even resolved to listen to some of the pre-'88 stuff in my record collection, free from the prejudices I've built up over the years against the musicians who've spraffed the accompanying mundane bullshit.'

Mission accomplished, a classic feature and another convert. Plus an invaluable new member of the extended Scream family, who would later join them in a couple of ventures. I didn't know at this time that three years later I would count Irv as one of my closest mates and be in a band with him too! The man is remarkable – brilliant company, a no-holds-barred attitude to enjoying himself whatever the cost and, above all, a top mate.

That interview was conducted when the Scream were in rehearsal for the upcoming tour. Before that took off I was booked to do a UK jaunt with St Etienne – both playing with Secret Knowledge and DJing. Kind of a warmup for the Scream really, although those boys and girls do like their dressing room rider. Which brings us to a sore point. In Dublin Bobby and Innes showed up, having flown over from London. However, they didn't watch any of the show, being content to sneak into the dressing room and nick all the group's rider, except for a bottle of Jack Daniel's. It didn't go down well with St Etienne's legendary tipplers, but it was a good omen for the upcoming Scream tour!

So it's about time we said hello to the other key members of the 1994 Scream Touring Party (or STP) who boarded that tour bus on 22 March, 1994. Tour manager Phil 'Trigger' Hamilton, once with PiL, a Chelsea fan, is unflappable in the face of an eruption and still with 'em, so he must be doing something right. The mighty Harte was still along, helping Trig, and proved to be a nutcase prone to prancing around hotel rooms clad in large nappies made of sheets while bellowing opera. Murray Mitchell, in his capacity as production manager, lived for Primal Scream

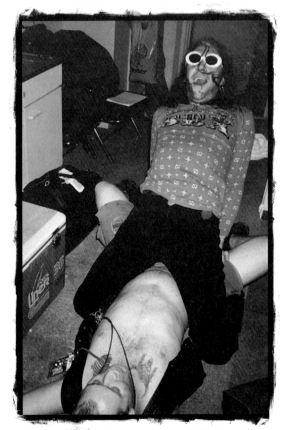

Post-gig hotel dressing room frolics with Throb and Steve 'Fatty' Molloy, '94 UK tour.

and was in turn much-loved for his inscrutable amiability, often in the face of mayhemic calamity. Steve 'Fatty' Molloy, the terminal punk who never sleeps, was in charge of security and also Throb's nurse-maid, which he still did even after cutting himself up by falling through a plate glass window. Nightingale was often along, and Grant Fleming, the hedonist hooligan who'd utilised his camera skills to become the band's visual recorder, ended up publishing the results in a book called *Higher Than The Sun* (Random House, 1997). There was also Jeff Barrett, still A&Ring the band during this time, in the self-enforced absence of Alan McGee.

Then there was the long-suffering road crew. Under Muzz's direction, guitar roadies Jason Caulfield and Chris Ridge, monitor man Jacko, soundman Oz and lighting designer Andy Liddle made sure that whatever was gonna hit the stage that night would sound and look brilliant. Of course, there were also the riggers, caterers, drivers and humpers who were just as essential a part of Primal Scream's rollicking carnival.

The actual tour started with two low-key warm ups which I wasn't doing: Northampton Roadmenders – where I saw Mott the Hoople in 1972! – and Ayr Pavillion. Then they did Belfast and Dublin, with David Holmes DJing.

My first proper gig as Primal Scream tour DJ was at Wolverhampton Civic Hall, which local officials had seen fit to plaster with anti-heroin posters. Whereas the *Screamadelica* tour had taken the form of a non-stop acid house party storming until the early hours, here they were playing venues which closed mainly before midnight. The first gig set a sort of precedent, a routine even, for the four Scream dates I'd be doing that year. First I was required to warm up the crowd with the non-house set similar to the one I'd played at the video shoot. Then I'd get the nod that the band were ready and drop a few they could sing along to in the dressing room and would wind up the crowd – stuff like 'Born To Lose' by Johnny Thunders and the Heartbreakers, the Pistols' 'Holidays In The Sun' or 'Jail Guitar Doors' by The Clash.

The band would duly stagger on to a heroes' welcome and limber up. Bob would shout a quick 'hullo' and it'd be into 'Jailbird'. Innes leaning against his Scottish flag-draped

Running order for my first gig, at Wolverhampton Civic Hall '94

amp. Throb slashing his guitar with hair swinging down. Duffy caressing the keyboard he was also using as support. Bobby clapping and hollering in the black satin shirt he favoured for most of that tour. Denise lending her silky soul-tones, wearing a huge grin, while the Sidelnyk-Olsen rhythm section weighed anchor. With the Scream sun logo beaming down through Andy Liddle's black-and-white drapes it was an awesome opener, before the momentum was carried through with 'Rocks', 'Movin' On Up' and 'Don't Fight It Feel It', where Denise took over and Bob scooted off for a quick break. (This is where I'd usually meet him and Fatty to discuss the evening's progress, the state of the crowd and all that, over a few light refreshments.) Bob would then skip back on and carry on into the ballad section, which was usually 'I'm Losing More Than I'll Ever Have' and 'Everybody', before picking up the pace with 'Funky Jam', 'Call On Me' and 'Come Together'. The first encore was twin slowies 'Cry Myself Blind' and 'Give Out But Don't Give Up', before they'd come back a second time for 'Higher Than The Sun', which visited 'A Love Supreme' and 'Don't Call Me Nigger, Whitey', 'Loaded' and a molten version of 'No Fun', originated by the Stooges and taken on by the Pistols. There'd sometimes be a reprise of 'Rocks' too, just to put the lid on it. It was always a job getting back down from the lampshade when I had to play afterwards.

That first night I just remember thinking that this was rock 'n' roll as I hadn't heard it for years. Bludgeoned by years of shameful abuse, rock 'n' roll had been left for dead, but that night – and over many more to follow – Primal Scream had a riot of their very own.

NME's Ted Kessler was at that date and, obviously not bowled over by the album, gave it a bedgrudgingly good review. After expressing concerns for the band's health – 'these are not well-looking men' – he was forced to admit that the place went bananas. Ted ends up: 'Tonight Primal Scream do a fine job of erasing the knowledge that their album sucks a fairly large one by doing what they've always threatened, and rocking convincingly out with just the right amount of mysterious soul . . . Check them out before one of them dies.'

In 1994, touring with the Scream developed its own warped timetable. A daily ritual with

Innes, Bobby, me and Fatty lounging backstage during the Japan tour.

things like days off, eating and often sleep being considered something of a pain-in-the-arse by the group's hard core. At lunchtime Fatty, who never went to bed, would be noisily rounding up the troops and, within an hour, the bar would be filling up rapidly as last night's wreckage filed in, ordered pints of Guinness and started cranking it up again. The merriment would then spill onto the luxury tour bus as the fridge was ransacked and the video turned on. *Carry On* films – particularly *Abroad* and *Up the Jungle* – plus *The Sweeney* were faves on this tour. By mid-tour we knew all the dialogue and little bloke Kenneth Connor's trademark 'Phwoar!' had become a band catchphrase. By the time we hit the gig everyone was in bits again, except for the session people and Bobby, who'd be taking it easier (sometimes).

The soundcheck was always a Scream delight as they ploughed through old faves to warm up. I could almost make a soundcheck set list – a lot of songs they started playing for fun ended up as encores: 'No Fun', 'Jail Guitar Doors', 'Cold Turkey', 'Kick Out The Jams' by the MC5, which ended up in the 2000 set, and Johnny Thunders' 'Born To Lose', which was much favoured at the 2002 gigs. They also do gorgeous versions of Sister Sledge's 'Thinking About You', Marley's 'No Woman No Cry' and Curtis Mayfield's 'People Get Ready'.

The half of the band I was hanging with didn't have much need for catering – I think Throb managed it once during the entire tour – so it was hotel/bar/pub until gig time. While I did my warm-up set the raucous cavorting in the dressing room proceeded to gain steam. Sometimes Bob would come and crouch behind the decks, rifling through tunes and coming up with suggestions. It was funny seeing the crowd's reactions when he got noticed. Squeals, waves, pointing, the odd roar perhaps.

There's no dressing room routine for a Scream gig. They loaf, wait, drink, laugh and do whatever else comes naturally. The gigs could either be outrageously great, pure Scream magic or, on actually quite rare occasions, bloody awful, depending on how excessive the day's activities had been or whether there were any technical hitches. But they were never boring or just going through the motions.

After the set the dressing room would invariably be packed with dodgy mates, fans and crew, all whooping it up and getting warmed up for further festivities. We'd either go to a club or simply repair back to those much-abused hotel bars. And so it would go on until the next day. Curious incidents and chaos have always followed Primal Scream – especially around this time – but the general 'Carry On Screaming' hedonism is often simply a side-clutching way of side-stepping on-the-road drudgery. Not to mention a way of life.

After Wolverhampton the tour would go on to take in Nottingham then Manchester. I was quickly learning that the band have certain strongholds where the mayhem quotient is stepped up. In Manchester they conveniently had a show booked on the same day as a United game. Along with Celtic, that's the team for the Scottish trio, along with Muzz, so they duly hotfooted it to the

ground after the soundcheck, getting back just in time for the gig. That's the one where a few morons shouted, 'Primal Scream are shite!' at the band. Bob turned round with a disdainful glare and the reply, 'Yeah, but rich shite.'

That gig got a top review from Mandi James in – of all places – dance bible *Mixmag*. 'Herein lies the essence of Primal Scream. They make their fuck ups and their foibles their virtues,' she wrote in nail-on-head style, ending her review with 'Primal Scream, they mean it maaan. For those about to rock, we salute you.'

It was some night. Back at the Britannia Hotel the bar was full of foreign Man Utd fans, including the Norwegian Manchester United Supporter's Club. They were treated by Marco Nelson, sometime Scream and Paul Weller bassist, reeling off a Jerry Lee Lewis medley and my version of 'Swing Low Sweet Chariot'. Next morning I woke up on the end of Throb's bed. He was in it with his girlfriend of the time, Anita. Good job it was a day off, even if me and the guitarist ended up slightly off our faces at the infamous Hacienda's fetish/gay night Flesh. And he was wearing a cowboy hat! By now Throb and I had been christened the Toxic Twins, and occasionally sported Burger King crowns with the name amended to Bugle King.

Meanwhile, Martin Duffy would burble ceaselessly and with great passion about his current obsession. On this tour it was still patenting a line of brown corduroy

Keith Moon in classic pose on the '94 UK tour itinerary.

*The infamous Dave Beer, of Leeds'
Back to Basics.*

underpants with caramel piping. One night in Cambridge Duff went missing, and was eventually discovered by Muzza sleeping in the drum riser. Innes watched all this stupidity with a satisfied smile while Bobby would usually sit quietly at the front of the bus, listening to music or reading. Although he'll cane it with the best of them and constantly guffaws at the antics of his mates, Bob's thing isn't swinging from the chandeliers. He'd rather turn inwards and revel in a glorious musical heritage which, to him, will never be anything less than a bottomless well of discovery.

The fun continued as we proceeded to Liverpool, where I played at Nation – superclub Cream's venue – with Justin Robertson after the Scream gig. A few of our party bowled in, with Nightingale marching around the dance floor, holding up his red tour pass card if he thought anyone looked particularly ropey.

Next day was home city Glasgow, and we had to drive over 200 miles to get there. It was also the anniversary of Marvin Gaye's death, so Bobby paid tribute by sticking up a photo in the bus and playing his Motown tape. Tonight he would dedicate the gig to Marvin.

You can imagine the state of the crew which staggered off the bus at the other end. Glasgow was always a good one, as many of the Scottish trio's relatives would turn out for the party and this one was being broadcast live on Radio One. And the Barrowlands is home turf madness. During the soundcheck I dueted with Bobby on 'Wild Horses' and forgot most of the words, while he didn't, of course. Afterwards I met Bobby's dad and quite a few Scream relatives – all lovely and proud. At showtime the roar that went up when the band walked on was just like the terraces. Over 2,000 nutters getting their communal rocks off. Afterwards was a party at Alan McGee's sister Susan's flat, where they set up decks. I started playing at six in the morning and finished up at ten, with Bobby and Throb lolling back on the sofa in front of me.

Another 200-mile drive, this time to Leeds. We were a week in and, finally, a few people weren't being too loud. That didn't last for long. For the first time on the tour I utilised one of the sleeper bunks and felt rough. Plus we were a bit late, but we soon perked up. I played Suicide's 'Cheree' before the band came on and Bobby walked on humming it to himself and dedicated the set to me, so I was quite touched.

Some of my closest friends in the clubbing community are Dave Beer and the city's notorious Back to Basics crew. If clubland has a Primal Scream equivalent it's Dave, DJ Ralph Lawson and the gang, who had arranged an aftershow knees-up at a local Mexican bar. I was pissed as a fart on Throb's new invention, Jack Daniel's and Purdeys – 'It's healthy!' – and ended up playing a set consisting almost entirely of punk classics, which had both Scream and Basics camps dancing on tables and punching the air. Festivities continued back at the Hilton hotel and ended up in the jacuzzi at seven in the morning. Throb demonstrated how to hide your can of beer underwater before getting locked in the ladies' changing room. He later insisted I stole his underpants when, in fact, it was my own that had gone astray.

Next morning there were even sorer heads as we drove nearly 150 miles down to Cambridge. I seem to remember the gig went off okay – that's the one where Duff was found asleep in the drum riser when the crew were packing up. It was also notable for Jason Donovan turning up and hanging out in the Holiday Inn bar afterwards. Took me at least half an hour to work out who the wired fellow in the woolly hat was. 'Throb's new mate,' was how Innes explained that one. Then it was a much-needed day off – this time I went home to Aylesbury – before it was off again to Southampton and an aftershow jacuzzi party, Cardiff, and finally back to London for the big one.

One of the best bits of this tour turned out to be that three night stint at Brixton Academy, the realisation of a show that had been talked about for months. It was an obvious move that Nightingale had been working on for about a year: Primal Scream sharing a bill with George Clinton and his P-Funk All Stars. The Scream's London all-nighters were already infamous but this would be extra special, although few could have predicted one event that would cloud the whole weekend.

Roaring back into London the day before the first of the gigs, I realised how cut off from the outside world we'd become. All we'd seen was motorways, hotels, venues and bars, but now we were back among familiar surroundings, mates and reality. It still felt like a bunch of marauding outlaws riding into town though, with the Stones' claustrophobic *Gimme Shelter* on the video.

Halfway through my set at Brixton Academy on the first night, Bobby came running over and shouted in my ear.

'Needsy, guess what? Kurt Cobain shot himself!'

Blimey.

I didn't know if the crowd knew at that point, but launched into a brace of Sex Pistols and Clash classics in tribute. Then I walked off stage and straight into George Clinton, who we'd last seen in New York. He'd flown in a day early and was hanging out with the band backstage, so there was a curious mixture of shock and elation in the air. The Scream went on to play a blistering set, with Bobby dedicating songs to Kurt and George getting up for 'Funky Jam'. But everyone was saving themselves for the big one next night.

There was a good omen during the afternoon, when Throb borrowed 50 quid off my mate Stuart to put on the Grand National – and won 300 quid! Arriving at the Academy on Saturday afternoon, it was immediately apparent that this wasn't going to be your average Scream gig.

Backstage was mayhem as there were about fifteen people in George's band, with just the P-Funk girls taking over three of the dressing rooms. It was cute watching the whole troupe queue up behind George by a sidestage flight case as he dished out the pre-gig bugle like school dinners. The fact then dawned on me that I was opening up for one of my all-time heroes.

Gulp.

So I did my funk set, and it went fine before the whole crew trouped on and proceeded to play for over two hours. While George exhorted and led the mass singalongs like a deranged ringmaster in Technicolor biblical robes, his group immaculately cruised through P-Funk classics like 'Tear The Roof Off The Sucker', 'Mothership Connection' and 'Flashlight'. The bass player was wearing a huge nappy! It was prime funk which dipped, exploded and did indeed tear that old roof off. Towards the end, both road crews started anxiously looking at

Backstage pass for the historic Scream/Clinton gig, Brixton Academy, April 9, 1994.

TRINIFOLD TRAVEL

CLIENTS: THE SAUCHIEHALL STREET CHORAL SOCIETY PARTY B

HOTEL: MARRIOTT, LEEDS

ROOMING LIST

GUEST NAME	ROOM TYPE	ROOM NO	DATE IN	DATE O
PHIL HAMILTON *	SINGLE	350	11 DEC	12 DEC
ARTHUR BLACK	SINGLE	302	11 DEC	12 DEC
CHARLIE ABODI	SINGLE	307	11 DEC	12 DEC
JACK KOWALSKI	SINGLE	311	11 DEC	12 DEC
RON SANOVICH	SINGLE	314	11 DEC	12 DEC
HENRY LAYCOCK	SINGLE	102	11 DEC	12 DEC
DENISE JOHNSON	SINGLE	106	11 DEC	12 DEC
STEVE SIDELNYK	SINGLE	120	11 DEC	12 DEC
STEVE MOLLOY	SINGLE	101	11 DEC	12 DEC
GRANT FLEMING / PAUL HARTE	TWIN	323	11 DEC	12 DEC
KRIS NEEDS / JOHN NOAKES	TWIN	331	11 DEC	12 DEC
PAUL ROGERS (6PM RELEASE)	SINGLE	319	11 DEC	12 DEC
MARK NEWMAN (6PM RELEASE)	SINGLE	226	11 DEC	12 DEC

* TOUR MANAGER

*Hotel rooming lists for the '94 UK tour.
Some aliases afoot . . .*

their watches as George had a gig in Europe the next night and had to go straight to the ferry. Me and the band just stood in the wings, pinching ourselves in disbelief. Then they were gone and everybody knew they'd witnessed something very special. Never let it be said that Primal Scream don't do things in style. That was some support band.

Still paying tribute to Kurt, my between- bands set consisted mainly of Pistols, Clash and Stones. By now the place was going mental. Fired up on the buzz, the Scream didn't take the stage until about three in the morning and turned in a wired-up stonker of a show. Bob dedicated 'Cry Myself Blind' to Kurt in the encore, followed by 'Give Out', 'Higher', 'Rocks', 'Loaded' and 'No Fun'. There was just no stopping 'em that night. Afterwards I had to come on again and take it home for the diehards with some banging electronic stormers until six.

The festivities still didn't stop there. Around seven in the morning a major shower staggered into the foyer of a posh Kensington hotel, sneaked into the lift and commandeered Hartie's room to continue the carnage. It was to be the night of the infamous 'Hat Session', featuring one of those Scottish 'Jimmy hats' with tartan beret and orange hair. It sounds stupid in cold print – and most definitely was. Eight grown men trying on this hat, then falling about giggling helplessly for half an hour. 'The fun you can have with a hat!' bellowed Throb. Before long, two grim-faced hotel security blokes turned up. Hearing the knock, Hartie stripped off his clothes, wrapped a bath-towel round his waist and answered the door. I thought I was gonna die laughing. We promised to keep it down, but then Hartie continued with a towel-clad opera performance. The morning's entertainment climaxed with Throb disappearing to the bathroom for a while, then springing out sporting the Hat and shades while giving it loads on Rod's 'Do Ya Think I'm Sexy?' Security appeared again to complain about the racket. Apparently some guests were getting their early morning calls a few hours early. A couple of hours later they appeared again with grim faces and opened the wardrobe – only to be showered in a chest-high pile of empty champagne bottles. After that we just toned it down to sitting on the floor and talking bollocks. So it went on, until my sides could take no more and I sloped off to my own room.

It was about ten o'clock in the morning and we had another Brixton that night so I decided to have a bath. Next thing I knew Fatty was shaking me. I'd fallen asleep and was about to go underwater in an unwakeable state. Worried about the lack of response from my room, Fatty had got a house key. And just in the nick of time! Just as well too, because that night former Clash man Mick Jones turned up backstage. I introduced him to Bobby for the first time and the two got on like a house on fire. Bobby was well made up that Mick liked his group. The effect of that meeting was felt the following August, when Mick joined the band onstage at the Reading Festival for a few songs, including 'Jail Guitar Doors'. Good one.

Incidentally, much to the band's amusement, I'd been booked in under the name 'John Noakes', after the former Blue Peter presenter. It's a band tradition to book into their hotels under surreal aliases. On this tour Bobby was William Bonney, Throb was South American chang-psy-

Fly Scream Airways. Bobby with his handiwork in the 'Jailbird' video.

cho Pablo Escobar, Innes was Jack Kowalski from the movie *Vanishing Point*, and Duffy was, erm, Martin Dauphin. John Noakes, though?

Select's Andrew Harrison called the Clinton-Scream show "94's best night out yet,' adding, 'Just as Bob, Innes, Throb and Denise cut loose a frantic, indistinguishable jacuzzi of hair, legs and guitar-necks, so the band stab right to the heart of the songs . . . if this is dance treachery, bring on the tumbrils!' Forget all the negative press that surrounded this period and the band's later near-dismissal. Forget 1994. This was one of the best nights I'd ever had in 35 years of gig-going.

After the Brixton stint it was Brighton for – gulp – the last night of the tour. They were playing the Event with a two o'clock curfew. That would have been okay but, at the time, Brighton also happened to be home to Bobby and Throb, as well as Nightingale's mum.

It was an uproarious gig even by this tour's standards. Afterwards we bowled over to the house that Annie Nightingale was moving out of for a wrecking party. I found myself playing that punk set again. Then it was on to the suite at the plush Grand Hotel, which was bombed by the IRA when Thatcher was in power. Shoulda seen her coffee table! Eventually we hung the Confederate flag over the balcony at nine in the morning and toasted commuters with champagne, before returning to Annie's for further frolics. Or maybe it was Throb's?

Apart from *NME*, I also did a tour report for long-time Scream allies *Jockey Slut* and found myself scrawling, 'During that tour I watched as the Scream became one of the most magnificent, full-on live celebrations I've ever witnessed. Celebrating what? All the great music that's been made in all those man-made boxes. All shoulders, knees and nether-regions in a joyous cacophony of love, soul and sheer groin-level rauncherama interspersed with ballads that can turn your heart into a huge, billowing teardrop before drop-kicking your ass clean through the ceiling with euphoria.'

Give Out But Don't Give Up sold well, debuting in the album chart at number two. I wrote a tour report for *NME*, which would have been on the front cover if Kurt Cobain hadn't died. The next single was to be 'Jailbird', that feisty slab of filthy rock-funk with its rousing refrain of 'I'm yours, you're mine, gimme some of that jailbird pie.'

The video, shot by Douglas Hart, showed the band reclining aboard a Led Zep-style customised plane, which Bob had sprayed graffiti-style with the New York gang message 'PRIMAL SCREAM L.A.M.F.' That's derived from a Lower East Side street-gang tag – 'Down To Kill Like A Mother Fucker,' which was also adopted by the Heartbreakers for an album title in 1977. This was eventually intermingled with footage from the European tour. Douglas had also recently made a film called *Goal!*, which focused on the 1970 Brazilian World Cup squad. It was shown on BBC2 as part of a Bank Holiday Monday football evening on 30 May. The Scream's music popped up throughout. They're big Brazil fans.

After the UK tour I was due in the Ladbroke Grove studio with my partner Ben Recknagel to work on a 'Jailbird' remix. I turned up around noon, and who should open the door with the words, 'You're late!' but Throb. Instead of going home to bed he'd come straight from the video shoot with Douglas and Bobby.

Uh-oh, I thought, as we did the offy run and various other supplies were procured. Within an hour yet another party had broken out, Throb was adding new licks on the battered old five-string he'd found in the corner, and I'd decided to mix in sound effects and records live instead of using the usual sampler-computer approach. Hence the chaotic nature of the mix, which ends with two minutes of classic gospel group the Swan Silvertones. (Incidentally, later, at the insistence of everyone, Creation actually managed to track down their songwriter in New York and handed him a nice cheque to avoid any potential legal problems.)

We were happy with the mix though, which emphasised guitars and a Meters-style funk-vamp donated by Throb, who literally took me up to Honest Jon's record shop and bought it for me. It's that humping bongo break round about the middle. As I tried to liven up our killer groove, Bobby clapped along and made a few suggestions, and later I was caught mixing in live police sirens from an ancient sound effects record and *Jerry Lee Lewis Live In Hamburg* – one of the best albums ever made. I wanted the Killer and I got the crowd. In other words, I miscued and got some severe handclap action. It was no-holds-barred that day in poor Ben's studio. Eventually he became used to Scream antics. This mix got christened 'The Toxic Trio Stay Free Mix', after us three and a particularly favourite Clash tune – the that one that goes, 'We met when we were in school / Never took no shit from no one, we weren't fools.'

The band had to shoot the video while I remixed the track, along with Andrew Weatherall and the Dust (later Chemical) Brothers, who were also doing it. The Chems turned in a rabble-rousing big beat stormer topped with bits of Bob and a well-known hip hop sample. The Sabres did two versions: 'The Sweeney Two' – that must've come from Innes – and 'Weatherall Dub Chapter Three Mix'. Both were stark, stripped down and atmospheric, with the latter's thirteen minutes ending up on the twelve-inch. 'He's back,' commented Innes.

Roy Wilkinson's *Select* review was somewhat condescending, bringing up the old Stones comparison chestnut but praising the remixes: 'OK, Primal Scream's rock archaeology may be as risible as it's vibe-perfect. But the transfixing remixology coming with "Jailbird" scores heavily by freeing them from Bob's comedy soul lexicon.' He claimed their current direction would never catch on, but the album was still riding high and the single popped into the charts at number fifteen.

There had been more snide press when we'd been on tour. *Melody Maker* had brought in Simon Reynolds to try to destroy Bobby in a convoluted stitch-up. He hated the album and made sure he said so – in paragraph after paragraph of pseudo-intellectualese. This was a bloke who

Bobby in Manchester, '94.

Bobby in San Francisco, '94 US tour.

wanted *Screamadelica Part Two*, and it was almost like Bob had been placed in the dock and had to defend himself as to why not: 'You are charged with dance treachery, Mr Gillespie.' But Bob refused to be shot down, constantly pointing out that there was humour in there as well as emotion and soul. He also gave some insightful quotes which cast him in a good good light:

'[On *Screamadelica*] we were experimenting with sound, working with friends like Andy Weatherall and Alex Paterson who were dub-wise. That record happened because that was what we were involved in then. Then we went on tour for a long time and got off on the energy of playing live. We started jamming and that's how the songs for the new album came about . . .

'It wasn't a particular sound, it was a particular feel we wanted. Most of the songs we'd written were real soft ballads. They had to be played very sensitively, and that's why we hitched up with Roger and David, and that's why we wanted to work with Tom Dowd, because he always goes for feel over technique. That's just the way we play . . . we try and feel the music from the hips as well as the heart . . .

'I don't believe there's a sell-by date on emotions.'

Of course, Reynolds also brought up the drugs.

'I don't think we play on it really,' retaliated an unfazed Bobby. 'Maybe in the past, around *Screamadelica* we were talking about hallucinogenics a lot, but it went with the music. But I felt that if you spoke about drugs openly, it would kind of demystify them. They were part of our lives and we were being totally honest. People buying our records, coming to our gigs, they were all getting wasted. We come from that culture, all the kids we knew were doing a lot of drugs. And, back then, Ecstasy did help put a lot of people in contact with each other, like us and Weatherall and Paterson. So that's why we spoke about it. Back when it was real Ecstasy and not cut with barbiturates and strychnine for a cheap flash. It generated a lot of energy, creativity, contact.

'What you've got to understand is, we live the way we live but we don't cultivate that image.

This record we've made, so far people have focused on the rockers, the party songs. But most of it is ballads, soft and soulful.'

Reynolds also picked up on how 'Rocks' was supposedly derived from the Stones' 'Rocks Off – forgetting that the Stones got their very name from a Muddy Waters song.

'I think it's funny. It makes me laugh. It's a party record. You can't get too self-conscious about it. Sometimes it's good to smile when you're dancing.'

Bob's Keef t-shirt also got targeted.

'Oh, that's a good t-shirt. And it's also taking the piss, taking the piss out of people who say, "you sound like the Rolling Stones." This fucking Stones thing, I don't know . . . I love 'em. I mean, how many great rock 'n' roll bands have there been after the Pistols? Fucking none. To me, that's the truth. There's only been the Mary Chain. And maybe Suicide.'

Game over then. In the end the poor interviewer was forced to vent his hang-ups in a rant at the end of the feature. I've never seen a journalist win an argument with Bobby Gillespie.

Throb working up to his collapse onstage in Gothenberg, '94. The last known photo of my hat, before it blew off on the rollercoaster.

Only ten days after the UK jaunt it was on to our next target – continental Europe. 'Business as usual,' as Innes liked to call it, for the best part of the next three weeks.

The same mob all convened at Heathrow and immediately hit the bar. It didn't seem like the partying had stopped since the end of the UK jaunt. We started in Oslo then drove overnight to Stockholm. With these long drives over foreign terrain – sometimes in overnight sleepers where those capable of sleep could crawl into little pod-bunks – it became even more insular. One far-fetched idea for the band and crew to share one extra-large coach was scrapped two days in, after protest from the hard-stretched crew. The party-inclined members were often more fucked when they hitched up for an opening gig than most groups would be after an entire tour! The festivities would simply roll on amidst the road ritual. Such unabashed hedonism made for some uproarious incidents.

By the time we'd bulldozed Oslo and Stockholm, Throb and I still hadn't slept. It continued on the overnight drive to the quaint city of Gothenberg, where I finally nodded off on the coach – only to be awoken at around ten in the morning by Throb, shouting, waving a bottle of Jack Daniel's and playing Aerosmith or someone like that at top volume. We lolled about a bit at the gig, while the crew were setting up, still a bit miffed about their sleepless night on the coach. Fatty informed us that Gothenberg had the biggest rollercoaster in Europe, so we decided to give it a whirl, hitting the bars on the way and nearly getting into a few fights with bemused local lager monsters. Throb had nicked my new top hat and we must have looked a real sight, with the guitarist staggering about all over the place supported by a similarly zonked yours truly and bellowing Fatty, still sporting the same leather waistcoat, army officer's cap and old baggy shorts he'd worn on the UK tour. He loved it just as much as the band. If anything, he was worse, but still kept it together. We found the rollercoaster and Throb immediately lost my new hat.

Finally we made it back to the gig and staggered into catering, cackling wildly at a toilet seat we were waving about. This did not improve the road crew's mood. They feared a gig shambles and got it. All the band were fairly wired and tired, and it was one of the few occasions where they couldn't wing it on stage and things went pear-shaped. The sound wasn't great and there were a few problems. By the third song, 'Movin' On Up', Throb was playing sitting down. Finally, he disappeared

★ After-Show Party   Mon, 25.04.
                       Soulution Club

Primal Scream

Soulution Club open Wed. - Sat. / Simon v. Utrecht Str. 42, St. Pauli Hamburg

Don´t be a part of the problem - be a part of the Soulution !

INVITATION -

- To get your ass out of the 🪑

Aftershow party invite, Hamburg, '94.

off-stage altogether and the group soldiered on, with Innes gamely handling all the guitar parts.

After the show nobody was allowed in the dressing room, as Throb had collapsed with chest pains and was lying on the floor in agony. A doctor was called. Later he seemed alright, clutching his bourbon and Coke as we made for the overnighter to Hamburg in Germany and a much-needed day off. The local paper later had a field day on its front page, with all sorts of unbelievable allegations about suspected drug taking under the headline, 'ASHAMED!' Not really – it was an industrial accident. Later the band got an 800 quid bill for a smashed dressing room mirror.

A day off? In theory. Throb, Fatty and me ended up dancing like the Village People in a local bar. Well, those two still had their hats and leather waistcoats. I unfortunately ended up dropping my strides to show off some smart new leopard-skin underpants. We only found out afterwards that it was the local gay hotspot. The morning ended up in a coffee shop by the autobahn with Throb and Fatty nursing the tattoos they'd just acquired and the latter lying in the middle of the road.

The Toxic Twins on the Scream bus. Throb and me had customised our Burger King hats with penis cutouts and 'Bugle King' amendments. Certainly livened up our journey from Nottingham to Manchester, anyway.

108

God, we were only four days in!

On to Berlin, where Douglas Hart turned up to film some more footage for the 'Jailbird' video. He filmed the local sights and Bobby chatting to fans outside the gig. Apart from Gothenberg the shows were going fine, mainly selling out at similar capacities to the UK. Audiences weren't as mad though.

Next came another overnight drive to the picturesque city of Prague. Not content with sleeping in the hotel, the usual firm embarked on a bar crawl around the city centre, stopping off to buy military regalia. Innes acquired a white furry Russian army officer's hat, which he insisted on wearing for the rest of the tour.

The gig was a lovely old 2000-capacity joint. This was one of the big ones. Douglas was filming the live set, Annie Nightingale turned up with then-boyfriend Nikki Sudden and Alex was back on the firm too. The level of our current mental activity might have been illustrated by the fact that we spent 40 minutes decorating the passed-out Sudden – who was a bit of a Johnny Thunders wannabe – with the dressing room fruit. And that was at only five in the afternoon. The gig was a stormer though, the best of the tour so far, even if the band were on at eight in the evening.

The mighy Fatty shares a drink with Euro '94 tour mascot Eric the Gnome . . .

Then there was another day off, spent driving to Munich – and the first quiet night in of the tour so far! They made up for it at the gig though, which was held at the Zeppelinhalle by the airport. This is the spot where the Manchester United squad suffered fatalities in a terrible plane crash in the seventies, and the band were duly respectful. In fact, a photo of Denis Law adorned the tour itinerary. Innes had taken that day off to fly back to London to supervise the cut of the upcoming single, and I was well pleased when he showed up during the soundcheck with a couple of slates of all the new mixes. The Weatherall excursions were as titled but mine came with 'Needs United' scrawled on it, with the Dust Brothers' mixes inscribed 'Dust My Scream'.

Next it was the city of Berne, in Switzerland. This particular overnight drive stands out. We made a pitstop at the German-Swiss border and availed ourselves of the services. Trigger, for reasons best known to himself, invested in a massive cow sellotape dispenser, which I believe still sits proudly on his desk. Then there was the football match in the car park, which saw an obviously on-form Trig capsizing into a distant bush. I swear I have never seen Primal Scream laugh so much at anything. He just went sideways trying to catch one of Fatty's curve balls. Talking of Fatty, he thought he'd outdo Trig and acquired himself a garden gnome. From here on the gnome, whom Fatty called Eric, was the tour mascot. He rode in the front seats of cabs with a seat-belt, tried a sauna, and sat on the

109

desk of one hotel for the duration. He also ate in restaurants and it was a bit of a pisser when Eric, sporting a Scream t-shirt, got blown up at customs on suspicion of carrying illegal substances.

The gig was halfway up a mountain and reached via an elevator. It was also notable for the capers at the hotel where me, Throb, Innes, Fatty and Eric the gnome hit the sauna to sweat it out. Throb kept a fag on the go the whole time – even in the sauna! Then we cleared the swimming pool as Eric was thrown in, and other guests were treated to the sight of Fatty's arse when his shorts remained in the pool as he hoisted himself out. Of course, by the end of the night all the toxins we'd sweated out had been replaced by new ones.

Then it was Milan, Frankfurt and Cologne, before an overnighter took us to Amsterdam, another Scream stronghold – and one of their favourite places, for some reason. The Paradiso was one of the best gigs I've ever seen the group play. They were glorious, almost as if it was on home turf. They even got rave reviews in the UK music press. That gig is often remembered for Nightingale, semi-comatose at ten in the morning outside his hotel room, trying to open the door with his tour-laminate pass. It turned out he had about six room cards in his pocket.

'Jailbird' video run-through.

A rare moment of calm for Duffy in Brussels, Belgium, '94

NME's Roger Morton covered that one and said that I was leaning over the balcony flicking v-signs at the punters. No, that was aimed at Jacko the t-shirt seller! Roger – one of our favourite writers – encountered the band in the hotel bar and described them as looking 'like the remnants of some weird Scottish clan taking brief respite from marauding'. He's half right there! Roger went on to give the show a rightful thumbs up, calling it, 'High-powered, freeflowin', stumblin', tearjerkin', brilliantly blowzy entertainment, the Primals are everything that they're meant to be tonight.' Seen.

Just as well the next day was free. Certain members of the party didn't go to bed. There was only a late departure for Lille in France to worry about, a low-key one, then Brussels – cue Duff for sprouts imagery – and, finally, Paris. Le Bataclan was the last night of the tour. A worthy gig, even if Paris cool prevailed. Afterwards the band were supposed to go back to the hotel before the long drive and ferry home.

Present at the gig was one Nick Kent, the greatest writer to honour *NME* with his presence. He wrote classic articles about the Stones, Lou Reed, Brian Wilson and Syd Barrett, with a flair and ability which put him on a par with America's late, great Lester Bangs. Nick had come out of a period of prolonged drug abuse and knows a kindred soul when he encounters one. So he invited the Scream back to his flat. Trig had the address and we had to be on the bus, so I wandered off into the night with a mission to extract the missing members of the touring party. When I finally arrived at the Kent abode, it was a nice, pine-ish kind of place, with the boys all gathered round listening to Keef stories and good music.

A few hours later, we embarked on the end run of another mad tour. I always remember wishing these things would never end. It's more fun than a person's suppsosed to have in one whole life, encapsulated in three weeks. Duty (free) bound, we got on the bus and ended up snorting an Irish Bailey's equivalent off the rear room coffee table. Duff took to wearing Fatty's officer's cap and making Hitler moustaches out of green gaffa tape.

But that was it, in effect. I left them shouting outside the Shepherd's Bush Hilton and waving noisy goodbyes.

Seven

Big Jet Plane

'It's a rock 'n' roll guitar band. It's always been one and it always will be.'
– Robert Young

I missed the next expedition and, from all accounts, am quite glad I did. The Scream were booked to do two months around the States with Depeche Mode, who were big fans and had asked them a year before. It was a disaster. Primal Scream means dark nights, blaring lights, and their own crowd. Not playing half their normal set in a stadium on a sunny afternoon with hordes of American 'rawk' fans wolfing hot dogs and swigging Budweiser while waiting for the star attraction. They did manage to whack in a few one-off club dates, which couldn't be advertised until the arena shows sold out, and even then only locally on the day. But that triumphant Scream team that traversed Europe was now on the dreaded support band trail. Primal Scream had never supported anybody before. Now they were subjected to lengthy drives through desert heat, just to whisk up a bit of crowd reaction and get the odd shot in the arm from their own crowds. Cramped, dirty, disgusted and busted – there were incidents aplenty, recounted in Mr Fleming's immortal *Higher Than The Sun* tome. In a gruelling jaunt which seemed to veer from one extreme to another, the customary Scream whoopee was played out on an American scale. On one hand, the band were in complete despair over the crappy support gigs, and the massive distances, on the other.

Plus, Andrew Perry from *Select* joined them and submitted a gritty eyewitness account of smashed-up, blood-splattered dressing rooms, Throb walking about with two unnoticed cracked ribs for ten days, Fatty snorting MD20/20 wine and the massed reprobates going for an unwitting midnight swim in a Texas cesspool, for which they were busted. Another tale I heard had Duffy staggering into the soundcheck at one of the band's headline club gigs in Baltimore, totally pissed, with two broken fingers and a sign around his neck saying 'no martial arts'. It's hardly surprising that *Apocalypse Now* was the tour bus video fave on this jaunt. Despite the piss-offs, Bobby would later say that the whole experience had made them a better band, although Depeche Mode's Dave Gahan had the nerve to call them a bad influence! Not bad from someone who, at the time, was on smack and had his own medicine cabinet carted about on the tour. Obviously, the Scream had to investigate it. Gahan would tell journalists that 'the more out-of-it you become in their company, the straighter they seem to be getting.'

While the group were away, Creation held an acoustic showcase gig at the Royal Albert Hall which they called 'Undrugged' – possibly a reference to Alan McGee's recent detoxification. I went to represent the Scream as they were away on tour, and witnessed a string of earnest blokes

Sacramento, California, '94: Throb and Bob hitting the daylight Depeche Mode hordes.

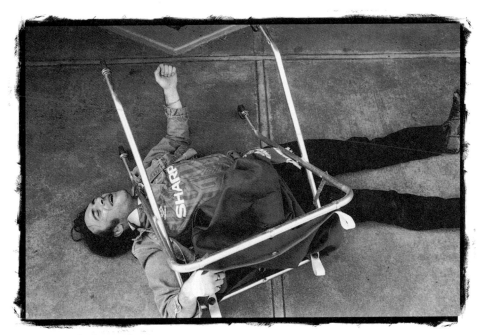

Throb takes a break in San Francisco.

with acoustic guitars. It reminded me of the first time I went to the Royal Albert Hall to see folk-hippie Donovan and T.Rex – then called Tyrannosaurus Rex. It was the same old sit-down warbling to a crowd apparently under mass sedation. I've seen wilder vicar's tea parties.

Then they showed the Scream video for 'Jailbird'. As I was missing them a bit, I was made up. Bobby spraying 'PRIMAL SCREAM LAMF' on the side of the plane was the most rock 'n' roll moment of the night – and it was on video!

The American tour finally drew to a knackered close. But now it was time to hit Japan! Just the tonic. The band were coming direct from Chicago, so I was flown out alone on 12 July. After the thirteen-hour flight I arrived the next afternoon. Heading for immigration, I suddenly heard a familiar voice. 'NEEDSY!!' It was Fatty, accompanied by a band who looked liked they hadn't slept, washed or stopped going for it since the last time I'd seen them. The usual suspects were all rat-arsed from the long haul, but suddenly perked up to embark on yet another ten days of bad behaviour. It was obvious that the band were pissed off by the US outing and glad to be in another country. So we duly celebrated that night after checking into the plush Rappongi Prince Hotel, ending up in an absinthe bar.

The gigs were mainly centred around Tokyo, so that was our base for most of the tour, while gigs outside the capital were reached by a bullet train that put the UK rail system to shame. It was one big exotic barrel of laughs, what with a whole shop devoted to the Stones, and the band being followed everywhere by screaming teeny-fans, often bearing gifts like cuddly toys. Poor old Bob. Every time he showed his face outside the hotel they'd be there, and start chanting, 'BOBBEEEE!!' One night Throb had to hide in the wardrobe in my room – fag and drink in hand, not helped by my farting in his general direction – to escape one young lady's attentions.

The gigs were a bit strange because curfews were very strict – which is a bit tricky for a band traditionally late taking the stage – and the audiences sat politely during my DJ sets. But when the band came on they went bananas.

Another night we were sitting in Throb's room when the phone went. There were two blokes in reception who wanted to see him. 'Tell 'em to come up,' he said. It turned out to be the legendary besuited Iceman, with his briefcase of goodies.

'You Kris Needs?' he asked.

'Er, yeah,' I replied, maybe a tad shakily, knowing the man's connections.

'Ah, Secret Knowledge!'

Phew.

As the morning wore on, bed became another distant memory.

We got banned from this hotel too, in the end. All the touring had got to Innes, who hated Japan. He ended up seeing snipers on the roof and, one night, vaulted over the reception desk to get his room keys. It all came to a rousing climax with the final night at a place called Club Citta. This one didn't start until midnight, and the band came on about three. This was totally different as the place was more like a dance club and I got to play a banging techno set at the end. End-of-tour celebrations raged on through the night at a nearby hotel, with Bobby and I getting mobbed as we left to get the bus to the airport. There I found that I'd lost my plane ticket and, despite being booked on, had to fork out two grand for a new one. Basically all I had earned for the tour.

When I eventually arrived at Heathrow, on a later plane after a gruelling thirteen-hour flight, the band were in the airport bar. Waiting for me and still going strong.

In August, two days after we got back, I DJed at Throb's wedding to Anita in Brighton. The Archbishop had presided in full regalia, Fatty wore a ten-gallon hat and it was the expected Scream clan riot. Also in attendance were all the crew and the Judge – Bobby's brother Graham – who ran the Creation warehouse and, as I've said, never took no shit from no-one.

The band spent the summer doing festivals – Dublin's Feilhe Thurles, Glasgow's Big T, some in Europe, plus headlining the last night of Reading on 24 August. Another triumph which saw them joined onstage by Mick Jones, plus Dave Gahan from Depeche Mode, who supplied off-key

'BOBBEEEE!!' Me and Bob escaping Club Citta at eight in the morning, '94

harmonica on 'Loaded'. (We also found out around this time that the Rolling Stones were play-ing 'Rocks' before their live sets!) The band's caravan was next door to gangsta rapper Ice Cube and his crew, who must've been either perplexed or simply scared stiff of the raucous mob whoop-ing it up next door. They didn't come out much anyway.

Next day I was playing at a new club off Great Portland Street called the Heavenly Social. Jeff Barrett and his gang had started it as an antidote to four-four beat-dominated superclubs and the Dust Brothers were residents. It was in this amyl nitrate-soaked basement that the whole big beat thing kicked off. Initially it was to be for a four-week run with a guest DJ every week: David Holmes, Dean Thatcher, Paolo Hewitt and yours truly.

You could play anything you wanted, within reason. Everyone was going for it and the Scream soon got into the swing of things. They were obviously still going from the night before, with Bobby in his same new shirt, and took great delight in standing behind and guffawing as I tried to play. 'Sympathy For The Devil' was okay, but maybe 'School's Out' by Alice Cooper wasn't such a good idea in retrospect. Anyway, the club went on to become huge, moving to the bigger Turnmills in Clerkenwell where I was resident. And this anything-goes punky-party attitude seemed to suit the Scream, and the new direction they would eventually head in. Just to cap the weekend, some of us adjourned to techno club Strutt afterwards. I emerged on Monday morning and there was Bob perched on a doorstep, chatting.

In October, Bobby, Andrew Weatherall and I appeared on the cover of *Melody Maker* in sup-port of an EP we'd contributed tracks to under the collective banner Retribution. *Repetitive Beats* was released on the Sabres of Paradise sister label Sabrettes, and protested against the incoming Criminal Justice Bill. The Scream had knocked up a new tune at producer Youth's Butterfly stu-dios in Brixton, based on 'Know Your Rights', after The Clash song of the same name. It was a sleazy, slightly 'Jailbird'-ish rocker, which would later end up on the 'Kowalski' twelve-inch too, after becoming a live fave, where Throb would smear on the riff from the Stones' 'Undercover Of The Night'. For my track, I purloined Keith Richards shouting, 'I want 'em outta the way, man' from the stage at Altamont for a psychedelic house version called 'Take No Prisoners' and, apart

Bobby and the Stones, Tokyo, '94

from the Sabres, on fine form as ever, there were tracks from the Drum Club, Fun-Da-Mental and reggae figurehead Bim Sherman.

The *Melody Maker* session was a fun day out in the photographic studio of the mighty Tom Sheehan, with all concerned convening to drink Red Stripe, be photographed looking moody and agitational, and then do an inter-view about it all.

The Criminal Justice Bill threatened everybody's way of life. A few weeks before, Bobby and a few people had gone to a demo against the bill and afterwards went back to a mate's house. They were playing music for a while, shut it down and the police turned up. According to David Bennun's feature, Bobby was slammed against a wall with a truncheon to his head and the mate – an epileptic – was manhandled into a police van and beaten but not before they'd had a blast of 'Know Your Rights'. Next day the judge threw the case out of court but, to Bobby, it looked like the

Duffy, Fatty and Throb frolic in the dressing room of the Liquid Room, Tokyo, '94. Fatty is being mummified in toilet roll, by the way.

shape of things to come. 'I don't think they liked that mix,' he later commented.

The Bill basically gave the police powers that the more brutally-inclined revelled in. Loud music could be shut down, public assembly denied, squatting eliminated, and a few kickings could be given, to boot. Police now had the power to bust gatherings of ten people or more 'listening to music with repetitive beats'. Obviously this had come about after the rave explosion, but sound systems at 'illegal' parties – of which the Drum Club were an integral part – had been in operation for years and to this day, fortunately, still happen every weekend.

Mr Weatherall made a good point when he said, 'Next time there's a Horse Guard's parade and they've got a band with the big bass drum, we should phone the cops. Just say there's a mass gathering of people and they're all marching along to repetitive beats. Flood the police switchboard – there's a load of mad fuckers wearing coats and banging drums outside my front door!'

For obvious reasons, Bobby was most concerned about the increased police power. 'I don't trust those powers in the hands of the kind of police force I've seen over the last three days. The lack of intelligence has been really predominant. They were just like gang members, real thugs.'

Andrew came up with a suitable headline when we were talking about the general crackdown on groups of young people having fun, especially from self-righteous media elements: 'KILL A RAVER AND WIN A METRO!'

Whatever, this draconian legislation – probably drawn up by MPs whose idea of a public-funded night out made ours seem like going to *Riverdance* – did jackshit to stop people having fun. Just look at the Scream. They simply got more agitational. Overall, the free parties got better organised. We just felt at the time that we had to say something. Primal Scream might be painted as the ultimate hedonist hooligans with little more than a drug-fuelled racket to impart, but behind the image beats a heart born out of Bob's solid trade union background. In 1994 they might have been getting their rocks off big-style, but later lyrics would show increasing frustration

Depeche Mode's Dave Gahan pitched in at the Reading Festival for a spectacularly out-of-tune harmonica solo on 'Loaded'.

with grey New Labour Britain. 'Know Your Rights' was the first overtly-political Primal Scream song, but by the millennium they'd be rampant.

The third and last single to come from *Give Out But Don't Give Up* was going to be 'Cry Myself Blind', that beautifully melancholic ballad. It was to be lead cut on a ten-inch EP, but, true to form, the rest of the contents comprised a Screamic field day. I was enlisted for a remix of 'Rocks'. Tall order. After much deliberation Ben and I decided against an obvious dance pump-up, and I was into this dub and funk thing with Bobby. Underneath the Westway we slowed it down, tried a vocal take which didn't quite sit, then embarked on a sinister boom-bass hip hop roll with just snatches of Bob dubbed to hell.

This initially saw the light as a promo ten-incher, flipped with a sultry Portishead remix of 'Give Out But Don't Give Up' and ten minutes of Brendan's 'Struttin' (Back In Our Mind)' expedition. The released version – which added 'Cry Myself Blind' – featured a cover photo of Bobby sitting head-down on stage at a Manchester soundcheck – either deeply into it or deeply out of it. The picture was taken by Pennie Smith, the brilliant photographer who worked for *NME* in the seventies and was photographer-of-choice to The Clash. She was now doing the same for the Scream. As for me, when I saw those sleeve credits I thought, 'Fuck me, I've just remixed Tom Dowd!'

Just to round things off, Primal Scream announced another UK tour for December. Entitled the 'Cry Myself Blind Drunk' tour on the itinerary, it would navigate assorted entertainment venues around the UK, starting in Exeter and moving on through Cambridge, Leicester, Portsmouth, Stoke, Sheffield, Warwick, and then into an Irish leg.

The only pisser was that I was only going to be on half of it. Those Heavenly Social darlings the Dust Brothers – who are a lovely pair of chaps – had been roped in for the last half of the tour. Fair enough. I'd had a good innings, etc. But it did hurt to have to unceremoniously abandon my year of fun mid-flow and not see my best mates in the situation I liked best. Kind of like getting dumped for the bloke with bigger muscles. No sand got kicked in my face, and I did give Tom and Ed my copy of 'Ball Of Confusion' by Undisputed Truth, as a guaranteed pre-Scream crowd builder. It was all up to the Scream, and I'd been flattered to succeed Mr Weatherall and Dr Paterson. Whack that baton, baby!

The Scream were obviously delighted and relieved to be playing in the UK again. They copped a good review in *Melody Maker* from Andrew Mueller under the headline, 'Mr Bobby!': 'You will grin like an idiot, you will bounce up and down. You will forget all about it as soon as it stops. Then they'll play another one.

'If there is a point to Primal Scream, it is surely that they are a band who prove that the generic cross-pollination that has made the last few years such good listening is complete. They can still, for all the accusations of neanderthal rockism pelted at them this year, embody the disconnected hedonism of club culture like no-one else. All things to all people, tremendous, unadorned good fun. Primal Scream must be the best band in the world to be in. They still do all right as one to go and see as well.'

Then came the Irish episode. Belfast was simple at first, as we hit Throb and Fatty's favourite pub. It's over the road from the Europa hotel, the most bombed place in Europe, and does a mean Guinness (so much better in its home country, with a slight chaser – whiskey, as I recall). Anyway, two hours later, Throb sat proudly in his room sporting the nearest lampshade on his head. That was alright, but then we hit Dublin, the fine S.F.X centre and a mighty Scream gig. Afterwards, back at the hotel, we encountered the inspirational presence of B. P. Fallon. This man is a rock 'n' roll legend, who started off doing press for Roxy Music, and hanging with Marc Bolan and Led Zep, before a long stint with U2. He's a lovely bloke and knows a good group when he sees one. It was only natural that myself, Throb and Beep would be swinging off the balcony around three am . . .

Guest pass for Reading, '94

but on acid? Plus booze. We were still orbiting the lampshade several hours later.

This became the controversial *Top of the Pops* incident. While us three, and the odd visitor, were cavorting about, the rest of the group and the crew had to wait endlessly in the bar for certain members to, quite literally, come down. But we all got slaughtered and missed a plane that had been chartered to take them to *Top of the Pops*. *NME* said that the group reckoned they were 'too rock 'n' roll' to land at Luton Airport, but that was bollocks. They were simply bollocksed. In the best possible sense of the word. But they had missed an important promotional opportunity and pissed off the record company. It was one of the few times I'd seen the eternal party bubble burst and heard raised voices.

We went on to Cork and then over to Glasgow, where I'd share the bill with the Dust Brothers. It was weird, handing over to someone else. I did my last show in Leeds. After a certain Mr Beer turned up, Throb and I stayed sitting in a room with him until the sun came up. Then I realised I had to go back to Aylesbury to play the grammar school dance. That's the place I'd been expelled from 25 years earlier. After a distress call to Aylesbury, good old Bern the Gurn showed up with his girlfriend, dragged me out of bed and ferried my lifeless, Scream-addled body to the gig. There I stood, proud and defiant as the first chords of my 'Jailbird' mix rang round an old school hall more used to the strains of 'Jerusalem'.

After shows in Manchester and Norwich, the group did two nights at the Shepherds Bush Empire where they were joined onstage by Paul Weller and Noel Gallagher. I was gutted to miss all of them but a last-minute burst came with another Brixton all-nighter. I DJ'd for the last two hours after my band, Secret Knowledge, had played a set following the Scream. More hotel room drama included the Bishop knocking on my door and leaving the entire floral display from the foyer in the corridor outside, and a fight in the bar next day between some of the Scream team and a well-known football squad. But it ended up with a lovely, civilised Chinese meal with Mr Throb and his then-missus next evening. The guitarist then proceeded to get a cab – all the way back to Brighton. I love that man.

And that was it. Probably the maddest year of my whole life. A couple of years later I did a month with the Prodigy, which was a vicar's tea party in comparison (albeit a very pleasant one).

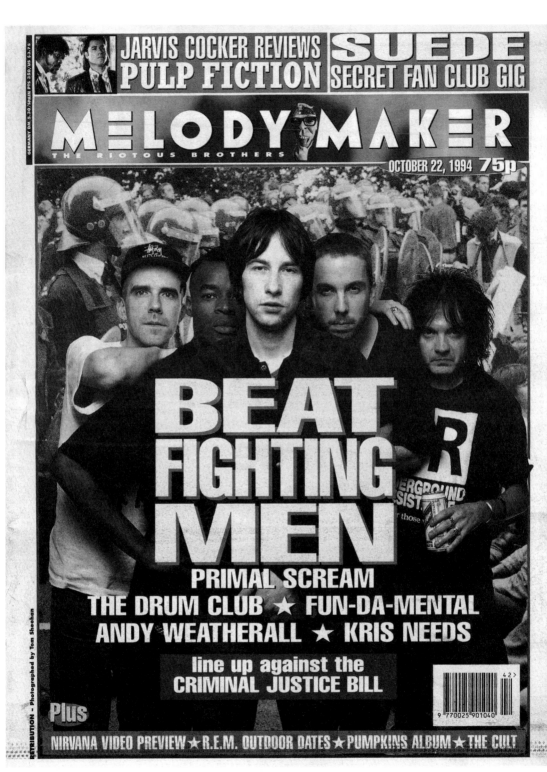

The Melody Maker *cover for the Criminal Justice Bill protest EP. Participants from left to right, Drum Club's Lol Hammond, Dave of Fun-Da-Mental, Bobby, Weatherall, yours truly.*

It wasn't quite over for the band yet though. They still had the Big Day Out tour lined up in Australia – nine dates in twenty days. Along for the crack, and for *Loaded*, was Mr Granty Fleming, who is just as bad as all of the band put together basically. He's also a loyal, lovable bloke who's been there from the start and remains a frothing fan (often literally). He was on a lot of these dates, taking photos which eventually turned up in his *Higher Than The Sun* book and the *Loaded* feature. Surprisingly, he seems to remember more than I do!

The cover for 'I'm Gonna Cry Myself Blind' featured Pennie Smith's hauntingly apt shot of Bobby, taken at the Manchester Academy soundcheck.

I didn't go myself, but still couldn't escape the ghost of the Scream. In January, I had to go to San Francisco to do a gig with Wonder as part of some major music conference-type affair. We walked into the hotel bar, and straight into a bunch of expatriate Brits who'd come up from LA for the shindig.

'We've just left the Scream in LA,' said one.

'Nah, that's impossible,' I said. 'They're supposed to be in Australia.'

Not so. Apparently an eventful plane trip, mainly involving the contents of the drinks trolley, had led to Throb, Duffy, Fatty, Trigger and guitar roadie Jason Caulfield being frog-marched off the plane at the LA pitstop. Now they were banned for life from New Zealand Airways, and had to stay in LA for two days, and fork out fourteen grand on plane tickets on to New Zealand. There was a happy ending – though not for the more well-behaved members of the group, who remained on the flight and got strip-searched by alerted airport officials. But the publicity had proceeded them, and had been so good for the gigs that the promoter agreed to foot the bill.

There were more incidents, of course, and then, just to round things off, a final mission to Japan, back to the Bobby-girls, the Iceman and . . . then, they finally stopped.

Paul Weller and Throb onstage during the two-night stint at Shepherd's Bush Empire, London, '94

The Scream in Melbourne, Australia's Big Day Out, '95

Throb and Bob, Big Day Out, Australia, '95.

Bobby tries to Fukuoka in Japan, '95.

Out Of The Void

'I was born to have it and have it I shall!' – *Mani*

ne solid year on the road and the Scream were done in. Even after the second UK jaunt, they'd swept off on that New Year mission to Australia. And that had come straight after another one of Alex Nightingale's mammoth birthday bashes at Fatty's Bar and Grill, aka the Fortress studios in North London. This time I didn't finish playing until around noon, while Bob did his thing standing by the door like a vicar, shaking hands with disheveled hardcore survivors as they left.

Post-tour exhaustion after Australia was attended to by some, while the partying carried on for others. Innes was up for a bit of recording. After all, it had been a year since the release of the last album and by the time the next would be finished it'd be two. But Primal Scream albums don't just happen to order. They evolve slowly, then find a path which turns into a running track, until they're on a roll and it's the home stretch. Creation had started nagging for a follow-up to *Give Out* during the world tour, but the group simply weren't ready when it finally wound up. There had been a brief interlude the previous summer when Bob, Throb and Innes had gone to Ibiza, of all places, to write. Needless to say, nary a chord was strummed, and Innes fell off his motorscooter. The Scream are not really ones for sitting quietly in hotel rooms, composing new songs on acoustic guitars, and soundchecks are just built for cover versions.

Then Throb had a motorbike accident and broke his leg badly. He was out of action for months, which further hampered proceedings. And Bobby was going through a depression, which had started during the world tour, and sometimes quizzed himself if the band had indeed run its course.

In early 1995 I was still working at the studio under the Westway, where I'd remixed 'Jailbird' and 'Rocks'. The group were already familiar with the place, and genial engineer Ben, so Bob, Innes and Duff tried coming in a couple of times to see if they could bang down a few song-germs. I'd start a beat and the band would jam but, invariably, things would degenerate into a drunken Rolling Stones singalong. Bobby did strike up the vocal line which eventually became 'Medication' at one of those sessions, although then it went 'gimme all your lovin' to save my soul.' Other highlights included a wailing 'Wild Horses', a tear-jerking 'Dark End Of The Street', the Bee Gees' 'To Love Somebody', the Stooges' 'Search And Destroy', a languid version of Bob Dylan's 'Knockin' On Heaven's Door' dueted with Wonder, the Stones' 'Time Is On My Side', Clinton's 'Testify', Jimmy Cliff's 'The Harder They Come' and the MC5's 'Sister Anne'. The stu-

Another man down! Soundman Oz offers help while Throb laughs and tour manager Trigger turns the blind eye of familiarity. Primal Scream tours always had a few casualties. (Melbourne Airport, Australia, '97)

Duffy and Innes imbibe at the Ship Inn, Aylesbury, '95.
The start of my two-day birthday bash.

dio would become a hotbed of early-hours jamming with the Scream at the loosest I've ever seen them. Mick Jones turned up once and joined in. I've got most of it on tape too and it's not bad, but having a top laugh isn't going to get any new songwriting done.

Later that same year Primal Scream started building a recording studio in a disused dance studio down a mews off of Primrose Hill's main drag. It was a stone's throw from the Creation offices and situated conveniently between two pubs, which became secondary headquarters when tours and duty didn't call. The band would pop into Creation occasionally, if only to give themselves more things to get pissed off about. At the Chalk Farm end of Primrose Hill, there was the Pembroke Castle pub, a spacious conversion favoured by the Creation office staff and a gaggle of degenerates including Bob's brother Graham, who ran the Creation warehouse, and Paul Mulreany, a Romford boy who would become the band's drummer for a short spell later that year. The band also favoured the Queens pub, up the road facing the park. Here it wasn't uncommon to see Robert Plant propping up the bar. The restaurant was dynamite, and the toilets were also very popular.

Innes had fondly dubbed the new studio the Bunker. At this stage, it was little more than a place to thrash out tunes and put ideas down on the computer. The big mirrors were a reminder of the room's past as a dance studio, but it had been Screamified with photos of their heroes (Maradonna, the Stones, De Niro, etc), Celtic and Man Utd banners and models of Stukas hanging from the ceiling. But the place suited the band, and they ended up recording the whole of the next album there. It was a very slow start, although they did manage to turn in a stomping cover version of 'Understanding', for a Small Faces tribute album organised by longtime band mate 'Big' Bob Morris. The track was also notable for featuring veteran soul songstress P. P. Arnold, of 'The First Cut Is The Deepest' fame.

Although Innes and Duffy turned up every day, they usually only had Murray Mitchell and Paul Harte for company in those early stages. Throb was in Brighton recovering, and had also been producing a project with his guitar roadie Jason Caulfield, which never saw the light of day. Bobby was still in Brighton too, but would visit London, either popping into the studio or going out. His visits got more frequent as the Scream germs were sewn in that little place but, until about May 1996, I sometimes wondered if there would ever be another Primal Scream album, or even a Primal Scream anymore.

As Bobby would later explain it to *NME*'s Paul Moody, 'Between the last LP and last summer, I wasn't very well. I was pretty depressed, and I had to ask myself why we were doing this. I wasnae sure we were going anywhere, and we weren't making any music at all really. And anything we did try and do wasn't going anywhere. We were in a hole . . . It didn't sound new and it didn't sound exciting . . . it was devoid of energy. And I guess we stopped for a while and went away and . . . I guess what makes a good band is what any individuals bring to the band, right, and I think we went away and everyone got a lot stronger and came away with new ideas. And listened to a lot of stuff on our own which we then brought back to the band. We just remembered why you get into music in the first place.

'After that it was like a new band. But up until we recorded *Vanishing Point* last summer I gave it six months . . . if by the end of 1996 nothing had changed I thought we had to split up . . . I mean, if you've got nothing left to say, give up . . . just don't say it. Otherwise it's just career rock, and we ain't career rock, we're punk rock.'

I had quite a few phone calls from Innes throughout these months. We'd become close after the touring madness had subsided into this feeling of *ennui*. It's okay to have a rest after a gruelling year, but it would be nearly eighteen months before the whole band was really firing on all cylinders.

The 1994 experience more or less made Innes decide to become the Scream's backroom man. He'd always been a major backbone in terms of organising production, remixes and stage shows anyway. 'I hate all that promotional shite,' he'd often protest. Even now he doesn't take part in photo sessions or interviews, and took to wearing a jet-pilot's visor for the 'Kowalski' video. He's more into pushing out the boundaries in the studio than in the pub, which made him all the more frustrated when he'd go in every day and band members wouldn't show, or Scream mates would turn up with assorted refreshments and everyone would end up in the Pembroke. Great fun, but another unproductive day with just a hangover to show for it next morning. Most of the time he'd be waiting there with a couple of people, just tinkering. He'd do music on his own sometimes, and by March 1998 even had enough for a whole album under the name the Completion. Entitled *Electronic Music For The Cinema*, it sounded exactly like it said, being all instrumental mood pieces with titles like 'They Were Expendable'.

For three months in spring and summer I was making my first album with Secret Knowledge at Youth's Butterfly Studios in Brixton. Innes was glad to come along with the ever-keen Duff to contribute some supremely funky guitar to a couple of tracks, 'Love Beads' and 'Dear Johnny'. Apart from sublime keyboards, Duff found himself supplying the intro to one track after we miked up the toilet and recorded him having a piss! Another time, when we'd nearly finished mixing, Innes, Duff, Muzz and Hartie turned up just to see how the album was progressing. I was

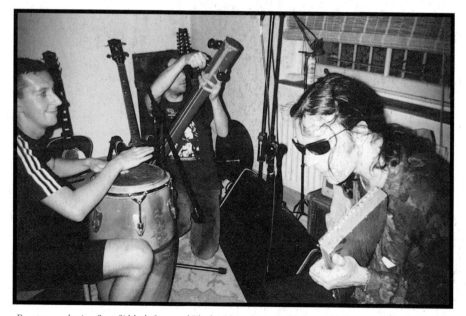

Drummer at the time Steve Sidelnyk, Innes and Throb raid Youth's studio store-room during a Secret Knowledge recording session, '95.

127

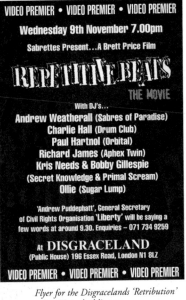

Flyer for the Disgracelands 'Retribution' party. Not a bad line-up . . .

made up when Throb – who I hadn't seen for months – arrived on crutches with his foot in plaster. It ended up with the boys all grabbing items from Youth's collection of Indian instruments and hammering away with Duff on piano. Throb sitting there with the sitar echoed the inner sleeve of *Screamadelica*. Even the dreaded Jimmy-hat made an appearance, but Muzz and I ended up doing a banging techno track.

During those hours spent hanging about in the hope of the others showing up, Innes, Muzz and Hartie often found themselves spinning records on the studio decks, although Innes and whoever was about were doing some remixes for Ruby and the Aloof. It was quite a logical move to do a spot of DJing, and they started spinning at an uproarious regular Friday night hoedown in the Disgracelands bar in Islington. On many a Monday morning I'd get a call from a hungover Innes describing the weekend's events, which had usually kicked off at Disgracelands, and its DJing free-for-all. The words 'very messy' were often used. I tried it myself and it was, indeed, all over the place, with most of the Scream's dodgy mates in attendance and untold scenes of debauchery.

Before long we had a DJ squad called the Scream Team and played the Heavenly Social at Turnmills, Clerkenwell, several times. Innes would play hip hop and funk, Hartie favoured dub reggae and punk rock, while Muzz and I broke out the disco classics. We even landed a few out-of-town gigs, with varying results: only eight people in Liverpool, but a belter at Leeds' Back to Basics – with all the hospitality that only Dave Beer, the promoter, can offer – and a weird one at

Bobby and yours truly lay on the dub and have some fun: behind the decks at the 'Retribution' launch, Disgracelands, '95.

On top of the world: the Scream Team (Muzza, Innes and Bobby) at UXI-95 in Iceland, '95

a several-thousand strong rave at Cardiff City Hall, where we held court in the backroom. The boys even popped up to Aylesbury in June to play my birthday bash at my local pub, the Ship. With a single red light on the small stage and the chaps belting it out, the regulars must have wondered what the hell was going on. Those who did know it was half of Primal Scream up there couldn't quite believe it. With Alex Nightingale down too, my ensuing housewarming party didn't finish until the Monday morning, with Duff and Muzz the sole survivors. Muzz and Nina from Sabres even presented me with a live giant rabbit, who I called Janet.

Then, in August 1995, there was Iceland. The country's tourist board had organised a three-day outdoor 'Glastonbury rave'-style festival called UXI-95 to promote the country, and booked the Scream Team to DJ alongside performances by Bjork and the Prodigy, with a bunch of journalists in tow. This turned into a mighty adventure as myself, Bob, Innes and Muzz, plus Grant Fleming, boarded a plane for Reykjavik and, after a night on the town, headed out on the hour-long coach ride to the site. We could see why the festival was called the Journey to the Top of the World, as we traversed what seemed like the surface of the moon to get there. You'd have probably had more chance of getting a drink on the moon too, as the event was alcohol-free. That meant everyone on the site was shit-faced by the time they staggered past the security guards wearing red jackets with 'milk is good' emblazoned on the back.

We had another night there before having to play the following day. By then all our duty frees had gone but some acid had turned up. Grant Fleming ended up go-go dancing onstage to DJ Craig Walsh and the rest of our crew simply staggered around giggling. Bobby and girlfriend Emily went on a jaunt up one of the local mountains to see the fjords with the UK contingent, but hated it because of the cold, and apparently Bobby demanded to be flown back down in a helicopter. When I saw the slightly shaken singer later on he came out with a classic: 'First time

Scream-mates Irvine Welsh and the indominitable 'Big' Bob Morris horse about during the 'Kowalski' video shoot. Bob is dressed up as a cleaning-lady for the occasion, so Irvine can't resist a grope.

the coming down was better than the going up.'

Asked about the helicopter request in *Q*'s questions section, Bobby said that he panicked because he thought the bus was going to topple over the edge into the glacier. 'It was really cold too! I just went, "Get me fucking out of here!"' So he came hurtling back in a jeep at 90 miles per hour. 'That was really exciting, like being in some crazy road movie. As for demanding the helicopter, yeah I probably did. Hey, that's fair enough. I'm lead singer in a fucking rock 'n' roll band! Why not?'

The Scream Team got to DJ in the afternoon when there weren't many there. But they didn't complain, as the blonde models doing a fashion show had to use the DJ booth as a changing room when I was playing. There were scratched heads as I opened up with the Smurfs and followed through with Barry McKenzie's 'One-Eyed Trouser Snake'. The quite small crowd was also somewhat puzzled when Innes made me play Jeff Beck's wedding classic 'Hi Ho Silver Lining'. We weren't taking this DJing lark too seriously.

The group were knocking about increasingly with *Trainspotting* author Irvine Welsh, who they had met when he interviewed them around the time of *Give Out But Don't Give Up*. Obviously they got on like a house on fire, and shared many similar hobbies. He asked them to contribute to the soundtrack of the film version of *Trainspotting*, and this might have been what rekindled their studio fire. The Scream – minus Bobby – went into Oronoco Studios in South London, where Andrew Weatherall did all his stuff with Sabres of Paradise colleagues Jagz Kooner and Gary Burns. The result was a cool after-hours guitar instrumental, with Duff on melodica, which they simply called 'Trainspotting'. It was the first completed track, which would appear on the next album, and, provided the closing minute of the soundtrack, even though the original was ten minutes long. And it was a sly indication that the ties with Weatherall had never been severed, even if Andrew hadn't quite been able to get his head around the *Give Out But Don't Give Up* material.

In early 1996 the Scream attended a media preview of *Trainspotting* as Irvine's guests, and afterwards repaired to the Ship in Wardour Street. Here the boozing raged like a forest fire until they got thrown out. As it happened, the Heavenly offices were just up the road, so the drunken gaggle staggered to the front door and began chanting, 'Fuck you!' outside. One of the girls in the office recorded it for her answerphone message and, once Innes had got hold of a copy of the tape, he had the inspiration for the track they'd been asked to do for Euro 1996 and the *Beautiful Game* soundtrack. Irvine and the Scream shared a mutual love of football and, even though Irvine supported Hibernian while the Scottish Scream members favoured Celtic and Man Utd, they both jumped at the chance to make a football record.

The result of this collaboration, which also included On-U Sound dub legend and fellow footie fan Adrian Sherwood, was billed as 'Primal Scream, Irvine Welsh and On-U Sound Present . . . The Big Man And The Scream Team Meet The Barmy Army Uptown'. It came out on Creation as kind of a semi-Scream record, probably to bridge the gap more than anything. And anyway, the FA had deemed it unsuitable due to Irvine's expletive-spattered lyrics, which concerned the sad state of football, alcoholism, and outrage at Rangers scoring a goal. These were ranted over a dubby funk-groove with production handled by Adrian Sherwood. Innes' 'fuck you' chant appears at the end, encapsulating the general sentiments of the track. There had to be an instrumental promo for radio. Eventually, the single was released for one week only in June 1996, the same week as the England-Scotland game. The Scream Team weren't too happy when Scotland lost – the run-out groove is scratched, 'If you hate the fucking English clap your hands.'

Innes: 'We were making a football record and we phoned [Sherwood] up and he said, "I know how to make football records, I've made loads of them." And he has – he's made loads of West Ham records. He makes about four a year I think.'

It was a good laugh and certainly puzzled a few people, while offending a few others, but still charted at number seventeen. These two Irv-related projects seemed to have kick-started Primal Scream back into studio action, and by June a new album was getting off the starting blocks.

It was as if someone had just turned the light on. Innes' phonecalls changed from ringing me up out of frustrated boredom, to excitedly reporting the birth of a new record. After months in the doldrums the wheels were turning again. Bobby was coming in the studio regularly and songs were starting to emerge. By now he'd moved to London and, away from the distractions of Brighton life, was totally focused on the group's new music.

The songs kept on coming, and Bobby's promise to himself that the band would split if nothing was happening by the end of the year went out of the window. A lot of the non-activity on Bob's part had been down to his refusal to rehash past glories to make a fast buck. Bob would rather go off and listen to other people's music for a year than simply regurgitate *Screamadelica*. An easy option and guaranteed success, but, as he kept on saying, 'we're not a career band . . . we're a band that has just kept changing. Some people want you to make the same record over and over again, but there's no time for nostalgia.'

Every time I visited the studio there was something new afoot. Paul Weller sound wiz-

Promo poster for the Scream-Irvine Welsh collaboration, 'The Big Man And The Scream Team Meet The Barmy Army Uptown'.

Augustus Pablo, the reggae legend who played melodica on 'Star'. Big bong, big silence, big tune.

ard Brendan Lynch was helping Innes with the production and mixing. Adrian Sherwood was getting involved in the production. Bass player Marco Nelson, also from the Weller camp, played on three tracks. Brass section Duncan Mackay and Jim Hunt came in for a couple, and even former Sex Pistol Glen Matlock showed up to play on the album's only out-and-out rocker, 'Medication'.

Another time reggae legend Augustus Pablo turned up to play on a track called 'Star', which had originally been demoed for *Give Out But Don't Give Up*. A gentle, calming ballad, it concerns itself with the need for unity, self-esteem and equality. It's one of the most touching things the Scream have ever done, and Pablo's melodica was perfect topping. Of course, it was via the Sherwood connection, but this is the first, and so far the only, time that this has happened with a British rock band.

A word about Augustus Pablo. A dread playing a melodica might not seem like the weightiest of dub-wise projects, but this man has made some of the most beatific, haunting reggae music ever. Especially during the late seventies when, then in his early twenties, Pablo breezed in on a Technicolor smoke machine playing an instrument more associated with the school orchestra, but slashed with expert dub trickery from greats like King Tubby. Pablo – real name Horace Swaby – was a veteran of the Channel One studios, working with such greats as Hugh Mundell on *Africa Must Be Free By 1983* plus artists like Jacob Miller, Dillinger and the Heptones. He also shoved out pre-releases on his own label, including two of the greatest reggae tunes ever in 'Up Wareika Hill' and 'King Tubby Meets The Rockers Uptown'. I unashamedly nicked that title for my 'Rocks' remix a couple of years earlier.

So Augustus Pablo walked up Primrose Hill, into the Bunker, planted a massive bong in the middle of the floor, smoked out the studio, heard the track twice, blew some lovely melodica and left without saying a word. That track also featured Andrew Love and Wayne Jackson, better known as those Memphis Horns. Yup, this was going to be a good one.

And then, the finishing touch blew in from Manchester. On 9 November 1996, *NME* announced that legendary band the Stone Roses had split up. Bassist Mani issued an official statement: 'After much speculation, I've decided, along with Ian Brown, that it's time to end the Roses saga. I will be joining Primal Scream, who are one of only three other bands I would ever consider joining. I am absolutely delighted and am relishing the opportunity of playing with Bobby and my friends.'

Mani – real name Gary Mounfield – had grown up in Manchester, getting his inspiration from similar sources to the Scream, but also soaking up local groups, like a militaristically innovative and unhinged outfit called Joy Division. They were a perfect foil to his obsession with PiL, whose bass player Jah Wobble prodded him to start mating that dub-funk boom with the symphonic rumblings of Joy Division's Peter Hook. From 1985 he played as bassist with the Stone Roses. They appeared at indie clubs, and got an early review in *NME* in August 1987, which said, 'their dulcet, simple songs make them sound like a smart, verve-ridden version of Primal Scream.' This suggests an element of jingle-jangle. But the following year – just like Primal Scream – Mani and the rest of the band got into the acid house scene. How could you not if you lived in Manchester? Now combining their rock background with the wide open acid-house sensibility, they started turning out the anthems which would make them the biggest group in the UK by the end of the year. 'Made Of Stone', 'I Wanna Be Adored', 'I Am The Resurrection', 'She Bangs The Drums' and the amazing 'Fools Gold', a ten-minute wah-wah crawl through Sly Stone's back passage which was a Top Ten hit. In June 1990 the Stone Roses played to 28,000 people at Liverpool's Spike Island, coinciding with the 'One Love' single.

In retrospect, the parallels with the Primals are all there – to a point. There were no efforts made to conceal their prodigious affection for drugs. Their tour bus listening consisted of the Stones, Hendrix, PiL and Burning Spear, plus lots of acid house and hip hop. They would also come out with good quotes such as, 'It's like scoring the winning goal in the cup final . . . on a Harley Electroglide . . . dressed as Spiderman.' By the end of that year they'd be playing to 7,000 delirious punters at Alexandra Palace, North London.

Acid house had napalmed indie music. 'The E scene is just going to explode this summer,' said Mani in *NME* that June. 'People in the media just don't realise how massive it's getting in the provinces.'

But in January 1992, *NME* ran a story saying that the Stone Roses wouldn't be releasing any new material until the autumn. They blamed the previous year's court case when they'd been convicted of sloshing paint all over their first record company's office, as well as all over the boss and his girlfriend.

Despite no further releases, public interest in the band remained undimmed. In May 1993, *NME* ran a cover story on the long-lost Stone Roses with the headline, 'GOTCHA! The Stone Roses Hunted Down.' Writer Gina Morris had gone to Manchester with her Sherlock Holmes hat on, and,

Vanishing Point *tour squad, '98: [right to left]: Bobby, Mani, Mulreaney, Duffois, Throb.*

133

Promo shot of Throb, Bobby, Mani and Duffy, '97.

after questioning everybody from the guy in the chip shop to local pub landlords, tracked the group down to a rehearsal studio in the suburbs. She managed to speak to guitarist John Squire, saw Mani and briefly spoke to frontman Ian Brown, who said they were working and it was too early to talk. She later saw them through the window, hard at work playing pool! At least they were alive.

In April 1995, drummer Reni quit the Stone Roses to be replaced by Robert Maddix. They were booked in to play Glastonbury but had to cancel when John Squire broke his collarbone. The band tried to make up for it by playing the Pilton Village fete in a tent. *NME*'s Steve Sutherland appeared to be horrified by Ian Brown's vocals – 'he sings like he's shouting into a bucket . . . torturing these songs.' But the Stone Roses went on to do a world tour. Then in March 1996 John Squire announced that he'd left the band to go solo. It was not an amicable split. He was replaced by session-type bloke Aziz Ibrahim. They played the Reading Festival and basically killed their career. The main criticism was of Ian's singing, which, according to *NME*, was 'woefully, wincingly out of tune . . . just a horrible, hollering moan.' They called it 'an appalling, hollow charade . . . history being milked beyond tragedy and ending up as farce . . . desperately sad.'

A cult figure, Ian Brown would later redeem himself and defy past criticism, moving on to a successful solo career. And the Stone Roses story had a happy ending for Mani too. The Scream needed a bass player, especially for live work. 'We were both sending out signals,' he told me later. It soon became apparent that here was a marriage made in heaven.

Mani was a total shot in the arm for the Scream. Always up for anything, up to anything and pumping up the good humour with his constant quest for laughs. 'I was born to have it and have it I shall,' was his much-repeated catchphrase, and he couldn't quite believe his luck in landing in the company of kindred spirits. 'All roads have been leading to this,' he'd say, and sprout the biggest grin in the world. 'We're going to blow your fuckin' socks off,' was another fave. And he was right.

'I enjoyed my time with John, Ian and Reni,' he said. 'I got a good education from those boys. It was a fuckin' pleasure and I've total respect for them. It was a great ten years. I don't think I ever got any recognition in the Roses but I was happy to take a back seat. But now I'm with these boys and I'm fuckin' havin' it!'

£2.30   JUNE 1997

SELECT

ROCKS

BEASTIE BUSINESS
Inside the world's coolest corporation

EXCLUSIVE!

PRIMAL SCREAM
Who's going to stop them this time?

It's Mani from the Roses!

THE SEAHORSES
Full LP review plus track-by-track chat

MARILYN MANSON
The most dangerous man in America?

9 770959 836074

ALSO IN THIS ISSUE...
7 DAYS IN CYBERSPACE:
THE SELECT INTERNET
TOUR OF BRITAIN

We regret that for copyright reasons, this CD is not available to readers outside the UK. Sorry!

FREE CD
OVER 70 MINUTES OF
COLLECTABLE MUSIC
INCLUDING BLUR, SUEDE, DODGY, DJ SHADOW, LAMB, KENICKIE & MANY MORE
PLUS! EXCLUSIVE INTERNET SOFTWARE!

Duffy, Bobby, Mani and Throb on the cover of Select, '97

He could barely contain his delight about hooking up with his dream team. 'It was an easy decision for me to join the Scream. Ten years of sweating it out with the other band have just pointed to this. I've always known of 'em right from the early days.'

'He's just what we needed,' Bobby later told *Select*. 'Everything's there, know what I'm saying? The football, the rock 'n' roll, the politics, the spirit. And he's got those Slavic cheekbones. He looks like one of the Red Army defending Stalingrad against the Nazis. He's totally heroic.'

Answering readers' questions in *Q* nearly six years later, Bobby was still as enthusiastic as Mani about the coupling: 'He brought in this amazing new energy, enthusiasm and great musicianship on bass,' adding that, after the 1994 experience, he didn't know if he ever wanted to tour again. But, 'when Mani joined I thought, "Fuck it, we've got to get out on tour again. This is going to be atomic!" We've now got the greatest Primal Scream line-up ever.'

Another good thing about Mani is he doesn't give a shit what people think. When a Stone Roses tribute band appeared at London's Underworld, he was in the DJ booth giving it loads and signing autographs for disbelieving fans. DJing is one of his other sidelines, so it was predestined that he would eventually join the Scream Team and head for Ibiza.

Mani holds the distinction of being the only member of Primal Scream to appear in a top shelf men's mag. He looked quite happy lolling about with a nude model in *Club International's* 'Naked Interview' section, but the interview itself centred more on the group. Apart, that is, from questions like, 'What's the best offer you've ever had off a groupie?' Answer: 'To tell the truth if I was into shagging seventeen-year-old spotty boys I'd be quids in, but I'm not.' Or, 'Have you ever had sex in front of your mates? And could you?' Answer: 'No. I'm a Roman Catholic, of course not. I'm quite a secret person when it comes to that kind of thing.' A bit of bikini-line chat then: 'Have you ever read *Club* before?' Answer: 'Oh yeah, many times. I chucked quite a few over *Club* as a youngster.' 'Can you be a successful musician and an upstanding member of society?' Answer: 'Absolutely man. I'm upstanding right now.' End note: 'How would you feel if you found out that someone had wanked over this spread and some of the spunk had landed on you?' Answer: 'Hey, as long as I'm helping people to get off then that's the main thing.' Nice one, Mani. Going where none of the Scream Team has ever gone be-phwoar!

There was also the now-legendary hook-up with Germany's revered Can, which ended up with the two parties doing a cover version of sixties psychedelic band Third Bardo's 'Five Years Ahead Of My Time'. This collaboration came about when Bobby and Mani – who admitted to nicking a Can bassline for the Roses' 'Fools Gold' – went to Cologne in April 1997 to do some promotion, and phoned up Can at their Inner Space studio just outside the city. Can were about to release an album of remixes of their old stuff, which The Orb and myself had contributed to, and *Melody Maker*'s David Keenan was there to interview them about it.

He ended up reporting on Mani and Bob meeting Can in a Thai restaurant and hooking up to work with drummer Jaki Liebezeit and guitarist Michael Karoli. At that time the new album was all but finished, with Bobby talking about the Scream's new 'psychedelic dub' direction. The recording session happened shortly afterwards, when Can were in London to launch their album. The pair came into the studio one afternoon and played solidly until four in the morning. Apart from the unreleased song and two others, there's an hour-long jam featuring Innes on guitar, Bobby singing, the two Can guys and late arrival Liam Gallagher on piano. Bobby compares it to the psychotic free-for-all that was the early Velvet Underground.

If anything, Can were the German Velvets. They started at the same time in the sixties and advanced the course of rock music by harnessing the classical keyboards and advanced synth-tinkering of Irmin Schmidt, the metronomic pluckings of bass player Holger Czukay (later to be a Wobble collaborator), heavy-duty funk drummer Jaki Liebezeit and spider-fingered guitarist Michael Karoli. They were once described simply as the sound of a flying saucer's engine. Endless, space-foraging jams would get whittled down into truly groundbreaking records which made a tremendous impact on the young John Lydon and Bobby Gillespie. Vocal-wise, the first album, *Monster Movie*, featured a demented Viet-vet lounge crooner called Malcolm Mooney. After that it was down to a Japanese guy called Damo, who they'd caught hollering in the Cologne streets one night after chucking-out time. He didn't even know what he was singing as he syphoned out surreal gems like 'Hallelujah' and 'Oh Yeah', while the band refined a menacing form of improvisational trance music through albums like *Tago Mago* and *Ege Bamyasi*. In 1973 I saw Can play four hours straight like a runaway express train. No breaks, no talking, just a relentless electronic barrage of awesome proportions. There never was, and never will be, anyone like them.

Bobby and co had long championed Can. These men were nutters, musical innovators, out there on their own. Can with the Scream? Another logical progression. When the Scream were playing 'Five Years Ahead Of My Time' live in Tokyo, they used some of Jaki's loops, co-opting the Can engine room via technology. Can loved that idea.

The last track to be finished for the album, and the first Scream track that Mani played on, was a pummelling psycho-hiss dub-pile-up called 'Kowalski', or as Bobby put it, the sound of 'a junkyard having a nervous breakdown'. He came down from Manchester, heard the track a few times and was told to let rip. This he duly did, taking the mood of the Can-style drums and launching into a filthy bassline nicked from the same group. 'I like working like that, it's dangerous,' said Mani later. 'I like danger. There's not enough danger in music any more. On the edge. Risky. The Scream. Totally.'

Mani's barrelling throb is the icing on a very dark cake. Total punk rock for 1997. The track was immediately chosen to be the first single to come off the album, which was to be called *Vanishing Point*. Even Creation could see the monster that was being assembled around the corner. When the group brought 'Kowalski' in to play to Alan McGee, with the declaration that it was going to be their next single, he said it sounded like his nervous breakdown.

'Good,' said Bobby.

The title comes from an early seventies road movie, directed by Richard Sarafian, which centres around Jack Kowalski – ex-racing driver, Viet-vet and ex-cop, whose girlfriend was killed trying to surf while stoned. Now he's a rental car dealer who undertakes to drive from Colorado to California in fifteen hours for a bet. Loaded on Benzedrine in his white Dodge Challenger, he takes on all obstacles from rednecks and cops to naked hippie chicks. His progress is narrated throughout by the blind, black DJ Super Soul. When the film was shown at the Heavenly Social, the Scream picked up on it. Bobby called it 'a punk-rock speedfreak existentialist flick'.

He told *Select* that they wrote 'Kowalski' – which repeats the 'Loaded' technique of

Innes in full regalia for the 'Kowalski' video, '97. 'Luftwaffe: The gentleman's Man Utd,' says Big Bob.

Bobby salutes the camera at the 'Kowalski' video shoot, '97.

inserting snatches of film dialogue into the action – because they didn't like the original soundtrack. He went on to explain to *Select* that it needed 'something that captures the feel, the paranoia, the amphetamine, the claustrophobia, the way the guy's focused and locked in.'

Then Duffy made his contribution: 'My personal opinion of that film is that point . . . you could say it was death, you know what I mean, but it's too small a point. Small. The vanishing point is massive. If you had to try and describe all the shit that you're into, that's what it all boils down to. That point. Wham! You're dead.'

Yes we see. But between them, Bobby and Duff had perfectly described the new single. The video, which was scripted by Irvine Welsh, went even further by featuring a red Dodge Challenger and getting supermodels Kate Moss and Devon to drive it, as well as bumping off Bobby and the group. The shoot was a hoot. A pyjama-clad Fatty gets beaten up by the girls before getting his face rammed into a bowl of Cheerios. The group are sitting around their lair playing cards – actually Fatty's Bar and Grill. Irvine, Nightingale and new drummer Mulreany played press photographers who bust in on the grisly scene, flashes popping. The girls then turn their attention to the band. A magnificently malevolent Kate cuts down Bob and the others, then their lifeless bodies are stuck in the boot of the Dodge, before being unceremoniously dumped in a Kings Cross backstreet, only to vaporise sci-fi movie-style. *Faster Pussycat, Kill! Kill!* meets *The Sweeney* had been the brief, and it all fit the song perfectly.

After the shoot we started a party with Muzz, Hartie and myself spinning ludicrous records. I ended up playing flat on my back while Kate laughed her head off and danced to disco. Not content with all the shenanigans at Fatty's, some of the band, Irvine and myself adjourned to Nightingale's Maida Vale flat for further festivities. It was the first time I'd met Irvine, and that night we discovered a mutual love of disco which eventually culminated in the formation of Hibee-Nation, a band where he wrote the lyrics and I produced the music. Having been there at the birth, Innes came along and added guitar to our first single, 'The Keys To The House Of Love'. It was released on the tiny Bubbles label run by the lovely 'Big' Bob Morris, longtime friend of the Scream and the bloke who dressed up as someone's mum in the 'Kowalski' video. By now Irvine was firmly ensconced in the Scream's sanctum and grew to become one of my best friends.

Funny how this band seem to attract like-minded nutters like loony flies to a radioactive turd.

The single received glowing press reviews and reached number eight in the charts. With the late addition of 'Trainspotting', the new album was also finished, after a period of intense mixing by Innes and Brendan up at Ocean Colour Scene's studio in Birmingham.

Vanishing Point

It's funny how – after being written off by the press over the previous three years for the traditionalism of *Give Out But Don't Give Up* – the Scream were immediately back in favour with 'Kowalski'. *NME* made it Single of the Week and said it was 'the stuff of genius', winding up their superlatives with, 'It's about as well suited to commercial airplay as *Apocalypse Now* is to kids' TV, but Primal Scream still look set to rip up 1997 and redesign it in their own delirious image.'

The group were featured in the 3 May issue cover piece, with Bobby berating himself for letting his hair grow and the band for overpolishing *Give Out*, when it should have sounded 'bruised and broken' like the band at the time. He declared, 'We stand for experimentation again. High-energy rock 'n' roll. Psychedelic experimentation and punk music. We wanted to excite ourselves as well as everyone else and we have. The last record sounded dead compared to *Screamadelica* or *Vanishing Point*. It shouldnae sounded dead. It should've sounded nearly dead.

'I think this album is better than *Screamadelica*, much better. I love *Screamadelica*, but I think *Vanishing Point* is a pure Primal Scream album. I think we've really and truly found our voice.'

Mani chimes in succinctly, in one of his first interviews since he left the Roses. The wounds are clearly still open: 'I'm in a better band now than I was before. This Scream album pisses over everything by the Roses . . . I've come home to my real family.'

Vanishing Point is a remarkable album, especially considering those difficult birth conditions. If *Screamadelica* was an ecstatic high and *Give Out But Don't Give Up* fulfilled the Scream's rock 'n' roll fantasies in a druggy comedown haze, *Vanishing Point* was an insular punk-rock voyage which didn't give a shit and swiped at any music that took its fancy along the way. It was claustrophobic, beautiful, rocking, melancholic and totally in your face.

The album starts with 'Burning Wheel', a swirling, psychedelic mantra recalling the classic sixties West Coast sound, shot to hallucinogenic heaven with sitars and other exotica. First words you hear from Bobby are, 'Through my diseased eyes / I'm sinful, sly / I can't stop stealing / I will pay the price of being a thief when I stop breathing.' Bobby described it at the time as his favourite Scream track ever. 'That was my dream to make that record,' he told *NME*. 'It's totally LSD 25-strength through the centre of your skull music. It's like taking acid without taking acid.'

'Get Duffy' is a cool instrumental loosely based on the *Get Carter* theme which dates from the Bob-less sessions. The apocalyptic 'Kowalski' is next, followed by the gorgeously fragile 'Star' and that Pablo-Memphis horn magic. It's probably Bob's best vocal on the album, as he sings gently about solidarity, freedom and resistance: 'Every brother is a star / Every sister is a star.' 'If They Move Kill 'Em' homes in on another movie – *The Wild Bunch* – for its speech-sample, but the music wouldn't have been out of place in a seventies blaxploitation movie as Duncan and Jim parp heartily over a vicious hip hop-funk groove with *Dr Who*-type synth squalls. This was the sound of a band totally at ease with itself, who didn't give a shit about preconceptions and were enjoying life as sonic explorers.

'Stuka' rivals 'Kowalski' as heaviest cut on the album, with its crashing dub-bass skank, reeling effects and Bob's distorted vocal uttered through a Darth Vader mask. Dark, booming and very nasty, it could be the anti-*Screamadelica* in mood. Cop this: 'If you play with fire you're gonna get burned / Some of my friends are gonna die young.' 'Out Of The Void' is a downer-haze ballad which could be born from Bob's depressed period. It's desolate and haunting. Next comes the rock section as they blast into the Stonesy 'Medication', which started life when Bob was chanting 'gimme gimme gimme all your loving' back in Ben's studio under the Westway. Now it wouldn't sound out of place on *Give Out But Don't Give Up*. 'Motorhead' is out there – the original was Lemmy's greased-up speed tribute riding hotwired guitars, but in the hands of the Scream it sounds more like Suicide-meets-the-Stooges. Finally, 'Long Life' is a gorgeous, breathy lullaballad spinning off into the ether to close a remarkable 58 minutes.

Bobby on the cover of NME, *May, '97*

Vanishing Point was ready. How about the world?

After the controversial *Give Out* nobody knew what to expect. An album of German drinking songs, maybe? But *Vanishing Point* had sprung out of nothing. A void. Down in the Bunker and out of the glare. *Screamadelica* had been the toughest act in the world to follow and *Give Out* was the last thing people had expected. With *Vanishing Point* they could go anywhere they wanted to, and did. No flash studios, no top producers, a few mates and some top guests. Their music had grown, in private, nurtured by a growing will to keep the Scream flag flying. By now they were getting closer to the Parliafunkadelicment ideal of George Clinton – a hard core of central players and a stream of like-minded lunatics dropping by to add their input. This more wide-open attitude meant that it didn't matter if someone didn't turn up at the studio. Anything was possible – as then exemplified by the input of Adrian Sherwood and the gathering sonic storm cloud that was Kevin Shields.

'I want to deconstruct the idea of a group,' Bobby told Paul Moody. 'There's no given roles with us. We're not trying to copy Funkadelic but we're into bringing in new people and experimenting. Having that straight line-up is okay for some people but not us. What I'm saying is there's no conventions in this band. The only limit is the limit to your own imagination . . . it's always the unknown with this band. You never know what's gonna happen.

'They always want us to be out of control. But I like that about the band. Like, no-one knows what's really going on. Is he a serial killer or an assassin? How many serial killers are there in Primal Scream? I can't say . . . all I know is that we're the best we've ever been.'

The reviews were generally over the moon. *Select* called it 'a scarifying wakeup call for the chemical generation. It perfectly mirrors the time, like *Screamadelica* did. Now things are a bit darker.' *Melody Maker*'s Everett True described it as 'the ultimate road movie soundtrack', adding that *Vanishing Point* is 'arrogantly self-assured, confusing, bemusing: often on the verge of imploding under the weight of its own imagination . . . [the album] resonates with a love of the rock 'n' roll lifestyle, but owes plenty to the present. It's sprawling, vast, superb. Mad, bad and fucking magnificent . . . a truly breathtaking record.' He liked it then.

NME's Stephen Dalton called it 'a return to the cutting edge', adding that 'the Scream have finally stopped gassing away about soul and got loose enough to sound truly soulful.' In their end-of-year issue, *Mixmag* called it 'the comeback of the year'.

The Scream debuted some of the new songs on a Heavenly-hired boat going down the Thames on 21 June. It recalled the infamous Sex Pistols boat trip of 1977 – which just happened to be almost twenty years to the week. Originally, top American DJ Armand Van Helden was going to play the Heavenly Social on the Saturday but had another booking, so the club constructed the boat party around him on the Sunday afternoon. When the Scream heard about it they asked, at the last minute, if they could play too. The whole band plus brass section were set up in impossibly cramped conditions with no stage and played 'Burning Wheel', 'If They Move Kill 'Em', 'Out Of The Void', 'Star' and 'Stuka', with 'Rocks' as the only old number.

The first *Vanishing Point* gigs were unsteady. They weren't using a drummer, apart from Mulreaney on a few items. The set had practically been shorn of oldies. Innes was resolutely refusing to do faves like 'Come Together', following the line that the band had moved on and it was the new album that reflected the times and their new direction. 'Who wants to come together now?' he reasoned. But 'Higher Than The Sun' and 'Rocks' were still just as relevant – getting high and getting your rocks off always will be.

The first night in Portsmouth, on 24 June 1997, was okay but low-key, far from the soaring party euphoria the group could generate. They were basically trying out the new stuff, warming up for the upcoming big one at Glastonbury. However, 'Kowalski' was a blistering highlight with Mani really getting into his stride at his first proper Scream gig. Another added bonus was that Adrian Sherwood was at the mixing desk, dubbing things up and contributing to the necessary aural mayhem of the new material.

On to Southend and Oxford, which showed the band were warming up nicely with the new material. Of course, it was all the normal antics and raucous gang shenanigans of the Scream Team on the road. The Three Musketeers – Trigger, Fatty and Muzz – were still on board, doing their jobs in their own unique ways: Trigger trying to keep it afloat with dry aplomb, Fatty shouting and looking after the boys, and Muzz keeping the show on the road with quiet efficiency. The addition of Mani to the equation was like a dose of rocket fuel both on stage and in the dressing room. The man never stops smiling and cracking funnies. He can party as hard as the rest and still be fresh as a daisy. But why Duffy had developed an obsession for expounding on Mr Kipling's Bramley apple pies remains a mystery.

Then it was Glastonbury, headlining in the Dance Tent. It was the year that the rains had come and we had advance warnings that we'd be sailing into a sea of mud. This was found to be the case, as our coach ploughed through sodden fields of bedraggled, mud-caked punters. We were all getting limbered up in time-honoured Scream coach fashion, while Irvine Welsh was in the coach behind us on acid. I got off the coach and immediately sank into about a foot of mud.

Apparently, the previous night some bright spark had plugged a water-hose into the sewage tank and squirted several hundred Dance Tent ravers with raw shit. That's where we were appearing and I had the unenviable job of playing between Armand Van Helden and the Scream. Armand had seriously got it going , and was rocking the tent with Lil' Louis' classic 'French Kiss' when I made soggy steps to vibe things up for the Scream. The only problem was that the decks were situated right in front of the stage, so all through my set all I could hear were guitars being tuned, noises being tested and the old 'one-two one-two!' I couldn't hear a thing. It was okay, but the crowd, patient to the last, knew what was coming and were basically sinking – literally – into a Dunkirk spirit, soaked but spirited and waiting for the Scream. My set got slagged in *Mixmag* but praised in *NME*, who credited it to Armand Van Helden!

That night the Scream were a great tonic. Ben Wilmott praised the gig in *NME*, saying that the crowd was 'wetting its collective pants with joy', continuing, 'Little wonder, seeing as the Scream are a rampantly heaving, devilishly swoonsome proposition from the off . . . Clearly, Gillespie wishes to make a weird, protracted dub-rock opera from his music this time around and it's nothing short of fantastic news.' He continues about this 'effortlessly beatific performance', finishing up with 'as the crowd staggers off to track down the best all-night sound system it can find, the noise left howling through our heads says that Primal Scream have returned with perfect timing, capturing the mood of the moment in infinite detail.'

Meanwhile, Bobby and Mani had formed a top interview tag team and were on fine form delivering their own quotes. Speaking to Michael Bonner in *Melody Maker*, Bobby called *Vanishing Point* a 'punk rock album for 1997', while Mani added that it was 'a soundtrack to life'. The paper itself described the album as 'one of the most audacious and spectacular comebacks in recent history'. Bobby: 'It's like Phil Spector said – "you can always come back but you've got to come back stronger" . . . We wanted to make a great album. We had a lot of ideas and a lot of energy . . . We went into the studio every day and experimented with sounds and ideas. There was such a joy there. That's why it sounds so alive. It's bursting. We've got a lot of music inside us. There's intensity of focus too – musically, lyrically, attitude-wise, everything. The clarity of thought is incredible on this album.

'I think the songs on *Vanishing Point* are about life in Britain at the end of the nineties in much the same way that *Metal Box* caught the mood of the country at the end of the seventies. That damp, dark, alienated feeling.'

Talking in *Jockey Slut*, Bobby said he'd been listening to lots of reggae, soul, Velvets, Electric Prunes, Nico, Joy Division and, yup, *Metal Box* when they were making the album – 'a lot of stuff that we listened to when we started the band really.'

During our frequent talks about music, Bobby would usually come back to the same names and influences. They simply got shuffled about in the Scream's sonic card-pack. He was proud about the mutations swimming about in *Vanishing Point* but disagreed with the magazine's Paul Benney when asked if the new album was a return to *Screamadelica*: 'Nah, it's completely different. We'd never return anywhere. It's just different. The only similarities are that we've started using samplers again. The last album was a live band recorded live in the studio kind of album. But I think we fucked it up. It could have been a lot better. With this album it's live musicians and loops and drum machines and samplers and stuff, so we're marrying the two again.

'We really enjoyed making this record, just fucking about with sound again . . . I love the record. I'm really proud of it and we've got a great band.'

But then the *Vanishing Point* tour started to hit the rocks. First of all there was a gig cancella-

Getting revved up at Oxford Zodiac on '97's Vanishing Point *tour.*

tion, so that the band could work at the new material, sort out the big screen visuals and reorganise after the departure of Mulreany. Also, one of the group needed some hospital treatment.

NME carried it as a lead news item under the headline 'Primals Vanishing Act', amidst rumours of personnnel shake-ups, illness and band uncertainty about performing the new songs. The official statement cited 'health reasons', with the band spokesman commenting, 'Absolutely nobody has left Primal Scream. Nothing like that has happened. Somebody in the band has simply got to have some treatment which means they can't do all the dates at this time. It's just down to one person and it's a private matter. It's not up for discussion. It's nothing to do with drugs, mental health problems or anything bad like that. It's just that sometimes people have to go to hospital. It's boring and unfortunate, but it's a personal thing.' Another spokesman added that the band weren't in any great trouble, and would still be playing after a good Glastonbury showing, including a Swedish festival at the end of July. 'Maybe it might persuade people that the band haven't split up. Then again, Martin Duffy was replaced by an animatronic robot about a year ago. Maybe they're having time off to replace his head.'

They were indeed soon back in action and, apart from Stockholm, the next gig was the Scream on the Green all-dayer on Glasgow Green on 24 August in front of 7,200 people. I was DJing that day and it was great to be playing to the Scream's home crowd, with the band rising to the occasion. It had to be 'God Save The Queen' before the band came on.

They still managed to hit the headlines when some asshole went around stabbing the audience with a syringe. Around twenty punters were hit and had to be vaccinated against Hepatitis B. An official Scream statement said, 'We are all collectively shocked and disturbed by this sick, degraded behaviour and our thoughts are with the people who were hurt and their families. We are frustrated and annoyed that this happened at a hometown gig which, for us and our fans, should have been a time of celebration and that these people, who had gone out purely to enjoy themselves, ended up getting injured by one stupid, irresponsible idiot.'

Dates set for the end of the summer were also cancelled, for mysterious reasons, and rescheduled. These included Manchester and two shows at Hackney's Victoria Park on 5 and 6 September, which were postponed after Princess Diana's death. The band were miffed that the music press carried a story saying they'd cancelled the Victoria Park gig 'out of respect for Princess Diana', when it was just an irrelevant coincidence. As Bobby commented, 'It's like being told the day before the cup final that it's cancelled, especially when it's some fucking scumbag who has nothing to do with your life.'

Eventually the Scream issued the following statement: 'We have no respect whatsoever for Diana Spencer or any member of the English Royal Family. We are totally opposed to the monarchy. With regards to the London shows, the Police refused to police the event which meant the council would revoke the licence. We wanted to play.' The band blamed the initial statement on promoters Metropolis Music.

Then it was the two rescheduled gigs at Victoria Park, on 13 and 14 September, where I was also playing. Of course, it was the usual fun and games backstage but the band weren't quite 100 per cent with the new set yet. Unsurprising, when you consider that much of the *Vanishing Point* magic had been created in the studio. They'd played about with the sound at their leisure, almost like creating a sonic painting, and were still getting the hang of translating it onto the stage with live instruments. There was still hardly any old material and that indefinable Scream magic was strangely absent.

The gig got panned by Dorian Lynskey – usually a fan – in *Mixmag*. He bemoaned the fact that the studio creation that was *Vanishing Point* translated sludgily to a big tent with no atmosphere, ending, 'For the first time, Primal Scream play like a band that doesn't want to be here.'

All that would soon change.

The band knew just what they wanted – and needed – to achieve. Even the usually retiring Innes had something to say on the subject. *Jockey Slut*, the one-time dance fanzine I'd written for in its early days, had grown into a literary hand grenade nestling in the racks of W. H. Smith, and was one of the few publications the Scream would open up to. The *Slut* actually got Innes, who never does interviews, to talk about the album. While he never spoke to the media or did photo sessions, he'd increasingly become the backbone of the Scream's music over the years. He supervises, remixes and orchestrates the volcanic creations which eventually erupt. The following quote explained a lot about the Scream-change between *Give Out But Don't Give Up* and *Vanishing Point*:

'The band's just getting better and better . . . We just want to keep working because if we get left with nothing to do we inevitably get up to no good . . . It's great having your own studio because you can just leave your old socks lying about,' he told Paul Benney. 'In your own place you open the door and you get on with it instead of waiting about for hours while they tell you they've got to line up the tape machines, sort the mixing desk out, plug everything in. I mean we don't actually do demos any more because what's actually our demo ends up as our record. When you do your demo you get the spark and then you have to try and recreate it in a big studio and most of the time it just doesnae work out. Whereas the way we work now, the initial idea is what goes down on tape. This album sounds like the spark's there whereas the last one we spent three months trying to get a guitar overdub right and it fuckin' sounds like it. You end up with all the life taken out of the record and there's quite a lot of life in this record. The last album should've sounded more like that but we let it get tarted up and made presentable. If you hear the actual original tapes that we scrapped you'd just think "they need hospital". You hear a group that is fuckin' dead. It's a shame that we just didn't leave it that way.'

When Bobby talked to Anthony Teasdale in *Seven* in November 1999, the controversial *Give Out* came up again. It was interesting to see how the band's views had changed in the five years since *Vanishing Point*. Bobby talked about the rocky road to the album's completion: 'What tore the band apart was heroin abuse, and cocaine, amphetamines and a lot of alcohol. Any drug you can name it was in there. We never hated each other. Everybody was just incapacitated. It was really hard to keep it together. In summer 1992 I'd arrive at the studio two hours before anyone to rehearse and people would turn up late, score and then fuck off again. The album was a comedown record, the aftermath of *Screamadelica*. We didn't have any energy left so every song seemed to be a ballad. What we were writing, there was a lot of emotion that got lost in endless retakes. But I like it because people expected another *Screamadelica* and got a Southern soul ballads record. At least we were being true to ourselves . . . We went on the road and it was great playing rock 'n' roll again. We'd stopped using samples, Weatherall had gone all hard techno, while we were going darker, heroin influenced, more ballady.'

The album still does sound really fucked. It was the Scream of that time, and I personally still think it's a great record. Not transcendental or menacing or challenging, but it works as a bunch of drugged-up nutters on the rampage with their heroes, gliding down from a big one. Maybe that's why *Vanishing Point*, a UK inner-city affair, came as such a stark contrast.

If Innes hadn't sat in that little studio every day, biting his lower lip, waiting for the boys to come back, it simply wouldn't have happened. He admits that his DJing brought home the power of the drum, and he focused on this, as opposed to polishing guitar lines. The reaction was to make it as fucked up as possible. But on speed, not smack.

'I call this album a drum and bass record because normally the hardest thing to do is to get the drums and the bass right and this time we got it right . . . We've learnt a lot over the years. If you work with people like Andrew Weatherall, Hugo Nicolson, Jimmy Miller, George Clinton and Adrian Sherwood and you don't learn anything then you just need shooting.'

NEW MUSICAL EXPRESS

'Wheel' will rock you

PUBLIC FLOGGING!
U2's PopMart
live in Leeds

Introducing...
INDIE KYLIE
the Manic Ramsay
Street Preacher

EDWYN COLLINS ★ STEREOLAB
JONATHAN FIRE*EATER
SWEET 75 ★ TRAVIS
AUSTIN POWERS

9 770028 636086   36>

'No-one knows
what's going on'
**PRIMAL
SCREAM**
On the road and off your face
with the maddest gang in rock

The Vanishing
Point Effect

'I tell you, we dinnae give a fuck. We're doing our own thing. They can all get on with it. We can't be bothered with it. Who cares? there's no competition anyway.'
– *Bobby Gillespie, June 1997*

'Star' was the second single to be released off the album, in June 1997. One of the loveliest ballads the Scream have ever done, it was the lead track on an EP whose sleeve featured a photo of a black activist holding a rifle. The record also featured a Rebel Dub instrumental of 'Star', which boasted supernatural interplay between Augustus Pablo and the Memphis Horns. What other group could get that? There were also two interesting demos: 'Jesus', which later became 'I'll Be There For You' on *Give Out But Don't Give Up*, but appears here as pleading funereal soul, taken to church by a heavenly organ. The second was a drowsy ballad called 'How Does It Feel To Belong?', which must also have dated from the Brownhouse sessions – although no-one would probably remember if it did.

The record went down well, entering the charts at number sixteen, and was notable for the fact that it landed the Scream their first *Top of the Pops* appearance since the Luton Airport incident three years before. *Top of the Pops* with the Scream is obviously a hoot, as there's lots of waiting about, but they looked good: Bobby soft and cool, the rest augmented by the brass duo and Mulreany. It all went smoothly so Creation were content (and probably breathed a big sigh of relief).

The same month saw the outrageous Two Lone Swordsmen remixes of 'Stuka' released as a limited edition of 3000. The tracks had originally appeared on an extremely limited promo but were put out to satisfy public demand. Just as well. It was one of the best things that Mr Weatherall has ever put his name to, and showed how his partnership with Keith Tenniswood was becoming almost frightening. The first mix takes the heavy dub and interjects it between chattering electro-beats before drenching the whole lot in gradually-building melodies. The breakdown is a monster, the extra space emphasising Bobby's robot vocal to even greater effect, and it's dubbed out to the max. The other mix is an electro-wired floor-destroyer.

Everyone was after a piece of dancefloor magic. In September 1997, I had been drafted in by Alan McGee and Dick Green to start a new Creation dance music offshoot, which I called Eruption. They reckoned that, with my contacts through DJing, writing for dance mags and the knowledge I'd gained, I could find 'a new Prodigy or Chemical Brothers'. At the time, the label's initial rush of euphoria and money following the success of Oasis was starting to level off. There

Bobby on the cover of NME, *September '97.*

Guest pass for Scream on the Green, Glasgow, '97.

had been a veritable flurry of signings, but they needed that third Oasis album to keep it going while consolidating the existing stable of groups like Super Furry Animals and Three Colours Red, as well as new boys like ex-Suede guitarist Bernard Butler. That didn't stop a few red herrings still clogging up the net. There had already been some follies and now they needed cash. The new Prodigy? That'll do nicely.

As both label and Scream HQ were ensconced between the Pembroke Castle and the Queens, it was inevitable that I'd be seeing even more of Primal Scream than when I was on tour with them. Myself, Innes and some of the boys had been talking about doing a track for a while and it eventually became one of the first Eruption releases. The great lost Primal Scream single: 'The Desert Song' by Los Terrorpinos. This particular bout of astral-dub silliness took place on a Saturday morning in the Primrose Hill bunker. The magnificent seven aboard consisted of Innes, Duffy, Murray Mitchell, Hartie, Sarah-Jane Harrison of the Hibee-Nation, me and anybody else I can't remember.

The track was an epic, sweeping dub tribute to Spaghetti Western soundtracks. But you wouldn't have known it from the session. We met in the Queens and, after a while, adjourned back to the Bunker. We set up a slow-motion dub-throb with gentle drums and bottomless bass underpinning all manner of stupidity. I think it was Duff who came up with the wafting Mexican trumpets, while Innes definitely threw in the twanging Spanish guitar riff. We were all messing about. Sarah-Jane added atmosphere with a ghostly, soaring vocal. Then it was time for the choir. Hartie, Muzz and myself gathered round the mike and let fly with all manner of operatic howls, cod-Mex buffoonery and Spanish asides – while splitting our sides. Somehow Innes and Muzz managed to put all these assorted elements through the patent dub blender and emerged triumphant with a twelve-minute sonic desertscape on Mars, with all manner of dub trickery added. It wasn't exactly a peak-time floorfiller but we got some good responses from the chillout mob. It didn't get much press though and many only got interested when they found out the Scream were involved. We pressed a thousand one-sided twelves only. But 'The Desert Song' still makes me laugh.

My new job basically meant that I was seeing the band every day. In the paper shop, the cafe, the pub, the record company and in the studio after work. It was a rare evening that I'd leave the office and stroll straight down to Chalk Farm tube station.

But the Scream were not happy campers. *Vanishing Point* had done well – over 300,000 copies sold – but the general sentiments fluttering around in the Bunker were not positive. It was one of those doldrum periods again. They knew that the live gigs hadn't gone as well as they could have, and that the band still wasn't firing on all cylinders. Plus they felt they were taking a backseat to the precious soft-rock of Butler and a bevy of no-hopers. They didn't mind riding behind Oasis, but would sometimes gripe about Creation through gritted teeth, with talk of firebombs. I didn't feel that my label was getting full support either. Sometimes it'd take me two weeks to get an A&R meeting, a point rammed home when I licensed the Wamdue Project from New York label Strictly Rhythm. When I was sent a new mix it was passed on. So it went to another label – and promptly entered the charts at number one! They did support a new disco outing from me and Irvine though, but its failure was probably due to the public's good taste. Maybe basing the cover on a can of Tennent's Super lager didn't help. Also, my old mate Dave Beer – a mighty man in Scream eyes – got to release a single.

After Oasis's *Be Here Now* didn't match up to the critical acclaim and sales of the previous two albums, an increasing sense of desperation seemed to be creeping into the Creation offices. Jobs were going, morale was dwindling and Paul Gallagher – the other one – was in there, for obvious political reasons, as an A&R man with a large expense account. Most of the hard-pressed staff were lovely, but obviously a little scared of the label's longest-standing act. Pity anyone who has to control that lot. Some mornings or early afternoons I'd stroll in and often either Innes or Bobby would be there trying to stir things up. Innes was normally up to his usual production supervision, Bobby was there just to see what the fuck was going on, while his then-girlfriend Emily also worked there. Another beacon was Bob's brother Graham, aka the Judge, who would usually join me in a swifty at the Pembroke, where we'd also be joined by the band.

It was a funny time, creatively and socially. Innes, Muzz and the diehards had got used to the Bunker being a kind of party central HQ before and after the pub. There would be casualties showing up after a long weekend, which Innes would dread when he was working.

Liam Gallagher often came round and messed about before the inevitable pub visit. One time he strolled into the studio with a crate of beer on his shoulders and the party started up again. Next day Liam was in the Queens when I walked in at lunchtime and we embarked on an all-dayer, climaxing in the Pembroke watching the football. I think Mr Gallagher liked the fact that, apart from being very likeable nutters, the Scream had no pretensions or barriers when he was about. It was just fun and there no photographers or assholes in the area. We did end up at places like the Met Bar, occasionally, but it was anything but rock-star backslapping.

Paul Weller was another mate. The Scream loved winding him up by playing the 'soul music only' singer-songwriter mad, white rock 'n' roll records. When the Scream were invited to do a tune for the Jam tribute album, they chose to tackle 'Non Stop Dancing' in full-on Velvet Underground style with Hartie on vocals, and called themselves the Going Underground. Weller hates the Velvets and the Scream knew it. The track never made the album.

Around this time Innes, Brendan, Duffy, sometimes Bobby and engineer Max Hayes did a few remixes, including Massive Attack, 'Indian Vibes' by Mathur, and ill-fated Creation signing Ultra-Living from Japan, who were calling themselves the Gruesome Twosome. All were dubbed-out and warped.

In October the band released a novel artefact – *Vanishing Point* remixed in dub by Adrian Sherwood, and retitled *Echo Dek*. Who better to call than the UK's don of dub? Massive Attack had done it a few years earlier when they got in Mad Professor to do one of theirs, but the concept originally started in Jamaica in the seventies when artists like Burning Spear and Hugh Mundell were dubbed out and mutated by the producer. Those *Cry Tuff Dub Encounter* albums, which melted gravel-voiced Prince Far-I into a sea of bass and drum echo and sonic effects – with added doorbells – are one of Bobby's eternal inspirations. Old school roots reggae by the likes of Keith Hudson, Dr Alimantado, Far-I and Culture provides much of his home listening. Plus tons of dub. It was radical stuff, putting the Scream at the mercy of the UK's great dub innovator.

They had to add a touch of class though. *Echo Dek* first came as a limited edition brown box of seven-inch singles printed up like Jamaican pre-releases. Tracks were distended, distorted and given new names. The titles in the box were 'Duffed Up' ('Get Duffy'), 'Living Dub' ('Long Life'), 'Last Train' ('Trainspotting'), 'JU-87', 'Wise Blood'('Stuka'), which, to Bobby's great delight, features additional vocals from Prince Far I, 'Dub In Vain' ('Medication'), 'Revolutionary' ('Star'), 'First Name Unknown' ('Kowalski') and 'Vanishing Dub'. Only his version of 'Motorhead' didn't make it, as the album would have been too long.

In the same *Jockey Slut* interview, which had been notable for Innes speaking so candidly, the

PRiMAL SCREAM

ECHO DEK

Box cover for the Echo Dek *singles collection.*

band talked about *Echo Dek*. Bobby: 'I used to go to see him [Sherwood] mix people like Jah Wobble live and the bass would be trying to tear your chest apart, it was so fucking heavy. So, the dub album was an experiment. Me and Innes would go to his studio every day and just sit there. He said he couldn't get motivated to mix a record privately. When he was doing the dub mixes we had to be present, he was working off our reactions. He likes his light refreshments as well. He was like, "I thought this was Primal Scream, Bobby can you bring me something to cheer me up?"'

Talking in the same issue, Mr Sherwood, the great maverick producer of UK music, took a guided tour through *Echo Dek*, confessed that he was too into his old school reggae to be a big Scream fan but admitted that he wanted some of the boys there when he was doing it, to get 'their energy as well'. And that's unusual for a remixer.

'I think *Echo Dek* is going to stand up for years, it's that good,' he enthused. 'The old dub albums derived from existing songs so this album is like a proper traditional dub album with none of those ingredients . . . I play the album at home, which I don't with a lot of my things. I think it's one of the best dub things I've ever done – perhaps even better than that, and I've done a few very good dub albums. I think they're a really important band . . . They've got a very punk rock attitude – their approach is one of the best of any of the people I've ever worked with.'

However, towards the end of the year it was becoming increasingly more obvious that the Scream were embarking on a mission of extreme noise terror. Kevin Shields was becoming more involved, after his ear-melting remix of 'If They Move Kill 'Em' – which Innes took great delight in assaulting the office with first thing one morning. It was a wall of guitar overkill and shrieking brass building on Moroccan rhythms, and it was incredible.

In his legendary band My Bloody Valentine, Kevin's speciality had been total guitar overload and, even though that group hadn't made a new album for years, it seemed that in the Scream he had found a bunch of kindred spirits hellbent on aural destruction by any means possible. What with Mani, Brendan and the brass-men, the Scream seemed to be assembling a new firm built on total ear-bleeding danger. They also moved the Bunker from the seedy two-room affair, where they'd hatched much of *Vanishing Point*, to a newer annexe across the courtyard, which had a band room, windows and a new, state-of-the-art computer. To get in you had to walk through prison-style black iron bars. Of course, within weeks it had been Screamatised, with photos of everyone from Maradonna to Sly Stone. Like Keith Richards, the Scream like to turn any place where they're going to be spending some time into a homely environment – even if that means a Sooty charity box with a Hitler moustache.

The third single off *Vanishing Point* was 'Burning Wheel' in October, the psychedelic opener which is as close as the band has ever got to transforming that sixties Pink Floyd/Love vibe into modern psychosis. The EP also came with a Chemical Brothers big beat workout, coupled with the original on DJ promo, plus there was also a vamping sixties-style go-go instrumental called 'Hammond Connection' – cue Mr Duffy – and the original version of 'Higher Than The Sun' before Dr Alex got his extraterrestrial claws into it. Ironically, the camera-shy Innes got his photo on the front of the CD – albeit wearing a US flying helmet. That one came and went, entering the charts at number 26 while business went on around the corner in the new Bunker.

Meanwhile, *Screamadelica* still had no trouble staying in orbit – it was voted number 27 in *Q*'s '100 Greatest Albums EVER' readers' poll that January. 'Our music offers a sense of the infinite possibilities, not like you're sat in some bedsit in Grimsby, like some,' was Bobby's comment.

But knowing that they hadn't quite got it right live yet, the band recruited drummer Darrin Mooney, who provided the necessary beef downstairs. By the end of the year they were firing on all cylinders again. This was evident in the press that started rolling in around February 1998. *Melody Maker*'s Paul Naylor gushed, 'They articulate, and thus neutralise, our collective agony and then make us turn around and pogo like invincible fools.'

The band were back, strutting at Scream Level One – a fact corroborated by *Select*'s Ian Harrison when he covered a string of dates at Tokyo's Liquid Rooms in the February issue, part of a tour which also took in Hong Kong and Australia. You knew it was business as usual when you saw the photo of Innes and Duffy sporting bald, Bilko-style wigs. Andrew had also acquired a replica Luger 'to deal with those cunts with the lasers' – referring to the quaint Japanese sport of aiming a red beam at the performers from a pencil-thin laser.

It seemed that Darrin was the missing ingredient. Brass boys Jim and Duncan were present and correct and Sherwood was still at the controls. The set had changed too, as they opened with the ghostly 'Out Of The Void' and even went back ten years to revive 'Imperial'. There was also their version of sixties garage band Third Bardo's 'Five Years Ahead Of My Time', with Can loops, the sinister hip hop of 'Insect Royalty', which would be the theme tune for the new Irvine Welsh film *The Acid House*, 'Higher Than The Sun' and, for encores, they tore through 'Motorhead' and '96 Tears'. After a stunning show Mani was heard to comment, 'We're fucking enjoying it again, know what I mean?'

February 1998 also saw some Irish and British dates that confirmed the band was a major live force again: Dublin, Galway, Derry, Glasgow, Nottingham, Manchester, Sheffield and the traditional Brixton Academy knees-up on Valentine's Day, where I found myself playing in the upstairs bar.

Kevin's remix of 'If They Move Kill 'Em' was eventually released that month – for one week only. It wasn't eligible for the singles charts as it broke the stupid 25-minute barrier. It entered the album charts at number thirteen instead and still made *NME* Single of the Week: 'The truth is they remain as sharply relevant as ever. A killer, indeed.' The track would also appear on the next album as 'MBV Arkestra (If They Move Kill 'Em)', but there were other great tracks on the EP, a twelve-inch disco mix of the lead tune plus an ethereal trawl through the Jesus and Mary Chain's 'Darklands', complete with a dub track called 'Badlands'. The record was dedicated to Sam Peckinpah (director of *The Wild Bunch*, the cult film that inspired the lead track), John Coltrane, Ian Curtis and Rosa Luxemburg.

NME's Roger Morton went with the band to Dublin. His piece – one of the finest I've read about the group – is an insightful, hilarious account which perfectly sums up the Scream Touring Experience. As the stories unfold, Duff comments abound and much excess is reported. But it's the New Scream Attack which really shines through in the writing. Or, as he describes them, 'a bunch of connected, vital avant-rock pioneers reinventing

'If They Move Kill 'Em'

PRiMAL SCREAM
BRiXTON ACADEMY
SATURDAY 14TH FEBRUARY 1998

RUNNiNG ORDER MAiN STAGE
21.00	DJ PAUL HARTE
22.00	TRYPTAMEANIES
22.30	DJ PAUL HARTE
23.15	ALABAMA 3
00.00	DJ PAUL HARTE
01.00	PRiMAL SCREAM
02.30	SPRiNGHEEL JACK
03.15	SPiRiTUALiSED
04.15	DJ KRiS NEEDS
06.00	CLOSE

FOYER
21.00 - 23.30	VEGETABLE ViSiON DJs
22.30 - 01.00	ADRiAN SHERWOOD
02.30 - 06.00	VEGETABLE ViSiON

CiRCLE BAR
21.00 - 23.00	DJ KAREN PARKER
23.00 - 01.00	ASiAN DUB FOUNDATiON
02.30 - 06.00	DJ KAREN PARKER & FRiENDS

Flyer for Brixton Academy, February '98.

themselves as the coolest sonic-contact soundclash out there,' with a show he describes as 'unparalleled'.

Roger asks Bob if they were 'aestheticising mental illness' when they made *Vanishing Point*. 'Yeah, I think so,' replied the singer. 'Slightly. Because songs like "Burning Wheel", if you read the lyrics, that's very internal. It's about having your mind fractured. It's about psychosis. It's hallucinations you can get. It's that state. And it's drug-induced but you can go beyond that. So, yeah, I think so. But I'm not glorifying it, I'm just trying to explain it, or make sense of what's going on inside my head. That's why you write a song like "Burning Wheel" or "Stuka", you're trying to articulate . . . confusion, it's purifying, it's angry. It's like confronting yourself and trying to work out what's going on inside your head and what's gone wrong.

'I'm not saying I'm mentally ill or anything, don't get me wrong. I'm saying like a depression or whatever. But rather than writing songs like "Movin' On Up" or "Come Together" which are affirmations of communality, it's like trying to take away anger, the self-hate that you've got inside you and get it out whichever way possible, by screaming or writing a song.' Like Dr Janov's primal scream therapy, in a way then.

It's not all like this. A lot of the article is funny, like the story about the band spending three days in Dolly Parton's tour bus, lying in the pink double bed on crystal meth, watching videos of *The World at War*. 'Innes' idea of a good time,' apparently.

Bobby also came out with a perfect summation of the Scream's *raison d'etre*. 'We want our music to move people and tonight you saw it. We want people to come to the gig and fucking get out of their skins and have a good time, but in a good way. That wasnae a druggy audience tonight, that was just pure joy. And that's why we do the music. I want people to get off on our music.'

I got another taste of the uproarious chaos and twisted humour surrounding the band when I nipped up to the Glasgow Barrowlands show. Duffy insisted on wearing a plastic pineapple on his head all through the soundcheck, while gazing longingly at one of those cheap South Sea Island girl paintings. The soundcheck was the usual covers-athon with, among others, Sabbath's 'Paranoid', Bowie's 'Rebel Rebel' and a few Stooges tunes put through their paces.

After deranged country-techno terrorists Alabama 3 had opened up with their sleazy drug-sodden hybrid, the Scream bowled on to a heroes' welcome. The place was going mental with football-style chants and the kind of mayhem rarely encountered down south. It was their home town again, so it was doubly essential that the band play a corker.

This they did, as 'Out Of The Void' uncurled its eerie spell in classic calm-before-the-storm fashion, before a monstrously heavy 'Stuka' turned the heat up. When they launched into 'Burning Wheel' it was lift-off time. 'If They Move Kill 'Em' kept it going, and here I realised just what a formidable unit this Scream line-up had become. Massive power, huge noise, sheer raunch and a front man who was up there with the greats. They just kept climbing that night, and so did the crowd. 'Rocks' put the lid on it. After that it's a bit of a blur: the Keefarama of 'Medication', the soothing ballad 'Long Life', 'Come Together', 'Higher Than The Sun', a juggernaut rendition of 'Kowalski', and those encores – this time it was 'Motorhead', Iggy's 'I'm Loose' and 'Kick Out The Jams'. At the end there wasn't a dry high in the house.

This time *Melody Maker* sent the right guy, with Tony Naylor calling the gig 'a stunning victory', summing it up by saying, 'They've streaked from a whimper to a full-throttled roar.'

In May 1998 the band also stormed the huge Creamfields dance music festival, before repeating the exercise at Glastonbury in the summer. Creamfields was the largest dance festival of the year and boasted all the top DJs. But it took this band, who everyone had written off the previous year, to fire up the event, along with veteran rappers Run DMC. 'We were shit then,' deadpanned Bob later. But *Melody Maker* dubbed the Scream as the festival's highlights. Under a massive picture of Bobby in full flight and the headline 'SCREAMFIELDS!', Carl Loben enthused about 'their most white-hot set ever', testifying how, 'A year ago, Primal Scream could be complacent, half-assed and, at times, dangerously close to disintegration. Now they want it.'

This was also the year when Primal Scream went to Ibiza. The Earth itself tremored at that announcement. I'd done a track for Manumission, the famed club held at the biggest venue on the island and, indeed, in the world. The place was notorious for the wildness of its events, which attracted at least 8,000 people and always ended with a stage show. There were always party themes, and all these involved teams of strippers getting up to all sorts, with promoters Mike and Claire shagging on stage. I'd recorded them doing this very thing in a London studio and supplied music which they used as the soundtrack.

Mike and Claire asked me if I'd host the back room for four weeks starting in June 1998. I could have a special guest every week. Irvine came over and the Scream Team came over twice! Bobby had no desire to visit the White Isle, as clubs were no longer his idea of fun, but we did get Innes and Alison, Hartie and Louise, and Nightingale plus Jim the sax player. The lovely Mike and Claire spared no expense with the hospitality and gave me a palatial room at their newly-opened Manumission Motel, where all visiting DJs stayed. The place used to be a brothel and was still decked out that way, with waterbeds, huge baths and a bar called the Pink Pussy. Every night of the week there'd be a disco featuring performances by the Pink Pussies, the strippers who also took part in the Manumission show. The place was a madhouse, like the fall of ancient Rome every night, with room-hopping, lots of suitable refreshments and a disco bar which sometimes didn't close until eleven in the morning.

Of course, the Scream Team loved it and even they couldn't quite believe their eyes at the scale of the debauchery. They did a spot in the back room of the Manumission one Monday night. When I say back room, it's the size of a normal club with an amazing atmosphere. But somehow Innes and Hartie managed to find themselves DJing in the toilets. When I say toilets, they're the size of a small club. The group were taken by the friendly atmosphere, the total hedonism, the characters, and just the sheer fun of it all. I've never seen Innes smile so much and take to people so easily. How could you not? Mike and Claire were perfect hosts and the girls were always great. The toilet set had gone down so well that by the end of the season they were back, after telling everyone at home how much they liked it, this time with Mani and Duffy in tow. By then I was several weeks in, and having the time of my life, although I'd broken my ankle poledancing in the bar. The motel now had a roof garden village, which Duffy took a particular liking to. Duff in Ibiza was a frightening prospect, and he lived up to his reputation, regaling all and sundry with his surreal theories and philosophies.

Back home in late July there was the titanic coupling of Primal Scream and the briefly-reformed Jesus and Mary Chain at Glasgow Barrowlands. That was some night. Then in September the band contributed 'Know Your Rights' – the romp named after the Clash song which first appeared on the *Retribution* EP – to the *Rock The Dock* compilation, which supported the striking Liverpool dockers and came out on Creation.

Meanwhile, a new high-energy virus was gestating in Primal Scream's collective loins which would result in their most incendiary, confrontational record to date.

Would you buy a used Dalek from these men? Waiting for the Xtrmntr.

Ten

XTRMNTR

'I want to make a record that sounds like Britain feels to live in today. Concrete, steel, fuckin' spray paint, fucking violence, tower blocks, everything . . . claustrophobic, paranoid.' *— Bobby Gillespie*

While the Scream were promoting *Vanishing Point*, they had also been cooking up an amazing new racket. One of the first tracks to emerge was 'Insect Royalty', prompted by the group being asked to contribute a song to Irvine Welsh's new movie, *The Acid House*. Hugo Nicolson was back on board for the first time since *Screamadelica*, producing a malevolent growler which feels like maggots under the skin. Then there was the brilliant assault of Kevin Shields' 'If They Move Kill 'Em', and the shock attack of the track 'Accelerator'.

If ever there was a band who were wired, angry and intent on demolishing everything in sight, it was grindingly obvious on this apocalyptic slice of pure mayhem. Fuck levels, easing feedback or sandpapering the edges. This was aural napalm, which got a well-deserved hearing when it was released as a rare, one-sided, twelve-inch vinyl promo. It's the noisiest thing they've ever done, and no band have ever come so close to capturing the *Funhouse* attack without even trying. It's so hot it burns a hole in the deck, the stomach and the soul. I heard that even Iggy Pop was knocked against the wall when he first got a blast of this. Maybe he thought he'd found a new Stooges, the old devil. (Iggy is now in his fifties, but still just as mad, cutting down the young pretenders with one shake of that horse's tail stapled to his arse.)

To capture the raw power of the Stooges is one hell of a task. On 'Accelerator' Primal Scream not only managed it but, courtesy of a few more guitars and modern recording equipment, booted off into that 'next dimension through music' which Iggy had talked about when he stuck 'I Wanna Be Your Dog' alongside a ten-minute mantra called 'We Will Fall' on the first Stooges album. The Scream have loved Iggy Pop since the seventies. Now they know Iggy Pop loves them.

So, *Vanishing Point* done, the Scream had dived headfirst into the next record. It was the type of thing they'd been itching to do all along. Bobby said *Vanishing Point* was like the end of an era, girding creative loins and launching into the unknown. The *Exterminator* album – later mutated into *Xtrmntr* – was by far the densest, nastiest, angriest Scream record yet. Only one ballad, and the rest lurching between growling future-funk and blazing guitar inferno overkill, with a distinct jazz injection.

Take the title track – a lopingly nasty groove, which is trampled by a huge Mani funk bassline sounding like Godzilla with a bad case of the shits. Discordant noises and guitars hover above as Bobby cuts through with a truly evil vocal. He repeats the phrase, 'no civil obedience' ad infinitum, which co-producer Brendan manages to mutate until he's just saying, 'Fuck! Fuck! Fuck!' 'I love that track,' says Bobby. 'The chorus just sums up British culture. People are just happy to exist and take whatever shit they're given.'

The group's fascination with jazz broke out on this album. By jazz, I don't mean chin-stroking noodlerama. Bob had always been partial to John Coltrane – repeatedly namechecking him during live performances of 'Higher Than The Sun' circa 1994 – but now he was listening to Miles Davis, as well as appreciating such lesser-known parpologists as Albert Ayler and Pharoah Sanders. These men, in their time, were the Primal Screams of the notoriously insular jazz world. Black 1950s punks protesting through the emotions in their music. The outcry when Bob Dylan picked up a Fender Stratocaster in 1965 was nothing compared to the disgust when Miles Davis – who'd made his name in the fifties with birth-of-the-cool trumpet virtuosity – attached a gizmo box to his horn. He would be content to stand stock still with his back to the audience for ten minutes before uncurling just one long, chilling lunar-note. Meanwhile, his hand-directed backing band were funking, flying and chartering the unknown. It's all caught on the *Live Evil* album, beloved of Bobby. And it's no surprise that Miles was lined up to work with Hendrix, his guitarist counterpart, just before he died.

Meanwhile, Bobby's other favourite, John Coltrane, fought a different battle. Miles coined the cool and Coltrane played in his 1955 band – but took shit for it. The press called him 'raw and shocking' with his saxophonic assaults – 'a horrifying demonstration of what appears to be a growing anti-jazz trend.' The only guy operating in the same stratosphere round then was John Gilmore, of Sun Ra's Solar Arkestra, (who we've already visited on Planet *Screamadelica*). A longtime heroin addict, Coltrane got even wilder, released the classic album *Giant Steps* – on which Tom Dowd worked – and died in 1967.

By this time Miles had caught up and, beneath hippie clothes and impenetrable wraparounds, set about napalming the snobbery of jazz purists by going electric, experimental and street-funk aggressive on large amounts of cocaine. Apart from the fuck-you attitude, Miles and 'Trane's musical influences were riddling the Scream at this time. Alright, the Shields 'If They Move Kill 'Em' remix and the David Holmes-produced 'Blood Money' are the only two album tracks that really go for the jazz jugular, but inside the dissonance and attack the attitude is pure Coltrane – if he'd hooked up with the Stooges. In the late sixties, Iggy's gang hacked a similar groundbreaking freeform terror-squall on *Funhouse* and the MC5's guitar rock was way out there on *Kick Out The Jams* – even covering a Sun Ra song. There's a lineage here.

'We just want to keep going like this, pushing ourselves as far as we can in terms of experimenting,' said Bobby. 'We're not fucking scared of anything now. We're not in competition with anybody. We just want to make music. Nothing else has any relevance.'

The other looming spirit on the album is the MC5. It seems like the Scream haven't done a gig in the last five years without encoring with the Motor City Five's 'Kick Out The Jams'. Their influence is all over *Xtrmntr*. The insurrectionist sleevenotes on the *Kick Out The Jams* album, by group guru John Sinclair of the White Panthers, are uncanny if applied to the Scream (even if a tad late-sixties hippie-activist): 'The MC5 will drive you crazy out of your head into your body. The MC5 is rock and roll. Rock and roll is the music of our bodies, of our whole lives . . . We have to come together, people, "build to a gathering," or else. Or else you are dead, and gone . . . the music will make you strong, as it is strong, and there is no way it can be stopped now . . . Go wild! The world is yours! Take it now, and be one with it! Kick out the jams, motherfucker! And stay alive with the MC5!'

Bob also continued his fascination with Sly Stone, and Innes was still championing Asian Dub Foundation. Incidentally, that's Bobby, the Judge, Muzz and me bellowing 'Free Saptal Ram!' on the Scream's remix of ADF's protest record about their mate who'd been wrongfully banged up and treated like shit in prison. If there's anything that raises Bob's hackles, it's blatant injustice, police racism, and the fact that most prison warders are born arseholes. ADF were angry and that was rubbing off on the Scream. Bobby took part in a demonstration against Saptal's treatment with the rest of ADF and Irvine Welsh, chaining themselves to the House of Commons gates.

As the autumn of 1998 started closing in, the album was almost there, and was also becoming cloaked in darkness. However, I wasn't seeing so much of the Scream after September, as Creation had decided not to continue with Eruption. It had never really been given a fair crack anyway. I just walked in one morning and there was Paul Gallagher sitting smugly at my desk, having binned all my valuable archives. The Scream just nodded, sadly but knowingly.

Most of their new album was done with Brendan and Kevin, apart from the afore-mentioned David Holmes-produced 'Blood Money' and the only ballad, 'Keep Your Dreams'. If 'Blood Money' is a full-on jazz turmoil freakout, 'Keep Your Dreams' is one of the loveliest ballads the group have ever recorded. It recalls nothing so much as the Velvets' 'Sunday Morning', with its tin-kling, bell-chiming beauty entwined in Bobby's fragile vocal. Once again, Hugo was recruited to do the twiddling, making it the closest thing on the album to *Screamadelica*. 'It's a love song,' said Bob. 'Not towards one particular person. It's important to be a dreamer. I'm a dreamer.'

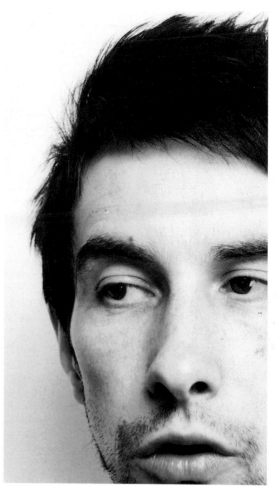

Bobby G.

As for the brain-ballooning 'Blood Money', he told *Jockey Slut*, 'We were working on this strange jazz instrumental thing that was quite filmic and soundtracky and we thought that David Holmes might be right to do some good work on it. And he was.'

David Holmes has always been a maverick in dance music. When he first started out in Belfast running the legendary Shine nights, Weatherall was his hero. It showed in epic creations like the Disco Evangelists' 'De Niro', and remixes of my own 'Sugar Daddy' plus the Sabres' immortal 'Smokebelch'. David, the Sabres' Jagz and Gary, and myself had a project in 1993 called Four Boy One Girl Action. The girl was Patti Smith. As David's career progressed, the cinematic element in his music grew through a series of solo albums like *This Film's Crap Let's Slash The Seats* and *Let's Get Killed*, where he walked around New York's South Bronx on acid taping the street sounds. It was logical for David to steer from DJing and remixing into movie soundtracks. He did the soundtrack for George Clooney's *Ocean's Eleven*, among others. Recently he has been pushing his new band Free Association, a loose, hallucinogenic funk ensemble which boasts Hugo on the knobs. Talking to *Jockey Slut* in November 1999, David spoke about how he finally hooked up with the Scream after he'd phoned up Jagz, who happened to be walking in the park with Bobby.

NME masthead text:

13 NOVEMBER 1999 £1.15 US4.75

CATATONIA
DEATH IN VEGAS
FOLK IMPLOSION
SHACK ★ KORN
WILL SMITH

SLAM PUNK!
PRiMAL
SCREAM
GET ANGRY ON YER ASS!
THE UK'S BiGGEST AND BEST GiG GUiDE

Duffy, Throb, Bobby and Mani on the cover of NME, November '99.

The pair started raving about similar musical avenues and found a lot of common ground. So Bobby asked David to do 'Blood Money', which he describes as '134bpm jazz-punk'. When he heard the demo of 'Keep Your Dreams', he asked to work on that too.

'It's fucking amazing working with them. There aren't many bands like Primal Scream around any more. There's too many bands playing it safe. The Scream wear their hearts on the sleeves. They've zero tolerance to being negative. It's pure punk. They don't give a fuck. They've got a vast knowledge of music. It's quite an education working with them.'

All the groups were big fans of Dr Octagon – aka Kool Keith from legendary hip hop outfit Ultra-Magnetic MCs – so they brought in his producer, Dan the Automator, for the funked-up psycho-rap of 'Pills'. Bob rants and raps his way through a major hang-over/comedown with lyrics like 'You ain't nothing / You've got nothing to say / Shine a light on you / You fade away,' culminating in just shouting, 'Fuck, fuck, fuck, fuck, fuck,' as the backing ebbs and flows in sinister Wu-Tang style. The Automator struck again, in even darker style than his 'Kowalski' remix.

'It's about a guy cracking up,' Bobby told Dorian Lynskey from *Select*. 'It's a hangover song. He's got a fractured head. He's schizophrenic. I walked in the studio feeling fucked up from the night before and just started singing, and that's what came out. It's a self-hate song, but it's quite a funny song really.'

He was more graphic in that *Slut* piece: '"Woke up, still drunk, throwing up, pissing blood, sick guts, sore skin, bunged up, pulled in, fade away . . ." It's a hangover record but . . . it's funny.'

'Shoot Speed/Kill Light' was produced by the Scream and Brendan, with mixing from Kevin Shields and Tim Holmes of Death in Vegas. It allows Mani to exercise the Joy Division fixation he shares with the band, as he unpeels a winding, Peter Hook-ish bass banana for this psychedel-ic-teutonic belter. When thinking about guitar sounds, one name came up – so they contacted none other than Joy Division guitarist and New Order frontman Bernard Sumner himself, who came down to add some atmospheric guitar shards. That summer Bobby would work with him again on the Chemical Brothers' 'Out Of Control'. 'To collaborate with friends who are doing good work and good music to come out of it is the greatest thing in the world,' Bobby said.

The first taste of extermination came with the single 'Swastika Eyes', released in November 1999. I first heard it in the studio one day after 'work'. It was the first time the Scream had used a 4/4 beat since 'Don't Fight It Feel It'. But this was no house re-tread or techno knees-up. It was a brutal, urgent pulse inspired by gay disco along the lines of Donna Summer, topped with acid house sirens and a claustrophobic barrage of noise. It made the perfect poison flower-bed from which Bob could let rip with the lyrics: 'Scabs, police and government thieves / Venal psychic amputees . . . You've got swastika eyes.'

Remixes from the Chemical Brothers, David Holmes and Jagz Kooner added to the impact of 'Swastika Eyes'. The video featured Sophie Dahl mowing down the band with a machine-gun. The band's idea to have the American stars 'n' stripes with swastikas instead of stars got pulled in case it offended the retailers.

A *Jockey Slut* piece was the first bit of press they'd done for a while, with the band smiling and gooning for the cover. But Innes was warning that the new album was 'a lot harder, fiercer, angrier.'

'It's an angry record,' agreed Bobby. 'We're angry ourselves and angry at what we see. Lyrically and musically it's about what it's like to live in a modern city. It's a hard, concrete fucking sound. We just want to make a record as hard and angry as the world.

'"Swastika Eyes" is about the new world order, American international terrorism. The Americanisation of the world. It's about control. It's a great image, a great insult. "You've got swastika eyes" – it applies to any authoritarian figure, a politician or a policeman – you see them everywhere.' When asked by the record company, the band refused to change the song's title.

Bobby's words during the interview now read as uncannily prescient. 'I don't think there's any bands – rock or dance – making any statements any more . . . we sell Indonesia all the arms. The fact that we can bomb Iraq every

Mani and Bobby on the cover of Jockey Slut, *November, '99.*

single day and nobody cares . . . Britain's part of the American empire, we're just an aircraft carrier for America. We're not even saying that we can make a difference, we're just saying what we feel. We can at least say that we're not part of that culture but we don't think any further than that. We're not an anarchist cell. This country's the shit hole of Europe. It's fucked. The drug dustbin . . . everybody's either smacked out or coked up . . . everybody's fucked. We live in such a negative culture that there's nothing better to do than to take drugs.' And that was before 9/11 – shortly prior which they'd write a song called 'Bomb the Pentagon' – and the 2003 Gulf War.

There was a similar attitude when Bobby appeared on the front cover of *Seven* – the now-defunct dance music publication. As he said of the album, 'It's violent, it's abrasive and dark but it's still hopeful. We wanted to make a record that reflects what it's like to live in Britain at the moment. Nobody's got anything to say in pop music any more. No-one wants to take risks . . . It's John Major making records instead of John Lydon. We want to jolt people's nervous systems, really change things.'

Reviews were overwhelmingly positive. *Mojo* talked about 'a rare kind of discordant anti-pop malevolence', but reckoned that 'much of it sounds like reworked outtakes from *Vanishing Point*.' (It doesn't, actually.) Dorian Lynskey's *Select* piece said, 'Against all the odds they sound all but unbeatable . . . It's a record about hope and despair, death and survival, and it's the first great record of the 21st century. Major bands aren't expected to make records this wildly creative, certainly not after fifteen years. But Primal Scream still sound desperately violently alive because they know what the alternative is.'

Probably the best critique came from Caspar Llewellyn Smith in the *Daily Telegraph*, who wrote, 'For all its stylistic diversity, there's a compelling and paranoid energy to the record, reminiscent of wracked classics such as Sly and the Family Stone's *There's A Riot Goin' On* or PiL's *Metal Box* . . . so this is the dark and incendiary sound of a group trying to start a revolution by themselves. Of course that's kind of risible, but it's always been what the best rock 'n' roll's been about. And on this evidence Primal Scream are the last rebels in town and the best rock 'n' roll

Bobby on the cover of Seven, *November '99.*

band in the world. They shame their young pretenders.'

NME gave the Scream the cover again, running a double spread where writer James Oldham opened by reporting Bobby flaring up at the photo-shoot location, and the fact that he was in the shit for daubing 'MC5' on a door. Bobby's anger had been sparked by Oldham bringing up the title of 'Swastika Eyes' and, as usual, the 'Stuka' track and artwork from the previous album. He seemed to miss the point that the song was actually anti-fascist, as are the band. They're just not afraid to use a normally taboo image, as on the *Give Out But Don't Give Up* album cover with its Southern flag.

The gist of this piece seemed to be that, in their musical experimentalism and psychosis, in their concern with the decay of the British social and political systems, they'd lost the mass appeal galvanised by *Screamadelica*. But *Screamadelica* was of its time – a loved-up acid-house revolution that was opening people's minds – as were 'Swastika Eyes' and the ensuing *Xtrmntr*, reflecting a country awash with discontent, dark drugs, escalating crime and a government fucking-over the public. There were still places to get loved-up, but it wasn't too fluffy next morning with a police boot in your head. The early nineties optimism had not risen like a cake with smiley face icing. On *Vanishing Point*, Bobby had started writing about personal rather than third-person issues. He always said that the records Primal Scream made reflected the state of the band at the time. So, going by *Xtrmntr*, the group must have been eaten up by a ferocious, twisted-nerve rage. *NME* was trying to say that, even if Bobby's lyrics had a message, the music was too extreme to get over to the masses. That idea was shot down in flames as a gigantic field of people went bananas when 'Swastika Eyes' opened their set at the Reading Festival in August 2000. And it still managed to enter the charts at number 23.

Bob got well heated on this one, basically reiterating the *Jockey Slut* rant, but ending with an ultimate payoff: 'We're a rock 'n' roll band and we sing about what we see and feel, so we wrote this song. It's saying, "I can see what's happening. I'm not going to be fooled by it. I'm anti-fascist. It's like fascism never went away," that's what I'm saying. Look, it's rock 'n' roll music. It's protest music. I think "Swastika Eyes" is a rebel song.'

The next single was the merciless 'Pills' in December 1999, while the album was finally unleashed in March 2000. It came straight in at number one, a new Scream album for the new millennium! It was accompanied by the uncompromising single 'Kill All Hippies', which saw Mani's bass bulging with evil funk, Bob intoning in a sinister falsetto and washes of Lynchian noise. On the intro they used a sample from Dennis Hopper's movie *Out of the Blue*. The single came with a dirty, sinister Massive Attack mix of 'Accelerator'. Those Two Lone Swordsmen were at it again on the promo, with Jagz on the B-side having a poke at 'Exterminator'. The single was dedicated to Curtis Mayfield, who had sadly died recently. The former singer with the Impressions was a major inspiration for the band, especially Bobby. His version of 'People Get

Ready' is utterly beautiful. The title *Exterminator* might sound deadly serious, but you still have to take into account the Scream's sense of humour – as when Innes phoned me up and told me the title, immediately launching into a Dalek impersonation.

Other times, I'd ask him what he was up to. 'Oh, just making a record,' came the easy-going reply. He must have known he was actually creating a monster. Incidentally, around about that time, I got back from the pub one night, turned on the answering machine and just heard the sound of a toilet flushing with someone shrieking, 'Help!' in the background. Could only be one person. And, on another occasion, Innes was surely on one when he rolled up to my local pub in his new Lotus, just to check out the Aylesbury Limbo Dancing Contest which was being held in the car park. The Lotus was a great source of fun for Innes, and we went for several high-speed spins in it. The band had somehow also acquired the Dodge Challenger driven by Kate Moss in the 'Kowalski' video. It was subsequently commandeered by Wayne, the Creation doorman/bouncer, a lovely West Country nutter who took Bobby, Innes and myself down Camden High Street and up Primrose Hill at a severe rate of knots. The young indie-kids cruising Camden couldn't help but get a little freaked by the sight of Bobby Gillespie blowing kisses out of the back of the 'Kowalski' car.

In the *NME* interview to tie in with the album's release, Bobby was firing on all cylinders. He can be the most charming, lovely person off-duty, but when confronted with an alien microphone he'll fire verbal bullets: 'We wanted the money. We wanted to travel and we wanted the excess. We wanted to escape. We didn't want to sell 5,000 records, we wanted to sell 500 million, okay?

'I saw The Clash when I was fifteen. The feeling I got from that and the Pistols still drives me, and it still drives Andrew, Mani and Throb. We were lucky enough to be around then. We saw those people and we picked up something from them.

'We're a rock 'n' roll group. We've got the soul, the feeling, the attitude, the electricity. We're fucking with styles and taking them somewhere new and different.'

Having already guested on the Chemical Brothers' 'Out Of Control', Bobby also sang 'Soul Auctioneer' for Death in Vegas on their *The Contino Sessions* album. That November, a newly-shorn Bob hopped out onstage at Shepherds Bush Empire with the band to give it some front.

There was definitely some wired-up attitude in the Scream camp, as if making up for the somnambulence of the *Give Out But Don't Give Up* period. Bob was on one, and partly explained the *Xtrmntr* spirit in the *Select* piece: 'Amphetamine has always been my favourite drug. I can function better on amphetamines. I can use that in the studio. What you hear on that record's pure fuckin' energy.'

The piece also carried a good Mani story. The large bass man had been in a Burger King at Preston railway station and spotted John Prescott. He strolled up in his normal cheerful manner and got the usual polite handshake and fixed grin. 'All right John?' said Mani. 'I'm Mani who used to be in the Stone Roses and I'm now in the Scream. Tell Tony Blair that if I see him in the street I'm gonna fuckin' leather him.'

He let loose his Scream *raison d'etre* near the end of the feature: 'I love making music with these guys. Without that I'd have nothing. Society's the way it is, so my sword and shield against the world has been Primal Scream and creating the music and giving people a good time and inspiring them in the way we've been inspired by bands like The Clash or Sex Pistols or MC5 or James Brown or Fela Kuti or Miles Davis. Their music makes my life worth living.'

Gig-wise, 1998 had seen the band play Australia's Big Day Out tour in January, with the Chemicals, Goldie, the Foo Fighters and the Red Hot Chili Peppers who, apparently, were horrified by the Scream's behaviour. Grant Fleming was covering the tour for *Loaded* in his inimitable style, i.e. getting more caked than the group, describing how Hartie sported an Elvis wig and how, in Melbourne, they dedicated 'Rocks' to Joe Strummer. The set list was sheer sonic bestiality, rather different from the previous tour: 'Swastika Eyes', 'Shoot Speed/Kill Light', 'Exterminator', 'Burning Wheel', 'If They Move Kill 'Em', 'Pills', 'Kill All Hippies', 'Blood Money', 'Rocks',

'Kowalski', 'Movin' On Up', 'Accelerator', and sometimes 'Higher Than The Sun'. Sounds like amphetamine nirvana. We'd see it all for ourselves pretty soon.

In August 1999 the Scream were doing the Reading Festival again, coming on before Oasis. For a little warm-up they did a last-minute gig at the Town and Country club in Kentish Town, north London. On arriving at the soundcheck I immediately sensed that something was up. From talking to Muzz, Trigger and Duff it became apparent that Nightingale had been dismissed as manager. Bobby and Innes had effectively brought in Alan McGee as a kind of caretaker. Fathoming out the real reason for it all proved impossible. I always thought of Alex as one of the band. If he'd been as wild as them in the past, he was really on the ball these days. Apart from Bobby and Innes, everyone was in a state of shock, with Mani and Duff particularly puzzled by the decision. 'He was the only bloke who could look after us,' said Duff in the pub before the gig. Eventually they started hanging out with Nightingale again – when he was around, as he ended up moving to Paris. I still miss him, and I'm not the only one.

Whatever the backstage traumas, the gig was a blinder. They were now playing a lot of what would form *Xtrmntr*, kicking off with 'Swastika Eyes' and blasting through new stuff like 'Accelerator', 'Insect Royalty', a shrieking 'Blood Money', 'Shoot Speed/Kill Light' and the Shields version of 'If They Move Kill 'Em'. Kevin himself was up there, playing on several songs. They even debuted a new song called 'Bomb the Pentagon', a rampant attack on multi-national corporations and American foreign policy, which would cause much controversy later on. There were still a few oldies, like 'Rocks' and 'Out Of The Void', with savage encores of 'Kick Out The Jams' and 'No Fun'. Bobby was now sporting a punk spiketop, while the spirit of the band was miles away from the 1997 gigs. It was now a barrage of unstoppable high-energy noise, not dissimilar to the MC5's live album.

Later that night we went back to Duffy's Chiswick abode for a bit of a knees-up. There was a hat contest between Duff, Mani and me, Wurzels records on the deck and fearsome consumption of refreshments. They were well psyched up for next day's Reading appearance.

It was a great day out. Nursing hangovers, Mani, Duff and I sauntered across the green to meet the coach outside a pub. As we turned the corner we saw that the whole squad was out in force. Throb, Trig, Fatty, Jim and Dunc, Darren and, eventually, a beshaded Bobby, who'd obviously been up all night. It was the dreaded 'business as usual' on the bus, and they were all obviously gagging to get on that stage, levels set on stun. Backstage was cordial fun, as Liam Gallagher breezed in and made for the fridge. Later, over in his own caravan, Liam sat hunched over an acoustic guitar while deep in conversation with Mani. He was enthusing about the new songs he was writing.

'How ya doing?' I enquired. 'Rockin',' he grinned, as he strolled off with his arm around new girlfriend Nicole Appleton. Then Liam Howlett from the Prodigy turned up with his new girlfriend – Nicole's sister Natalie. We all bowled *en masse* to the side of the stage when it was Scream-time and watched as Bobby greeted an endless sea of people, baying like wolves. Into 'Swastika Eyes' and it was instant lift off. It was a similar deadly attack to the previous night, and it basically slaughtered the place, a merciless, take-no-prisoners onslaught. Nobody else but Oasis could have followed that. Next day was the same again in Leeds, but the field wasn't so easy for the crew so the sound wasn't as hot. By that time I was done in and slinked off home. It was great to see the Scream back, exceeding the peak of their powers.

There was another Scream injury in mid-2000 – Duffy fell off a wall and broke his leg quite badly. Irvine and I turned up one day at Charing Cross Hospital, proferring grapes and Lucozade. It transpired that the wall had only been about a foot high!

Things remained eventful on the domestic front. In autumn of that same year, Throb became a dad. Love was definitely in the air, as I fell for a beautiful young girl called Michelle – the fact that she had all the Primal Scream albums was a decisive factor. Then there was Duffy and Della's

Bobby G, '99.

Liam Gallagher, Mani and mystery ligger backstage at Reading '99.

wedding bash – in a converted public toilet on Shepherd's Bush Green! The longstanding couple had been married in Hawaii so everyone was sporting flower garlands. I was DJing so I lent a definite Hawaiian flavour to the sounds too. The rest of the evening is somewhat hazy. I know Nightingale and Irvine Welsh turned up and we all ended up back at Duff's. Irv and Mani bellowed out football songs from the kitchen and I fell asleep under the grand piano.

Amidst all the merry-making, the next single from the album was released, the raging 'Accelerator', which came out in September 2000 and entered the charts at number 23. The flip was notable for two non-album songs – the long-awaited 'Five Years Ahead Of My Time', from the 1997 Jaki Liebezeit session, plus another called 'When The Kingdom Comes'.

But it came as little surprise when I heard, towards the end of 1999, that Alan McGee and Dick Green had decided to call it a day with Creation. Alan had been feeling dissatisfied with the label for a while. The last Oasis album had bombed compared to previous releases, and too many over-financed turkeys had dragged the roster down. He simply felt that the operation had got too big and wanted to get back to the roots of where Creation started. So he disbanded the label, sacked most of the staff, moved out of the offices on Primrose Hill and started the low-key Poptones operation. Alan and Dick had proved their point with a lot of classic records and, finally, the grand finger to the music industry that was Oasis. And, never let it be forgotten, they gave the world Primal Scream. *Xtrmntr* would be the last ever Creation album. Fitting, indeed.

Alan McGee issued an official statement on 25 November, which said, 'Creation Records has been our life for seventeen years. We started the company from nothing but it's the end of an era. It's the end of a decade, a new millennium and life begins at 40. I feel like trying my hand at some new things. I still intend to be involved with music but there are other areas that I am keen to investigate. It will be a sad day for both of us when we leave but the future is bright and I am genuinely excited about starting afresh.'

It was the lead story in the *NME* of 4 December. The headline read, 'SOME MIGHT NOT STAY – Shock reverberates round industry as Creation founders quit.' The story said Alan and Dick Green would be quitting the label in June the following year. The paper quoted one employee as saying, 'The first thing I knew was bumping into McGee this morning. He just said, "It's over, we're fucked." None of us can believe it.'

'I haven't been happy for two fucking years,' Alan told *Select*. 'Some of the bands and staff are pissed off at me for leaving . . . but I have to be happy for myself. The company just got too big. My ideal record company is six to ten people – get past that and it's not your people any more.' He also said that one of the decisive factors in disbanding Creation was when the label dropped my signings, the Wamdue Project, who subsequently shot to number one on another label with the same track I'd released a few months earlier!

Obviously, Alan's decision generally came as a shock and, indeed, a horror – to the music industry, the staff and a roster of artists suddenly without a label. Oasis and Primal Scream were okay though, with the latter now going through Columbia. It was a shame to see Creation go, but I respect Alan and Dick for riding off into the sunset instead of staying to climb up the tribal totem pole.

As 2000 melted into 2001, the Scream were already onto the next album. In February *Xtrmntr* won Best Album in the annual *NME* Carling Awards, beating Radiohead, Coldplay, Eminem and Badly Drawn Boy. Quite right too. Mani got up to receive the award and commented, 'This is reward for what we consider to be a great piece of music. The Mercury music people didn't fucking consider it to be a great piece of music, but what the fuck do they know? The people on the fucking street have fucking voted for this and that makes it even more fucking beautiful. This [holds up award] is going to keep the front door of my house open.

'We're our own worst fucking critics and we felt it was great. If we feel it's great we know people are going to feel it's great. And a lot of people seem reticent to recognise what this fucking band is. Well, here you go! And you'll fucking see us next time, ta-ra.' Added Duff, 'It's people's ears that voted for this, not a consortium of businessmen.'

John Harris's *Select* review had been accompanied by some good Bob 'n' Mani quotes about the new spirit which had coursed through the last two Scream albums.

Bobby: 'When we were making *Vanishing Point* we decided that it had to be spontaneous. Before that it was so laborious and painful – we sat jamming as a whole band trying to write songs. We don't do that any more. It's almost like instant compositions in the studio.'

Mani: 'I like working the way these guys like to work now – bang, bang, bang – really fuckin' immediate . . . We're just conscious of thrilling each other first. You've got to give yourself a hard-on before you can give the nation a hard-on. These guys do it. Better than Viagra.'

Harris asked if the band were proud that their music stood out as angrier and noisier than everyone else's.

Bobby and Mani in Dallas, Texas, June 2000.

Bobby: 'Yeah. Nobody's making rock 'n' roll records like "Accelerator" any more. I don't think they can. I don't think they've got the spirit. I think we've got the spirit of Detroit rock 'n' roll – the MC5 and the Stooges are in our souls. Our band are the last people that can actually play it. Us and Motorhead. Even beyond rock 'n' roll we do things that no-one else would dare. When we took "Swastika Eyes" to the Chemical Brothers we asked them to make a gay disco record. We all like Sylvester [the late transvestite disco icon] and Donna Summer, so that's what we wanted – a revolutionary gay disco record . . .'

Speaking now about the great influence that was dance music and club culture, Bobby said, 'I don't think I'm invigorated by any culture. I think I'm pretty disgusted by most of what passes for culture. I guess that's what we're writing about. I've not been going out to many clubs. I just talk about the culture that I see. It's a dance record, but our kind of dance record. It's not a conventional dance record – it's like a funk record. It's our kind of funk record – abstract, hard, fucking whatever . . .'

Gigs followed, but the group were mainly concentrating on working up the new album which they'd started the previous year. The Scream were on a roll and simply couldn't stop themselves now. It was a far cry from the extended mid-album slumps up to *Vanishing Point*.

In August, they played London's Astoria as a warm-up for Japan, and turned in a real firestorm of a set. Hartie's former girlfriend Louise was DJing and set the tone with a selection of coruscating punk rock. The band opened with one of the new songs, a rib-rattling blast of guitar-crash savagery called 'Detroit', and followed through with 'Bomb The Pentagon'. Kevin Shields was now onstage for the whole set, augmenting the fret-wrenched firepower, now deafeningly lethal, of Throb, Innes and Mani. The horn section got to let fly on 'Blood Money'. 'Rocks' was the oldest song they played. Not a sausage from *Screamadelica*. But with this amphetamined onslaught raging away, it would have sounded out of place. Other highlights were 'Swastika Eyes' (a personal favourite of mine), 'Accelerator' and a behemoth 'Kowalski'. And they finished off the place with 'Kick Out The Jams'.

That night, nobody could touch Primal Scream. Helen Mead agreed in her review for *Seven*: 'The

band looked, felt and sounded like they'd put time and effort into moulding the next giant leap into their evolution . . . The end was fantastic . . . the agitation, the rolling, active mass energy of the audience, everyone really pumped up and ready for action . . . It was really fulfilling, to let some real energy, some real fire, grab your belly. . .'

The last word on that remarkable album, and the Scream's new runaway adrenaline rush, belongs to Duffy in *Select*: 'You can call it what you want. Ultra cigarettes. Ultra everything. Ultra fucking psychedelic Primal Scream. All the way. Psychedelic storm troopers coming back through history.'

Xtrmntr: 'It's purifying, it's angry.'

19-TRACK GUIDE TO THE MONTH'S BEST MUSIC

Free CD!

THE CHARLATANS
Us against the world

UNCUT

NOVEMBER 1999 £2.95

MUSIC, MOVIES & BOOKS

PRIMAL SCREAM

Bobby Gillespie on 15 years of rock'n'roll madness EXCLUSIVE INTERVIEW!

BLAIR WITCH PROJECT
What frightens the people who made it?

BLUR
Damon Albarn looks back

BRYAN FERRY
As time goes by

STEREOLAB
Whatever happened to the future?

Plus NECTARINE No.9 **GORKY'S ZYGOTIC MYNCI** ATOM EGOYAN
COUNTING CROWS PHIL DAVIS **SHELBY LYNNE** JOE STRUMMER

9 771368 072039

11>

Bobby on the cover of Uncut, *November '99.*

167

Throb, Duffy, Bobby and Mani relaxing in 2002.

Evil Heat

'Every record we make I think this is the last one we'll do but a couple of years later I'm dying to do another one. I guess it's when you have nothing to say and the lifestyle can become too much. You can live the life but rock 'n' roll's worth living for. It's not worth dying for. Is that my maxim? It is these days.' – *Bobby Gillespie*

ust as *Xtrmntr* had been kick-started during the promotion for *Vanishing Point*, the next Primal Scream album began gestating in between the *Xtrmntr* gigs. They'd already previewed two new tracks at the Astoria in August 2001 – 'Detroit' and 'Bomb The Pentagon'. Then came the 9/11 atrocities and all hell broke loose. Columbia Records, the media and those who love to be outraged reared up on their back legs.

Bob later put the title into context as, 'just one line in a song. The song wasn't about bombing the Pentagon, it was anti-militaristic and it was about a variety of different subjects: alienation of work, drug culture, control. But when September 11 happened everyone went fucking crazy, trying to get us to explain ourselves. I don't have to explain myself to anybody. I'm a rock 'n' roll songwriter. When we recorded the song I didn't use the line, but then I change things all the time. I thought it wasn't that good a line . . . I just didn't feel like standing up and singing "bomb the Pentagon." It's dumb and boring and it would seem that I was really trying to push some violent point. I hate violence.'

He underlined this in the August 2002 edition of *Mojo*. 'It was never recorded, we only played the song four times. I took the line "bomb the Pentagon" out of the song. It was too sensational, too much shock value, it just didn't make for good rock 'n' roll. I wanted something more ominous. It was a great song – a lot of different themes: the pornography of militarism, the alienation of work, drug culture as control . . . and if I'd kept that line in the song would have been tied to a specific time and place. We got a lot of attention for that, but it's not the kind of attention we wanted. We hate militarism and we were starting to be seen as some pro-militaristic thing. There were all these stories in the music press saying we'd recorded it, it was going to be a single, it was on our album, the American record company had dropped us . . . All fabrication. We haven't had an American record company for two years!'

Mani spoke to *NME* shortly after the attack and said the band were 'mortified' by it, even if Bobby had told *Jack* magazine it looked 'spectacular'. Of course, what he meant was that it was an image that was so astonishing that you can never forget it. Mani said, 'I feel pretty numbed by it. It's a very strange scenario to find myself in. We're in a position where we could get fucking lynched, man, so I don't know.

Bobby Gillespie, Shepherds Bush Empire, June '02.

'We're obviously fucking mortified at some of the scenes of those poor people who have fuck all to do with somebody's else's politics. On the other hand, America has been the bully boy of the planet and it just proves that they're not infallible . . . it's very strange how they've been so lax to have been got at themselves. It's a great tragedy.'

The song was simply adapted by omitting that line and being retitled 'Rise'. It still makes its point, as Bobby chants the biting lyrics.

The as-yet-untitled album was recorded at the Scream's own Bunker and over at Jagz Kooner's place. Former Sabres of Paradise member Jagz had worked with the band before, remixing *Xtrmntr* singles 'Swastika Eyes' and 'Exterminator'. Innes was doing the basic recording along with Brendan and Jagz, while different producers worked on assorted tracks. Kevin Shields handled six, and Jagz produced 'Miss Lucifer', which ended up as the album's first single, while four songs were dealt with by Andrew Weatherall and Keith Tenniswood, aka the Two Lone Swordsmen. They spent a lot of time hopping between theirs and Jagz's studios.

Obviously, the Two Lone Swordsmen connection pricked up a few ears. 'Scream Back With Weatherall!' screamed one headline, with a hopeful fantasy footnote that claimed *Screamadelica Mark Two* was on the horizon. In fact, Weatherall had never been that far away. They never fell out, even when he didn't feel it was right to work on *Give Out But Don't Give Up*, and he'd still remixed 'Jailbird'. Later on he'd produced 'Trainspotting' from *Vanishing Point*, plus that epic Two Lone Swordsmen mix of 'Stuka'. For *Xtrmntr*, the Swordsmen had waded into 'Kill All Hippies'. The only difference now was that the band were cooking up new tunes while the Swordsmen stirred the pot. Electronic experimentation was firmly back on the agenda.

But it had taken Andrew a while to shake off the shadow of *Screamadelica*. In 1998 he'd replied to some readers' letters in *Jockey Slut* about that album. This was in the early days of TLS, when

Andrew and Keith were still developing their twisted, minimal, warped new sound, which has since blossomed into an electro-fuelled celebration.

Andrew explained, 'I've got all that baggage from years ago. Primal Scream and stuff like that. I still get people coming up to me in clubs and saying, "that record changed my life." That's a lot of baggage to carry around, a lot of expectations to live up to. Admittedly, it does mean I can rest on my laurels at times but it does my head in . . . that album was a total one-off that won't happen again for years. A random thing that fused. You can't recreate that.'

They didn't try. The Swordsmen tracks on the album simply ripple with innovation and the essence of the Scream when they're fired up and on a mission. That is the spirit of *Screamadelica*. It was another voyage of discovery, even if there was nothing like 'Come Together'. The four Swordsmen tracks are the furthest away from rock 'n' roll: 'Autobahn 66' and 'A Scanner Darkly' are underpinned with electro, lush and melodic, the latter track an instrumental. Both 'Some Velvet Morning' and 'Space Blues 2', with its Duffy vocal, hark to the past but beautifully push back the electronic boundaries. When Andrew Weatherall and the Scream are thrown together, the sparks still fly.

The record is also notable for Robert Plant playing harmonica on the dark and bluesy 'The Lord Is My Shotgun'. They may seem an unlikely team, but the Scream have always admired 'the Zep', as they affectionately call them. And not just for their infamous excesses in the seventies. That band packed a mean, sex-grinding wallop. John Bonham and Jimmy Page were like a rhythmic juggernaut. Robert Plant was the ultimate wailing rock god, but he also knew his music – from psychedelia to Moroccan folk.

When I was working at Creation we'd occasionally see Mr Plant at those after-work sessions in the Queens, always sitting at the bar rather than a table. There'd be a bit of nudging at the Scream table along the lines of 'that's Percy Plant, innit?' One night Bobby ambled up and struck up a conversation, which Plant recalled when the pair did a 'How We Met' interview for the *Independent on Sunday*. 'I was at a bar, feeling slightly self-conscious in my cowboy boots, and I

Jagz Kooner, another formidable aural cohort.

think Bobby came sidling up and said something like, "You're Robert, aren't you?" It was instantly clear to me that he'd got what I've retained; a ranting enthusiasm for music. He engulfed me with this warmth for Arthur Lee: "Hey man, you're into Love, Moby Grape, right? We met Arthur Lee and he played harmonica with us in the Chateau Marmont in LA." The idea of that being a moment he'll never forget is absolutely on it for me. There are so many experiences that I've had; if I get the opportunity to transpose them and send them down the line to someone with a like sensibility, that's magic . . . We just talk about the music we love. I can hear it coming through in his songs, but I was really gratified I guess, by the depths of his passion.'

Percy was also totally unfazed by the various states he's seen the band in during those nights in the pub. What did he make of Duffy? Shit, the guy's seen a lot more than a bunch of pissed rowdies shouting the words to cheese-rave biggie 'Cotton-Eyed Joe', Duffy's then obsession.

'You can hear Led Zeppelin and know we went and pillaged Howlin' Wolf's pocket. I heard *Vanishing Point* and I heard all the things I loved given a contemporary spin, plus I knew the guys were out there. I've met Bobby and the guys when they've been wired, and talking pretty quickly. I didn't hear a lot of punctuation. I thought, "Ah, I know where I am." But it's Primal Scream's points of reference that make their music really work . . . they have that essential quality of unsavouriness that marks out the true believers. Bobby's become a chum. He didn't need me and I didn't need him, but I'm glad we ran into each other. Though I think he could do with a good sandwich down him now and again.'

Then it was Bobby's turn:

'It was '94 or '95, a late summer evening in Camden. We'd had quite a bad year with the band; we were really down. We were smacked out and fucked up and not even sure we could continue. Walking back to our studio we heard this voice go, "Alright lads?" from across the road. We looked over, and it was Robert Plant. He was like, "How's it going?", just waving at us. Then he was gone. We stood there going, "Fucking Robert Plant! Fucking Led Zeppelin!" It was nice, it was friendly, and it was a real kick to get that kind of recognition when we most needed it.'

Bobby went to see Page and Plant play Shepherds Bush Empire, and took along a CD of Kevin Shields' blazing remix of 'If They Move Kill 'Em' to give them. It's the epic track that manages to work in a Moroccan percussion groove, incorporates a fatter-than-fat hip hop beat, plus dissonant free-jazz assaults and a mean rock guitar swagger. Bobby was rightfully proud when he handed it over to Plant after the show. A little while later, Robert called to say how much he liked it and asked if the Scream would like to support them in Europe. It fell through, but a bond had been established. Back to Bobby in the *Independent on Sunday*:

'I wouldn't go as far as calling him a friend but we've got so many shared musical reference points, it's sort of like a brotherhood. He's as far from being a dinosaur as you can imagine, which, when you think what he's been through, is remarkable. There's a kind of purity to what we both do, and an innocence as well, believe it or not; that wide-eyed belief in what you're doing, and giving your whole self to that music without irony. It's righteous, and it's kind of rare to find that these days.

'I was into glam rock as a kid, and it was punk that made me want to be a musician. But I remember going to discos and hearing this heavy stuff, not knowing who it was, and thinking, "I love this." I still love Led Zeppelin. They're sexy, flash, filthy rock 'n' roll. That's the kind of rock 'n' roll I love, and you can't fake it. He's playing harmonica on a track from our new album and we had a good laugh that day. He put his heart and soul into it. But there's no sense of him passing the rock baton to us. Though we are a pretty fucking good band.' It wasn't too far for Percy to stroll down to the Scream bunker with harmonica in pocket, and a good time was had by all.

The last song recorded for the album was a cover of 'Some Velvet Morning', a late sixties murder ballad by Lee Hazelwood and Nancy Sinatra. It sees Bobby trading lines with Kate Moss, an old friend of the band. The original was a dark, sinister country-style ballad with the immortal line, 'some velvet morning when you're dead.' Below Nancy and Lee's original lyric lurked a song of love and hate, covered in 1982 by Lydia Lunch and Rowland S. Howard as a piece of slow motion self-destruction – the latter still playing guitar alongside Nick Cave in the Birthday Party at the time, which gives an idea of where the song is coming from. Bobby was thinking more along the lines of Jane Birkin and Serge Gainsbourg: no heavy breathing, more sexual manners.

The band have known Kate for a while. She was in the 'Kowalski' video, and, years before that, went to gigs, hung out at parties, and we'd sometimes bump into her in the Queens on Primrose Hill.

'Kate's a good friend of mine,' said Bobby. 'We got drunk on the train to Paris in 2001 singing Velvet Underground songs. I asked her to do a duet. Her voice is really good, like a young Nico – really European and girlish but dead sexy. We wanted to make a sexy pop record and it was great fun.'

Handling the production were those Two Lone Swordsmen. It was actually touch and go whether the song would make it onto the album. The other tracks were all ready to go into production, and the advance promo CDs wouldn't even carry 'Some Velvet Morning'. But they got there in the end, and *Evil Heat*, as the new album was called, was now complete – even though the band still didn't have the title when the album's first single was announced.

Evil Heat started filtering through the air conditioning via its first single, 'Miss Lucifer', released on 22 July. First the single came as a CD promo, and it was obvious that the Primals had taken yet another path. This was one of the Jagz Kooner collaborations. Jagz describes the record as 'sonic terrorism at its finest'. He added that he'd got bored with four-on-the-floor beats, so on 'Miss Lucifer' he's messing about with an acrobatic sixteen-on-the-floor and turning 120bpm into 480. That explains the wild and wired beat anyway.

Electroclash was another ingredient thrown into the Primal stew. It had been simmering for years, but was a buzzword at the time, spearheaded by Chicago's Felix Da Housecat and a whole gang of Europeans with DJ Hell's International DJ Gigolos operation leading the way. The Gigolo label gave a home to Miss Kittin, a friend of Bobby's who'd applied her ice-queen sexiness to releases from both Felix and the Gigolo stable. Electro had been about since the early eighties, with studio trailblazers like Detroit's Juan Atkins and New York's Jay Burnett harnessing their Kraftwerk influences to hip hop and creating space-funk for the dancefloor. The term 'electroclash' soon became as derided as 'big beat', but the Scream simply sucked it into their creative mix and turned it into rock 'n' roll. Electronic punk, if you like.

It also showed the influence of Suicide, the New York duo of Alan Vega and Martin Rev, who launched their psychotic brand of electronic urban-terror carnage lashed with the spirit of Elvis in the early seventies. While Rev whipped up primitive jackhammer drum-machine beats and abused a massive synth he simply called 'Instrument', Vega howled his lyrics of love, death and decay. They were something genuinely new and frightening. When they supported The Clash on a 1977 UK tour they regularly got bottled off by the more conservative members of the audience. They're still at it too – 2002's *American Supreme* album was like a US counterpart to the Scream's, with its vicious grooves and tracks like 'Death Machine' throwing up walls of noise. Bobby has often cited Suicide as up there with the Velvets and the Mary Chain as one of the most important groups ever.

'Miss Lucifer' came in at just over two minutes as a single track on the initial promo CD, a short, sharp poke in the face steaming like a jackhammer on heat. Mr G demands, 'shake it baby,' while all kinds of sonic hell breaks loose around him, and the 'all night long' refrain is pure Alan Vega. The band weren't even in the video produced by Wiz, who'd made Flowered Up's 'Weekender' epic – just a load of she-devils having a party in a multi-storey car-park, causing havoc and disappearing in pools of oil.

Bobby was calling the new Scream music 'electronic garage band future rock 'n' roll', and he wasn't far wrong. Of 'Miss Lucifer' he said, 'it's a sexual song. Electronic rock 'n' roll. Yeah, it's quite short, but rock 'n' roll should be short, like Little Richard and Jerry Lee, you know?'

A vinyl promo came in with the near seven-minute 'Scream Team Hip To Hip' dub onslaught

– even more Suicide afoot as the drum machine overheated – with Jagz and Germany's Alec Empire supplying two granite-carved, more speedy hip hop versions – 'Bone To Bone' and 'Panther Girl' – on the flip. Alec fronts the hard-as-nails hardcore electronic punk outfit Atari Teenage Riot, and has been at the forefront of the German techno scene since the early nineties. The Scream were on one here.

In June 2002 the band were doing two nights at the Shepherds Bush Empire as part of a UK jaunt. It's their second home after Brixton, and both nights went off like a bomb: Bobby in white jacket, dancing more than I'd seen him do for years, Kevin Shields adding to the guitar power on the left, while Mani stalked his territory. Meanwhile, Innes, Throb and Duffy did what they do best – but better. Maybe it was Darrin Mooney's pummelling bedrock spurred them on to even greater heights.

They kicked off with 'Miss Lucifer', tore into 'Rise' and 'City' with MC5-style savagery, before revisiting the previous album with 'Shoot Speed/Kill Light' and 'Pills'. It was deafening and deadly, with Bob either dancing about or leaning onto the mike like Jim Morrison meets Johnny Rotten. An opiated 'Burning Wheel', then the cascading motorik of 'Autobahn 66' became an even mightier beast live. The slow section reached back to 'Out Of The Void', while they debuted 'The Lord Is My Shotgun', that Robert Plant hook-up from the new album. Back to the rock 'n' roll with a raunched-out 'Medication', inflammatory 'Swastika Eyes' and a demolition stomp through 'Rocks', which Bob dedicated to all the drug addicts. The encores put the cap on it: a pube-strafing 'Accelerator', 'Kill All Hippies' and 'Detroit', with Bob's old mucker Jim Reid sharing vocals. The encore's cover was Johnny Thunders' 'Born To Lose' before they finally bowed out with the thermonuclear detonation that is 'Skull X'. By now the guitars seemed to have taken over their owners and let loose a mutiny of unbridled sonic carnage.

Max Bell wasn't wrong in the *Hot Tickets* gig preview when he wrote, 'These days the Scream are more up and crazy than bitter and twisted. Old timers maybe, but definitely not old hat.'

They were on top form for both gigs, even if, that first night in the dressing room, my girlfriend Michelle and I made the fatal mistake of homing in on the one remaining full bottle of wine. There must have been some kind of 'additive', because next morning I regained consciousness zonked out in the doorway of the local post office, and Michelle found herself standing outside someone's house with her arm raised ready to ring the doorbell. That was scary, but raised a few chuckles in the dressing room next day.

Afterwards it was straight back to the Kensington Hilton to watch the World Cup final. In the bar we settled down and Fatty suddenly got up and drew a line down the aisle of the bar.

'Right!' he bellowed in endearing Fatty style. 'England on the left! Brazil on the right!' Of course, most stayed put on the England side or crossed over. Not Mani though. Sporting Brazil's yellow and green colours, he happily hopped over to their side. When the match wore on, as the dawn came up there were some bleary – and tear-stained – faces in that bar as England was defeated. When the match ended, Trigger was just standing silent with tears rolling down his cheeks, as were half the road crew. Not Mani though. He was as bright as a button.

NME's Alex Needham agreed that Shepherds Bush had been a killer. Under the headline, 'New Supermodel Army,' he reported the Scream's gig as 'a triumph, so much so that the ill-advised politics, weird fashion following [?] and drug rumours seem like mere side issues, burned at the crucible of incendiary rock 'n' roll.' He described them as a 'lean, mean sex-disco machine . . . Crucially they both sound and look amazing. Rather than the knackered husk of a couple of years ago, Bobby Gillespie now looks like a glossy-haired advert for hard drugs.'

The Shepherds Bush gigs were the first airing for the new album. Preceded by a five-track CD promo which gave a delicious taste of what was in store, *Evil Heat* itself arrived on 5 August. The album was in-your-face shock treatment, which roped in the new electro strains but, at the same time, harked back to the earliest Primal love for psychedelic 1960s rock 'n' roll, while keeping the

Shepherd's Bush Empire, '02.

high-energy levels of *Xtrmntr* for the rockers.

Mojo's Keith Cameron gave it a good one. After describing *Xtrmntr* as 'brilliant, but gruelling', he wrote: '*Evil Heat* is far more concilliatory. A year ago, Andrew Innes described its embryonic vibe as "Cabaret Voltaire meets Monkees", and inasmuch as it's full of tremendously melodic, malevolent electro-pop songs, that's not a bad place to start .. Less conceptually pure than its predecessor in terms of tone and motivation it may be, but *Evil Heat*'s bespoke tailoring pays dividends time and again. Indeed, its individual displays of brilliance are hit-the-repeat-button affairs . . . Vocally, the Scream mainman hasn't been so consistently switched on for a long time.' I think he liked it. I do too. There's a spirit of rampant creativity constantly threatening to boil over, coursing through an unearthly marriage of granite-hard beats and beautiful melodies.

The opener, 'Deep Hit Of The Morning Sun' (mixed by Kevin Shields), boasts airy West Coast harmonies over a squirting electronic pop groove, wafting along gorgeously in an opiated paradise of its own. According to Bob, 'We just try and make a really beautiful record that means something to us, and I think we've done it here.' Of the much-talked-about Two Lone Swordsmen hook-up on 'Autobahn 66', Bobby said, 'Aah, it's absolutely amazing. I think it's the best thing we've done since "Higher Than The Sun". I can honestly say, it's an absolute classic. So we're back with Weatherall . . . It's working, you know? While it's working, don't question it. It's as good as Kraftwerk. It doesn't sound like Kraftwerk, but it's got that melancholic, beautiful driving feel.'

It is a masterful piece of work: glistening, cruising along like another classic German-electro band, Neu!, with more West Coast-influenced vocal shimmer from Bobby. That was already lined up to be the second single.

The Shields-produced 'Detroit' bangs things up a notch. Amidst its unashamedly Stoogeville guitar barrage, it sports vocals from Bobby's old sparring partner Jim Reid. Bobby, true to form, simply thought that he was the right man for the job. 'I tried to sing it a couple of times and it really wasn't happening. He's got a really sexy voice, but it's also quite melancholy. He's a blues singer.'

'Rise' ups the ante even further. This is the notorious 'Bomb The Pentagon', now slightly remodelled to omit said phrase and coming on like a John Lydon eighties PiL whooper. PiL and Johnny were always major motivating influences, but this is probably the closest the Scream have come to PiL's early onslaughts. In fact, there's a mutated burst of 'Radio Four' from *Metal Box* at the end. That's Shields on the knobs again and the sound is sheer heart attack, with lyrics that lose none of their bite despite Bob leaving out the line that made grown men convulse. He says he wasn't out to shock, but the track is still a blistering sonic attack on political complacency. The band were wielding musical chainsaws by now. 'It's righteous, y'know?', asserted Bob. 'It sounds like the Plastic Ono Band. It's real glam rock meets PiL.'

Evil Heat

Then it's time for the low-slung, bluesy night-crawl of 'The Lord Is My Shotgun', with Percy Plant's most blues-wailing harmonica creating an atmosphere a bit like the Stones' 'Little Red Rooster' as the guitars moan.

Incendiary guitar antics again with the Shieldsed-up 'City' and its MC5-style punk roar, on which Kevin contributes 'skunk guitar' – derived from a David Holmes track called 'Sin City'. Things calm down for a moment with 'Some Velvet Morning', Bobby's aforementioned duet with Kate Moss. 'Skull X' is back into Shields mixed-mayhem territory, with a Joy Division-ish bassline and a wall of guitars which just builds into a searing skyscraper of sheer heart attack cacophony. This album's 'Accelerator'.

Bobby: '[Skull X] is short for, skull exploding. It's like a fucking guitar holocaust, incredible. Future rock 'n' roll. I love it.' Even good old Hartie joined in the axe maelstrom and is credited with 'stun guitar' on the sleeve.

'A Scanner Darkly' – named after a Philip K. Dick novel about a methedrine addict suffering mental problems – is another Swordsmen collision and is totally instrumental. The orchestrated pulse captures a mood not unlike 'Inner Flight' from *Screamadelica*, but a darker roboticised version.

'Really beautiful electronic music,' affirms Bobby. 'I don't sing on it. Big deal. Doesn't matter. The guys have made a beautiful piece of music. My ego, I don't feel like I've got to sing on it. That's how bands don't last. I know I don't need to be on this one. It's beautiful the way it is.'

Then a bit of a surprise. The closing ballad, 'Space Blues No. 2', features Martin Duffy on a poignant lead vocal. It's basically a revisit to his days in Felt and their 'Space Blues' single of 1988 and is quite gorgeous as a slow-motion final coda. With the Swordsmen on board, it leaves the album with a sense of calm like 'Shine Like Stars' on *Screamadelica*. It's as if you bask in the track's departure into the ether before you realise that this is quite a remarkable album.

April 2002 had seen Primal Scream placed at number 36 in the seemingly immortal *NME*'s list of the Top Fifty Artists of All Time. Not bad, when you consider they left out Hendrix and awarded top spot to the bleedin' Smiths. The Stone Roses made it to number three, while the Jesus and Mary Chain were at 29. In a short interview Bobby heaps praise on longtime Scream champion Jack Barron, a lovely man who remains one of the best writers the paper has ever had, and one of the first to spread the message of acid house. Bob also pays tribute to the great Nick Kent, whose articles inspired a generation and still put most of today's upstarts to shame.

Bobby added, 'I tell you what means a lot though, NME readers voting *Xtrmntr* their favourite album of 2000 – it's good to know people are listening. There's more to come.'

Bobby was on the cover of the *Evening Standard*'s *Hot Tickets* supplement for the week starting 16 August. Sporting huge black shades, red shirt and stubble, with arms raised, he looked as speed-mean as the Velvets circa *White Light/White Heat*. The headline said 'No Surrender', with the subtitle, 'Bobby Gillespie – I won't give up the rock 'n' roll lifestyle.'

Bobby told writer Tim Cooper that making *Evil Heat* had been a 'more joyful experience' than *Xtrmntr* and its dark, vicious reflection of UK life. 'I think there's a lot more love in this record. The last record was a bit angrier. But I don't like the term angry in music – it makes you think of really bad bands. I think this is more up, more joyous, more sarcastic, more sexy – that's what I think. With this record we were having good fun making it, and that's a good reason to make rock 'n' roll music.'

That said, Bobby alludes to some personal traumas during the making of the album, which he describes as 'just a few weeks of chaos'. Some of the lyrics – like 'Detroit''s 'I destroy everyone I love' – are dark in the extreme. 'Skull X' takes it even blacker with lines like 'Don't you find it hard to laugh / when your mouth is full of broken glass / Thoughts mutate to locusts, skull exploding / Come on baby, do it again.' 'I was quite unstable when I wrote that,' he says on reflection, but he obviously has a blast singing it now.

In 2000 Bobby had split with longtime girlfriend Emily and gone a bit wild. On the few other occasions I saw him around that time, he hadn't seemed like the old Bob. He seemed to be getting out there again. All that changed when he hitched up with Katy England, a pioneering stylist for fashion designer Alexander McQueen, who he asked to marry him over Christmas 2002. She said yeah. His son Wolf was born soon after, and now he's quite happy staying in or simply pushing the buggy around near their Islington home. I guess, if you'd said all this ten years ago, there would be some disbelieving looks, but Bob is genuinely happy these days. Anyway, he plays the baby Sex Pistols records.

I would never ask Bob or the group about drugs in interviews. For a start, I've hung out with

Bobby on the cover of Hot Tickets, *August, '02.*

them for over ten years! There is a level of trust between us, and everybody else is always on about it. Like the guy in the *Standard*, who got this response: 'I still love to do it. I just don't want to do it every day. It's unproductive really. That's the problem. If you put the whole band in a room it all goes off. We are what we are. We're drug addicts. We're not reformed drug addicts, that's the thing. That's the culture though. You look at people from 30 to our age who came through punk rock and acid house and that drug culture of the nineties – it's just so much of the culture now.' At least he's honest enough to say it. Most artists only agree to talk about drugs after they've been in rehab. The nearest the Scream ever got to that was Bob spending a couple of weeks in Alan McGee's country pile, to get over his chaotic period. Apart from associates like Hugo Nicolson, none of Primal Scream have been to rehab. What would be the point? When Throb was going a bit too far a few years back, he simply stopped and went fishing every day.

In *Mojo*, Bobby was asked by former *NME* writer Keith Cameron if the band were a 'rock 'n' roll Foreign Legion where men with "pasts" can find a sympathetic home?'

'I'm more romantic,' replied the singer. 'I tend to think of it as the Wild Bunch. Each time we go on tour I think it's gonna be the last bank job and we're gunned down by the Mexican army. Throb's gonna get captured and we're all gonna have to go an' get the guy even though we know we're gonna get massacred . . . I think we've got a good policy, musically. Because we've been honest about our drug use, a lot of times I think the music's been overshadowed by the lifestyle choices. And I think it's a testament to the musical ideology of the band that we've got people like Mani and Kevin Shields with us. Y'know, it's hard to get Kevin Shields to do anything. Ask Island – ten years and he never gave them a record.'

He was asked about Creation and if the Scream ever felt ignored in favour of Oasis.

'It was all right, because it was just timing. Whatever's successful people naturally gravitate towards. I don't have any grudges with anybody. On the whole, our relationship with Alan over the years has been amazing. There's only one time it wasnae so good and that's after he got ill. He felt that we weren't there for him. But we weren't there for him because we weren't there for ourselves, we were all having bad times. Everybody went a bit weird in the mid-nineties because of excessive drug use. Everybody was confused and isolated. I saw some strange things, things I never would have imagined would have happened. But it worked itself out. The support I've had from Alan, personally, has been incredible. I had a really bad time two years ago, I was a bit unbalanced, and Alan and Kate [Holmes, McGee's lovely wife] took me in and looked after us, sent me to their house in Wales and got us better. I had to get out of London because I had crazy things, some changes in my life that were too much for me to take. If you're going to do stuff, accept the consequences, deal with it and don't feel sorry for yourself and don't blame anybody else.' It does explain Bobby's ghostly demeanour around the time of that Reading Festival appearance. He was more withdrawn than I've ever seen him and nearly out of control backstage after the Town And Country warm-up. He looked thinner than ever, and clearly not a well man. It's amazing the difference that a couple of years can make. Maybe fatherhood had something to do with it.

'It's great. I've got a fucking amazing family. I love my girlfriend Kate and I love my son Wolf. The Wolf. He's a great kid. Mind you he's only six months old! Hopefully it's gonna make us less selfish. I just wanna be as good a father as I can. Not be a fuck up. I wanna be there for him, and love him, help him out. Make him laugh.' There ya go.

Another UK tour came up in December. This time the London date was Brixton Academy. The first night had been an early one which went okay, apart from sound problems. The Saturday was one of those Scream all-nighters. It wasn't a six in the morning job, but it carried on the three a.m. tradition established over ten years before. Messy.

Funnily enough, it was almost eight years to the day that I'd done Brixton and we ended up in the Shepherds Bush Hilton for that two-dayer. There were many faces from past and present: Hugo Nicholson, Jagz Kooner, Douglas Hart, Granty Fleming, Titch from the Pembroke, Big Bob, Mulreany, Trigger still holding the fort, Paul Harte, a reserved Fatty, Mani and Throb.

The gig was a stormer and had the packed house, who'd already been limbered up by the Black Rebel Motorcycle Club, going ballistic. Most of the set revolved around the new album, with momentum picking up as it roared on. The Scream at Brixton Academy is always an explosive combination. Coupled with the fact that they'd now settled into their new songs, it was sheer napalm scorching that stage. Bobby looked moody and vicious in black, while the band hacked and chainsawed a sonic holocaust. The place went nuts as they mixed classics like 'Higher Than The Sun' and 'Movin' On Up' with most of the new album. The aural assault was matched by the eye-blasting visuals. You can never go wrong with a good light show, but trust the Scream to up the ante. It was like a psychedelic war going on up there.

In June 2003, the momentum was still going strong as Primal Scream returned to Glastonbury, headlining the Other Tent on the Friday evening of the festival. It was a stark contrast to their static, drummerless appearance in 1997. The versions of 'Rocks', 'Swastika Eyes' and 'Loaded' that closed their set were probably the most noisy, strutting and amphetamined ever. Bobby was literally running across the stage, nearly bashed a BBC cameraman with the mike-stand, and repeatedly incited a crowd who went duly ballistic.

NME agreed, with Andy Capper writing, 'After today's totally insipid slew of grey, blank shit line-up, the arrival of the Scream is like the breaking open of the heavens. At last, there's a rock band onstage, blasting through their greatest hits at 500 miles an hour, blowing all the wankers that bored us to fuck today out of the water with a dirty bomb of electronic screaming stolen from a disused Soviet weapons laboratory in Kazakhstan . . . The combined age of Primal Scream is precisely 876 and they still make everybody else on today's bill look like old age pensioner hippy cunts. Kill all unbelievers.'

No sign of losing it yet then, obviously.

So we leave it with Innes and Kevin in an Old Street studio, mixing a live album from a recent Japanese tour for Japanese release only – 'we said we'd do it when we were off our heads!' There's also the greatest hits set *Dirty Hits* on the horizon, and the band have been plotting their next album in the Primrose Hill studio. That's good news. We probably need this group more than we do any other.

Not only for their constantly amazing music, but also for being rare individuals who show a consistent personal honesty, and are a constant source of entertainment via their antics and outpourings. I've had some of my most euphoric and hilarious times ever with the Scream, the best group in the world, who've made some of my favourite records. In the process I gained a whole new family. What more can you ask?

On the balcony at eight in the morning, Grand Hotel, Brighton, '94.

Epilogue

So, how are the wildest, most innovative group ever let loose on the world looking these days? Parenthood is still in the air. Innes had his second – a son called Syd, named after Syd Barrett. The baby was actually born two minutes into a Celtic game. Now Duffy and Della have had their first baby, Louis and Bobby's still buggy-pushing in Islington. Paradoxically, their music is fiercer than it's ever been.

Innes and Hartie showed up recently when I was DJing at a London gay club called the Cock! I'd also seen Innes at his birthday bash a few months earlier, and he was on fine form. The following week, we were all together again for a Andrew Weatherall piledriver obliteration set at one of his monthly Haywire Sessions parties. It was the first time my girlfriend Michelle had seen the great man in action. Now she knew what all the fuss was about. The fact that Bobby turned up and danced with her made her night, and I realised she was experiencing one of those Scream-family memories that live on forever. They get you like that, which is why I wrote this book. The best thing is, I know there's more to come.

We end by coming full circle. The news came in just before Christmas 2002 that former Clash man Joe Strummer – singer, guitarist and proverbial spokesman for a generation – had died from a heart attack at his Somerset home. Apart from my personally losing a good friend, Joe's sad, unexpected death had a profound impact on the music world. He's up there with names like Hendrix, Lennon, Morrison and Marley.

It was largely due to The Clash that Bobby formed Primal Scream in the first place. As he describes it, 'After that I never had a career plan. It just seems to keep happening.' So after guitarist Mick Jones had joined the Scream onstage at Reading in 1994, it was fitting that Bobby Gillespie was called up to present the three remaining Clash members with their *NME* Carling Godlike Genius awards in early 2003. Accompanied by Kate Moss, he joined Mick, Paul Simonon and Topper Headon on the stage after a short burst of vintage Clash footage.

That was some buzz for the kid from Glasgow who'd been inspired so much when he'd first heard The Clash over 25 years earlier. Afterwards, Mick Jones had this to say to *NME*: 'Bobby Gillespie is the perfect example of someone who has been moved emotionally by The Clash. The problem today is that the nature of the groups means they have no conscience.'

One final circle was completed when Primal Scream returned to the scene of their first gig in Glasgow, on 11 April 2003. The Venue is now called the Garage and the gig was part of the Carling Homecoming series. *NME*'s Barry Nicolson reported, 'Prodigal sons don't come more prodigal than this,' as he lavished praise on the Scream's 'dead-eyed, laser-guided, rock 'n' roll Panzer attack'. The set list was 'Accelerator', 'Miss Lucifer', 'Rise', 'Shoot Speed/Kill Light', 'Pills', 'Burning Wheel', 'Autobahn 66', 'Kill All Hippies', 'City', 'Rocks', 'Kowalski', 'Swastika Eyes', 'Skull X', 'Jailbird', 'Detroit', 'Movin' On Up', 'Medication' and 'Kick Out The Jams'. What a scorcher. Just looking at that list – despite the omission of classics in favour of the newer stuff – shows how many weapons of mass destruction are throbbing away in the Scream armoury. There really is no stopping them now.

In honour of The Clash, and Primal Scream, the group who've carried on their ethos, we dedicate this book to Joe Strummer. The evil heat is still burning and that light shows no sign of dimming.

Primal Scream Discography

In which I try and list all the records that Primal Scream have made. Obviously there are promos of various denominations, some overseas variations and the bootlegs that would be impossible to completely list. The Scream records are all on Creation, apart from where stated and not including the guest appearances and compilation appearances.

SINGLES

All Fall Down/It Happens
May 1985 – 7"

Crystal Crescent/Velocity Girl
May 1986 – 7"
Also 12" with 'Spirea X'. Jim Beattie nicked the title for his new band when he left Primal Scream.

Gentle Tuesday/Black Star Carnival
June 1987 - 7" on short-lived Elevation offshoot.
Also 12" with cover version of the Shadows of Knight's 'I'm Gonna Make You Mine'. The German version contained 'Gentle Tuesday' and 'Imperial'.

Imperial/Star Fruit Surf Rider
Sept 1987 – Elevation 7"
Also 12" with cover version of the Who's 'So Sad About Us' and 'Imperial' demo.

Ivy Ivy Ivy/You're Just Too Dark To Care
July 1989 – Back to Creation! 7"
Also 12"/CD with 'I've Got You Split Wide Open Over Me'. There was also a 12" promo with just 'Ivy Ivy Ivy'

and no info except a sticker with the title.

Loaded/I'm Losing More Than I'll Ever Have
Feb 1990 – 7" and 12" with version of the MC5's 'Ramblin' Rose', recorded live in New York City. The 12" initially appeared as a promo with 'Loaded' scrawled on it in black marker. A second 12"/CD swapped a Terry Farley mix of 'Loaded' for the original.
Original 12" run-out groove – A. Free Sly Stone NOW! B. Free James Brown

Come Together – Terry Farley/Andrew Weatherall Mixes
Aug 1990 – 7"/12"/CD. Second 12" featured 'Come Together' (Hypnotonebrainmachine Mix/BBG Mix).
Run-out: first 12" – A. You may say I'm a dreamer B. But I'm not the only one. Second 12" – B. Sing sing!

Higher Than The Sun/ Higher Than The Orb (both mixed by The Orb)/Higher Than The Sun (American Spring Mix by Andrew Weatherall and Hugo Nicolson)
May 1991 – promo 12"

Higher Than The Sun 7" edit/Higher Than The Sun (American Spring Mix by Andrew Weatherall and Hugo Nicolson)
June 1991 – 7"

Higher Than The Sun/Higher Than The Sun (American Spring Mix by Andrew Weatherall and Hugo Nicolson)
June 1991 – 12"
Run-out: A. LATER B. I get mine for 15's

Higher Than The Sun (A Dub Symphony In Two Parts) – Remixed by Andrew Weatherall with Hugo Nicolson/Higher Than The Sun (Higher Than The Orb) – Remixed by Dr Alex Paterson and Thrash
Run-out: A. QUALITY B. He's got what I want he's got what I need he's always there when I need some speed

Higher Than The Sun (7" mix)/Higher Than The Sun/Higher Than The Orb
June 1991 – CD

Don't Fight It Feel It (Whistling Mix)/Don't

Fight It Feel It (Scat Mix)
Promo. Both mixes by Andrew Weatherall with Hugo Nicolson.

Don't Fight It Feel It (7" edit)/Don't Fight It Feel It (Scat Mix)
Aug 1991 – 7"

Don't Fight It Feel It/Don't Fight It Feel It (Scat Mix)
Aug 1991 – 12". Both mixes by Andrew Weatherall with Hugo Nicolson. Run-out: There's a network B. it exists! A second 12" featured mixes from 808 State's Graham Massey.
Run-out: A. There ain't no crap . . . B. In a red and black cap

Don't Fight It Feel It (7" edit)/Don't Fight It Feel It (12" version)/Don't Fight It Feel It (Scat Mix by Andrew Weatherall)
Aug 1991 – CD

Screamadelica
May 1992 – promo. Same track both sides but misprinted one side as 'Movin' On Up'.

Dixie-Narco EP: Movin' On Up/[cover of the Beach Boys'] Carry Me Home /Screamadelica
June 1992 – 7"

Dixie-Narco EP: Movin' On Up/Stone My Soul/Carry Me Home/Screamadelica
June 1992 – 12"/CD Run-out: A. All the way from Memphis B. Kit off!

Funky Jam
Dec 1993 – 12" promo of mixes by George Clinton and Brendan Lynch.

Rocks (remixed by George Drakoulias)/Funky Jam
Feb 1994 – 7"

Rocks/Funky Jam
Feb 1994 – 12" Run-out: A. Oh ah Escobar B. Free Peter Packet

Jailbird (Original Remix by George Drakoulias)/(Dust Brothers Mix)/Jailbird (Sweeney 2 Mix by Sabres of Paradise – Weatherall, Jagz Kooner, Gary Burns)
May 1994 – promo 12"

Jailbird (Toxic Trio Stay Free Mix by Kris Needs, Robert Young and Bobby Gillespie)/Jailbird (Weatherall Dub Chapter 3 Mix)
May 1994 – promo 12"

Jailbird (Original Remix by George Drakoulias)/???
7"

Jailbird (Dust Brothers Mix)/(Toxic Trio Stay Free Mix)/(Sweeney 2 Mix)/(Weatherall Dub Chapter 3 Mix)
12" Run-out: A. Call In The Air Strike B. Once more over the wall, sir
(I'm Gonna) Cry Myself Blind/Rocks (live at Glasgow Barrowlands)
Nov 1994

(I'm Gonna) Cry Myself

Blind/Struttin' (Back In Our Minds) [Remixed by Brendan Lynch]/Give Out But Don't Give Up (Portishead Remix)/Rockers Dub (Remixed by Kris Needs)
10"
Free Scream graffiti poster saying 'wake the town and tell the people: Primal Scream, rockers galore!'

Rockers Dub (Needsy)/Struttin' (Lynchy)/Give Out But Don't Give Up (Portisheady)
10" promo

Primal Scream, Irvine Welsh and On-U Sound Present . . . The Big Man And The Scream Team Meet The Barmy Army Uptown
June 1996 – radio-friendly instrumental promo

Primal Scream, Irvine Welsh and On-U Sound Present . . . The Big Man And The Scream Team Meet The Barmy Army Uptown
June 1996 – mixed and recorded by Adrian Sherwood, vocals by Denise Johnson and Irvine Welsh. Versions: Full Strength Fortified Dub/Electric Soup Dub/A Jake Supreme. Released for one week only when the Scream contributed the 'clean' version to the Euro-96 Beautiful Game soundtrack.
Run-out: A. If you hate the fucking English clap your hands B. Who are you?

At this point there was an EMI promo for the Trainspotting *soundtrack, that coupled the Scream instrumental of the same name with Leftfield. It's very rare and some fucker nicked my copy, so I'm afraid it's all very dim and distant.*

Kowalski/[cover version of ? and the Mysterians'] 96 Tears/Know Your Rights
May 1997 – 7"

Kowalski (Original)/(Dan the Automator Mix)/96 Tears/Know Your Rights
May 1997 – 12" and CD

Kowalski (Original)/(Automator Mix)
May 1997 – promo

Know Your Rights
May 1997 – promo featuring Scream treatment of The Clash song, originally recorded in '94 for the Retribution *EP, produced by Steve Sidelnyk and Murray Mitchell. One-sided. 12" run-out: Paranoia is total awareness B. What do you need . . . speed! Promo run-out: First Name Unknown*

Star/Jesus
June 1997 – 7"

Star/Jesus/Rebel Dub (Adrian Sherwood Mix)/How Does It Feel To Belong?
June 1997 – 12", 12" promo and CD Run-out: A. GETTHEFUCK-INPAINTOUT! B. come alive with a DB5

Stuka (Two Lone Swordsmen Remixes by Andrew Weatherall and Keith Tenniswood)
June 1997 – initially scarce then issued as 3,000-only pressing.

Burning Wheel/Burning Wheel (Chemical Brothers Remix)
12" Promo

Burning Wheel/Burning Wheel (Chemical Brothers Remix)
Oct 1997 – 7"

Burning Wheel/(Chemical Brothers Remix)/Hammond Connection/Higher Than The Sun (Demo)
Oct 1997 – 12" and CD

LOS TERRORPINOS – The Desert Song
Nov 1997 – one-sided limited-edition Eruption 12" featuring Andrew Innes, Martin Duffy, Murray Mitchell, Paul Hart, Sarah-Jane Harrison and Kris Needs. Run-out: One more quack out of you and I'll cut your throat [courtesy of Graham Gillespie]

If They Move Kill 'Em (Original)/If They Move Kill 'Em (My Bloody Valentine Arkestra – Kevin Shields Remix)
Feb 1998 – promo 12"

If They Move Kill 'Em (My Bloody Valentine Arkestra)/Darklands
Feb 1998 – 7"

If They Move Kill 'Em (My

Bloody Valentine Arkestra)/Darklands/If They Move Kill 'Em (12" Disco Mix)/Badlands
Feb 1998 – 12" and CD Limited release for one week only – 10,000 CDs, 3,000 12", 2,000 7". Too long-play for the singles chart so it entered the album chart at thirteen. Runout: A. REHAB B. . . . is for quitters

Swastika Eyes (Chemical Brothers Remix)
Oct 1999 – one-sided 12" promo, only 500 copies. Run-out: It ain't all that.

Swastika Eyes (Chemical Brothers Remix)/Spectre Remix/David Holmes Remix
Oct 1999 – only 500 pressed

Swastika Eyes (Chemical Brothers Remix)/Spectre Mix
Nov 1999 – 7"

Swastika Eyes (Chemical Brothers Remix)/Spectre Remix/Edit
Nov 1999 – 12" and CD. Also a rare CD promo. Over-sensitive reaction to the title led to the track being retitled 'War Pigs' – its working title – in some parts of Europe. 12" run-out: A. USUAL RUBBISH? B. IT'LL ROT YOUR BOOTS

Pills (Original and Instrumental – both mixed by Dan the Automator)/Shoot Speed/Kill Light
Dec 1999 – promo 12" only

Kill All Hippies (Two Lone Swordsmen mixes one and two)/Exterminator (Jagz Kooner Remix)
Feb 2000 – promo 12"

Kill All Hippies (LP version)/Exterminator (Massive Attack Remix)
Feb 2000 – promo 12"
Both run-outs: Dedicated to Curtis Mayfield

Kill All Hippies/Revenge Of The Hammond Connection
March 2000 – 7"

Kill All Hippies (LP)/Exterminator (Massive Attack Remix)/Revenge Of The Hammond Connection
March 2000 – 12" and CD
Run-out: A. Curtis Mayfield B. Movin On Up

Accelerator
Aug 2000 – one-sided 12" promo

Accelerator/[cover version of Third Bardo's] I'm Five Years Ahead Of My Time/When The Kingdom Comes
Sept 2000 – 12" and CD

Miss Lucifer
Columbia, June 2002 – promo CD

Miss Lucifer (Scream Team Hip To Hip Mix with Jagz Kooner/Bone To Bone/Panther Girl mixes by Alec Empire)
Columbia, June 2002 – 12" promo
Miss Lucifer

Columbia, July 2002 – CD

Autobahn 66
Columbia, October 2002 – 12" promo

Autobahn 66
Columbia, Ocotber 2002 – CD

Autobahn 66 (Alter Ego Remixes)
Columbia, October 2002 – 12" promo

PRIMAL SCREAM FEATURING KATE MOSS – Some Velvet Morning (New Version, produced by Kevin Shields and Jagz Kooner)
Columbia, Oct 2003 – CD promo

Some Velvet Morning (Extended Version produced by Kevin Shields and Jagz Kooner/Two Lone Swordsmen remix)
Columbia, Oct 2003 – 12" promo

Some Velvet Morning (New Version)/Country Blues No.1
Columbia, Nov 2003 – 7"

Some Velvet Morning (New Version)/(Two Lone Swordsmen remix)/Country Blues No 1
Columbia, Nov 2003 – CD

ALBUMS

Sonic Flower Groove
Sept 1987 – LP and CD:
Gentle Tuesday; Treasure Trip; May The Sun Shine Bright For You/Sonic Sister Love; Silent Spring; Imperial; Love You; Leaves; Aftermath; We Go Down Slowly Rising

Primal Scream
Sept 1989 – LP and CD:
Ivy Ivy Ivy; You're Just Dead Skin To Me; She Power; You're Just Too Dark To Care; I'm Losing More Than I'll Ever Have; Gimme Gimme Teenage Head; Lone Star Girl; Kill The King; Sweet Pretty Thing; Jesus Can't Save Me
The LP featured a free 7", with early copies featuring demos of 'Split Wide Open' and 'Lone Star Girl'.

Screamadelica
Sept 1991 – LP and CD:
Movin' On Up; Slip Inside This House; Don't Fight It Feel It; Higher Than The Sun; Inner Flight; Come Together (Weatherall Mix); Loaded; Damaged; I'm Coming Down; Higher Than The Sun (A Dub Symphony In Two Parts); Shine Like Stars

Give Out But Don't Give Up
March 1994 – LP and CD:
Jailbird; Rocks; (I'm Gonna) Cry Myself Blind; Funky Jam; Big Jet Plane; Free; Call On Me; Struttin'; Sad And Blue; Give Out But Don't Give Up; I'll Be There For You; Everybody Needs Somebody [hidden bonus track]
Run-out: A. Why buy one – an 8 Balls Cheaper B. Do we weigh in now or do we get to fuck

Vanishing Point

July 1997 – LP and CD:
Burning Wheel; Get Duffy;
Kowalski; Star; If They Move
Kill 'Em; Out Of The Void;
Stuka; Medication; [cover versions of Motherhead's]
Motorhead; Trainspotting;
Long Life
Run-out: A. The question's not
when they're gonna stop B.
Some day this LP's gonna end,
son Free Titch C. Lee Is Love
D. Surf's Up

Echo Dek

October 1997 – LP, CD and
five x 7"
Living Dub (Long Life);
Duffed Up (Get Duffy);
Revolutionary (Star); JU-87
(Stuka); First Name Unknown
(Kowalski); Vain In Dub (Out
Of The Void); Last Train
(Trainspotting); Wise Blood
(Stuka); Dub In Vain
(Medication)
All tracks remixed by Adran
Sherwood.
Run-out: Most of my mixes
sound better through a wall

Xtrmntr

March 2000 – double LP and
CD:
Kill All Hippies; Accelerator;
Exterminator; Swastika Eyes;
Pills; Blood Money; Keep
Your Dreams; Insect Royalty;
MBV Arkestra (If They Move
Kill 'Em); Swastika Eyes
(Chemical Brothers Remix);
Shoot Speed/Kill Light

Evil Heat

Columbia, Aug 2002 – CD:
Deep Hit Of The Morning
Sun; Miss Lucifer; Autobahn
66; Detroit; Rise; The Lord Is

My Shotgun; City; Some
Velvet Morning; Skull X; A
Scanner Darkly; Space Blues
No. 2

Primal Scream Live In Japan

Japanese Sony, September
2003 – CD:
Accelerator; Miss Lucifer; Rise;
Shoot Speed/Kill Light; Pills;
Autobahn 66; City; Rocks;
Kowalski; Swastika Eyes; Skull
X; Higher Than The Sun;
Jailbird; Movin' On Up;
Medication; Born To Lose

Dirty Hits

Columbia, Nov 2003 – CD:
Loaded (7" Edit); Movin' On
Up; Come Together
(Weatherall 7"); Higher Than
The Sun (7" Edit); Rocks;
Jailbird; (I'm Gonna) Cry
Myself Blind; Burning Wheel;
Kowalski; Long Life; Swastika
Eyes (7"); Kill All Hippies;
Accelerator; Shoot Speed/Kill
Light; Miss Lucifer; Deep Hit
Of The Morning Sun; Some
Velvet Morning (New
Version); Autobahn 66

Dirty Hits Bonus Disc:

Come Together (Hypnotone
Brain Machine Mix); Higher
Than The Sun (Higher Than
The Orb extended mix);
Loaded (Terry Farley remix);
Rocks (Jimmy Miller remix);
Jailbird (Sweeney 2 Mix by
Sabres of Paradise); Kowalski
(Automator Remix); Living
Dub (Long Life Remix by
Adrian Sherwood); Stuka (Two
Lone Swordsmen remix);
Swastika Eyes (Chemical
Brothers Mix edit);
Exterminator (Massive Attack
Remix); Miss Lucifer (Bone To

Bone Mix); Some Velvet
Morning (Two Lone
Swordsmen alternative mix);
Autobahn 66 (Alter Ego
Remix)

SIDE PROJECT

THE COMPLETION – Electronic Music For The Cinema

Creation, March 1998 – CD
Little-known collection of
experimental instrumentals
by Andrew Innes, recorded
when he got bored in the
Bunker.

COMPILATIONS

The first two publicly-available
Scream tracks – 'Introduction'
and 'Circumcision' – appear
on the State Of Affairs cassette
(Pleasantly Surprised).
   A lot of early tracks like 'All
Fall Down' and 'Velocity Girl'
appear on several Creation
compilations. Best title: 1991's
Sorted, Snorted And Sported,
which featured the 'Dub
Symphony' mix of 'Higher'.
   'Slip Inside This House'
started life on a 1990 covers
compilation called Where The
Pyramid Meets the Eye – A
Tribute To Roky Erickson
(Sire). It eventually landed up
on Screamadelica, produced by
Hypnotone.
   When Creation made a concerted move to invade the
dance market in the early
nineties they whipped out a
double album called Keeping
The Faith – A Creation

Dance Compilation *(1991).* Included were the HypnotoneBrainMachine Mix of 'Come Together' and Terry Farley's 'Loaded' remix, alongside other dance acts on the roster like DJ Danny Rampling.

'Know Your Rights' was specially recorded for the Retribution – Repetitive Beats Remix *EP in 1994 (Sabrettes), appearing alongside Sabres of Paradise, Drum Club, Adrian Sherwood and myself. It also appeared as a one-sided promo disc in 1998.*

There's a live version of 'Don't Fight It Feel It', recorded in Tokyo, on Select *magazine's* Select Tracks 2 *cover-mounted cassette of 1994. Apparently it was taken from a Japanese bootleg DAT.* World's End Volume 11 *also featured a live version of 'Jailbird' recorded in Osaka, Japan, the same year.*

The Scream teamed up with sixties songstress P. P. Arnold for a version of 'Understanding' on a Small Faces tribute album called Long Agos And Worlds Apart *(Nice 1996).*

'Trainspotting', from the soundtrack to the film of the same name (EMI Premier 1996), also came out as a promo coupled with Leftfield and then popped up on Vanishing Point.

That same year, 'Higher Than The Sun' graced Dr Alex Paterson's Auntie Aubry's Excursions Beyond The Call Of Duty *CD of Orb remixes. Its eight-minute 'Higher Than A Kite' incarnation was the*

previously-unheard full monty. There's also the Welsh-Sherwood hook-up on Eurocup's The Beautiful Game *compilation – which appears, understandably, as an instrumental.*

'Star' appeared on The Jackal – Music From And Inspired By The Soundtrack *(MCA 1997) and 'Come Together' on the* Trainspotting Number Two *soundtrack (EMI Premier 1997).*

'Stuka 7' – an exclusive version from the Sherwood-mixed Echo Dek *sessions – was donated to* Jockey Slut *magazine and emerged as a cover-mounted seven-inch in 1998. The original version of 'Higher Than The Sun' appeared on the* Rock The Dock *compilation in support of Liverpool dockers and their families (Creation 1998). The first taste of 'Xtrmntr' came in the instrumental form of 'Insect Royalty' on the soundtrack to* The Acid House *(EMI 1998).*

BOOTLEGS

Where do you start? There's a load from the '94 touring blitz, revolving around the listed set.

One interesting title is Tomorrow Ends Today. *The first six tracks are from the first album, recorded at a gig at London's Clarendon Ballroom in October '85. But then it unearths that aborted first single, 'The Orchard', which was supposed to have been destroyed at the time, as well as demos of*

'Leaves' and 'Gentle Tuesday' with drum machines, and a live version of 'Gloria' from Holland in '86. These are followed by another ten tracks recorded live at Ziggy's, Plymouth, in '85.

Acknowledgements

DEDICATIONS, INSPIRATIONS, THANX & SHOUTS

To some of the people who have inspired the music of Primal Scream, made it happen in and out of the studio, on and off the stage, and kept the group going in some shape or form. My mates, who've either helped with this book, shared Scream-related activities in the past or I just happen to like. Obviously there might be some omissions amongst the emissions. Some are deliberate. But how can you not forget a name or two with the group who do it every time they break the guest-list record at Brixton Academy?

SCREAM-RELATED

Bobby Gillespie, Katie & Wolf; Andrew Innes, Alison, Eva & Sid; Robert Young, Jane & family; Martin, Della & Louis Duffy; Mani & Imelda Mounfield; Paul Harte; Murray Mitchell & Karen Parker; Andrew Weatherall; Jeff Barrett & family; Phil 'Trigger' Hamilton; Steve 'Fatty' Molloy & Ray; Alex & Annie Nightingale; Alan McGee & Kate; Dr Alex Paterson; George Clinton & the P-Funk All-Stars; Bob Morris; Irvine Welsh & ?; Brendan Lynch; Darren Mooney; Grant Fleming; Hugo Nicolson; Kevin Shields; Denise Johnson; Paul Mulreaney; Henry Olson; Steve Sidelnyk; David Holmes; Jagz Kooner; Mick Jones; The Chemical Brothers; Paul Cannell; Chris Ridge; Oz; Andy Liddle; Jacko; Jason Caulfield; Keith Tenniswood; Jim Hunt; Duncan McIntyre; Wayne Jackson & Andrew Love; Jim Dickinson; Roger Hood & David Hawkins; Marco Nelson; Augustus Pablo; Jim Beattie; Dan the Automator; Atari Teenage Riot; Massive Attack; Kate Moss; Toby Tobanov, Ivor Wilkins & anyone else who's sailed higher than the sun in the Scream-ship. The Jesus & Mary Chain; Dave Beer & the Basics family; Slam & the Glasgow massive; Graham Gillespie; Johnny Hopkins, Vanessa Cotton & Tones at Triad Publicity; Titch & the Pembroke Crew; the Queens; Robert Plant; Dick Green, Mark Taylor, James & the good ones from Creation; Wayne with the 'Kowalski' car; the Heavenly mob; Pennie Smith; Steve Schultz; The Archbishop; Tim Tooher; Sheer Taft; Simon Stephens; Anna Haigh; Liam & Natalie; Liam & Nicole; Asian Dub Foundation; Mike & Claire & all at Manumission, Ibiza; The Iceman; Wonder;

Richard Norris; Bent Recknagel; Richard Fearless; Tim Holmes; Bez; New Order; Kylie Minogue; Nina & Craig Walsh; Simon Stevens; Clare Orb; Roger Morton; Helen Mead; Jack Barron; The Jockey Slut; Andrew Perry; Michael Bonner; Siobhan Fahey & Wildcat Will; Sarah-Jane Harrison, Matty & family; Steph; Ardon O'Bugle; John Peel; Satpal Ram.

ADDITIONAL KRIS SHOUTS

Michelle, Abbey, Chloe, Jamie, Ellie & E-bunny; Mum; Julie & Adrian Needs & their families; Julie & Alan Long; Keith Richards; Robin Pike; Colin Keinch; Jo, David, Sara, Jeanette @ FML Management; Bernard Doherty & LD Publicity; Jo & Jack; Bernie & Sam; El Strongo & Mel; Vernon; Val Howe; Woz & Fay; Steve Mirkin, NYC; Parker DuLaney & family, NYC; Marc & Nancy Mikulich, SF; Leslie & Simon; Stuey; Jim Fyffe; Don Letts; Jodie & Steve; Gideon Millard; Henry Cullen, Justine & Alex; Guy The Geezer; Prodigy; Debbie & Gary next door; Aron, the S.U.F. crew & Ernie; Alan, Jackie & Paul Clayton; Jim & Wayne & The Cock, London; Robin Banks; Johnny Green; Youth; Chris Salewicz; Phil Silcock & Sara; All at Hotel Pelirocco, Brighton; Ashley Beedle & Katie; Chalkie & Suzette; Michael Parker. A big thank you to all at Plexus Publishing, especially Sandra Wake, Terence Porter and Paul Woods. A very special thank you goes to Chloe Lola Riess at Plexus Publishing, for coming up with the idea for this book, getting the show on the road, and then patiently putting up with me.

Enormous thanks are due to Grant Fleming whose photographs appear on the cover and in chapter one (page 22), chapter two (pages 24, 27, 28, 32, 33, 36, 37, 38, 39), chapter three (pages 40, 43, 45, 49), chapter four (pages 50, 52, 55, 56 x 2, 57, 58, 59, 60, 61, 62, 64), chapter five (pages 66, 68, 70, 72, 76, 80, 82, 84, 86, 87), chapter six (pages 90, 103, 105, 106, 110, 111), chapter seven (pages 112, 114, 118, 121, 122 x 2, 123), chapter eight (page 124). Many thanks also to Shelley Parker for supplying photographs used in chapter eleven (pages 170, 171, and 175). Thanks also to Bob Morris for supplying photographs used in chapters 3 (page 48) and chapter eight (pages 130, 137 and 138). All other photographs and memorabilia are from my personal collection and I would also like to thank the following individuals, publications and organisations for the use of their photographs: Glenn Luchford/Walkerprint/ Creation/Kris Needs; Gerard Malanga/Polydor/Kris Needs; William S. Harvey/Elektra/Kris Needs; Fierce Recordings/Kris Needs; Creation/Kris Needs; Creation; Jayne Houghton/Creation/Kris Needs; Hugo Nicolson; Marc Sammons/Kris Needs; Joel Brodsky/Elektra/Kris Needs; William Eggleston/Creation/Kris Needs; SJM Concerts & Metropolis/Kris Needs; Martin Duffy/Kris Needs; *The Face*/Kris Needs; Pennie Smith; Pennie Smith/Creation/Kris Needs; Eruption/Kris Needs; *Melody Maker*/Kris Needs; Kevin Westenberg/Heavenly/Kris Needs; *Select*/Kris Needs; Paul Kelly/Creation/Sony/Kris Needs; *NME*/Kris Needs; House at Intro/Creation/Kris Needs; Terry Richardson/Creation/Sony; *NME*/Kris Needs; *Jockey Slut*/Kris Needs; *Seven*/Kris Needs; *Uncut*/Kris Needs; Corinne Day/Creation/Sony; Tones Sansom/Triad Publicity; Columbia/Sony Music Entertainment UK/Kris Needs; *Hot Tickets/Evening Standard*/Kris Needs.

It has not been possible in all cases to trace the copyright sources, and the publishers would be glad to hear from any such unacknowledged copyright holders.

SWEET INSPIRATIONS
The Clash; The Rolling Stones; John Lydon, Keith Levene, Jah Wobble & Sex Pistols; the Velvet Underground, NYC; the MC5, Detroit; Brian Wilson; Can; Suicide; Marvin Gaye; The Byrds; Arthur Lee & Love; James Brown; Nico; Iggy Pop & The Stooges; The New York Dolls & The Heartbreakers; Roky Erickson; James Carr; Gram Parsons; Dan Penn; Chips Moman; Third Bardo; Ramones; Sly Stone; Jerry Lee Lewis; O.V. Wright; Donna Summer; John Lennon; 'The Sweeney'; Lemmy!

R.I.P.
Joe Strummer; Johnny Thunders; Jerry Nolan; Jimmy Miller; Tom Dowd; Sun Ra; John Coltrane; Kurt Cobain; Barry White; Weasel; Mickey Finn; The original 'Carry On' cast!

Kris Needs, October 2003